RIFE

TWENTY-ONE STORIES FROM BRITAIN'S YOUTH

EDITED BY NIKESH SHUKLA
& SAMMY JONES

unbound

First published in 2019

Unbound
6th Floor Mutual House, 70 Conduit Street, London W1S 2GF
www.unbound.com

To protect the privacy of individuals, some names and
identifying characteristics have been changed.

Lyric from *iLL Manors* on page 85 reprinted
with kind permission from Plan B.

Text design by PDQ

A CIP record for this book is available from the British Library

ISBN 978-1-78352-576-8 (paperback)
ISBN 978-1-78352-578-2 (ebook)

Printed and bound in Great Britain by Clays Ltd, Elcograf S.p.A.

For all our Rifers past and present: Shanai, Ryan, Jon, Adibah, Molly, Jess, Sham, Hal, Yero, Leo, Jack, Cai, Antonia, Grace, Ailsa, Aisha, Jazz, Holly, Kaja, Barker, Imogen, Euella, Alexie, Mikael, Ella, Tim, Lily, Asmaa and Sumaya.

CONTENTS

NOTES FROM THE EDITORS

In February 2014, I started work on a new magazine, funded by Bristol Youth Links and commissioned by Watershed, that was designed to amplify the voices of young creatives in Bristol. We were to create a space for them to tell stories and make films about the things that were important to them. We did this through six-month paid internships, stressing that they didn't need experience and they didn't need a degree. They just needed to have ideas and enthusiasm. We'd help them find their voice.

In the first team, Adibah, in one of her first pieces, wrote about the gentrification of an area in Bristol called Stokes Croft, which generated a lot of online discussion. We had arrived. I was impressed by how political she wanted to be. I hadn't expected that. I didn't know what the teams would want to cover – probably pop culture stuff and the occasional political thing. But there she was, bringing social issues to the forefront of what became *Rife* magazine.

We called ourselves *Rife* because we wanted to give the impression that we were everywhere. Through the years I worked on the project, we produced thousands of pieces of content, gaining us over a million views across all platforms, and I trained up just under thirty young people as well as commissioning hundreds more. It was the best time of my life because it directly challenged what I thought young people cared about. It made me realise what I had missed out on when I was young. This isn't a 'I believe the children are our future' editor's note. No. It's more than that. This country has repeatedly gone against the wishes of young people for decades. And a whole new politicised generation, coming up around the time of the tuition fees protests, have social media, all to arm themselves by giving them a space to come together.

We're going to get to a point where the country has moved so far away from what young people want they are playing catch-up, and the stress point will test the fabric of what we consider important. This book is about the cracks starting to form.

Nikesh Shukla, Summer 2018

When I did my *Rife* internship, I didn't know how important it was, to be honest. Plucked from my supermarket job, I was overwhelmed by the power handed to me by Watershed. They trusted me to write (and make very bad videos) about what I was passionate about, and they let me use their sizeable platform to shout about my thoughts and feelings to a national audience.

Now I'm one of the editors of *Rife*, I have a more in-depth view of the project. I'm trying not to be too cheesy, because when it comes to *Rife* I'm prone to gush – but to me it seems more remarkable every day. Young people simply do not see themselves reflected in traditional media (note the staggering decline of print papers, in which all you get are caricatures of kale-scoffing millennials and square-eyed Gen Z-ers). The young people I work with are alarmingly switched on to a world where they aren't properly represented. They're willing to think and reflect on big issues, and they really care about our country, however frustrated they get with it. They want to make the world better – they're just not being given the tools to make change. I hope *Rife* can act as a space to think about and express their views in a way that feels natural. That feels like a vitally important tool.

Because the world is, undeniably, pretty bleak for the average young person. When I think of having to live through this era, I feel an overwhelming instability. I've spun through rented flats, shared houses and rubbish jobs far faster than my parents did, and that's a national trend. My mental health has been rocky to say the least, and working that out over the past ten years through the NHS has been a challenge. But where there are massive gaps in the infrastructure that should be supporting us, I am surrounded by hope. I look around me and I see young people making it work against all odds, gathering strength by leaning on each other and forging their own outlets – zines, websites, books, even tweets – that breed optimism.

By showcasing these inexpressibly talented young writers, tackling twenty-one different topics that mean something to them – from gentrification to dating, and from the horrors of university to disability rights – I hope that this book can be a source of such hope, too.

Sammy Jones, Summer 2018

GENERATION SPENT: BRITAIN'S RENTAL CRISIS

Alex Diggins

For me, as for many others, the troubles began with an email. 'Dear Mr Diggins,' it read. 'As you know, your initial tenancy agreement is due to expire in two months' time. Therefore, we require you to pay outstanding fees of £2,600 for the next six months. If you do not make payment by 14 February [at that point, two weeks' time] we will unfortunately be forced to serve notice. Yours, Bristol Residential Lettings.'

Reading those words, my emotions shuttled quickly through shock, bafflement and, finally, to anger. The whole situation, and the threat of eviction, seemed completely unwarranted and absurd. When I finished university, after a brief, tedious period stuck at home in a small Devon village, I had decided to move to Bristol. Unlike so many of my friends, I was dubious about the bright lights of London; I'd heard far too many horror stories of graduates exploited at work as barely paid interns and at home by landlords who charged exorbitant rents for minuscule scraps of living space. I didn't want to be a part of that world. I was also realistic about my chances of making it as an aspiring freelance writer – I knew I'd have to pull a few pints and whip up some mean flat whites along the way to becoming a swashbuckling combo of Hunter S. Thompson and Tom Wolfe. Bristol seemed (just) cheap enough to sustain this lifestyle whilst also offering some of the same big-city attractions.

I moved without hesitation. When I arrived, though, this meant I didn't immediately have permanent work in place, which made renting a little difficult; letting agents are surprisingly reluctant to let to underemployed graduates, no matter how nuanced their understanding of Old English poetry. But my friends and I found a place eventually – I was allowed to move in on the condition I paid six months' rent upfront. This seemed fair enough, given my uncertain employment status, and I duly dug into my savings. Four months into the tenancy and all was going fine: I'd found a part-time job working at a publishing company, and I was writing and teaching in my spare time. The hurdles of adulthood that had seemed so unconquerably high – housing, employment, security – were, if not entirely surmounted, a little more in reach. Until, that is, that email arrived and the bottom dropped out of my world. I was plunged into a Kafkaesque nightmare of eviction threats, legal counsel, and fighting daily to maintain a roof over my head, where the mere fact that I tried to argue my case put me in danger of going to court and losing my home.

The letting agent maintained that I owed them another six months' rent in advance; I countered that as I now had a stable job, there was no need for this condition. Besides, I didn't have nearly £3,000 lying around, and paying them upfront again would mean taking out a loan: a very stupid financial decision. Most damningly though, there was no legal justification for their demands – under Section 5 of the Housing Act 1988, the tenant has the right to remain in the property after the initial tenancy agreement has run out. Thereafter, unless either the landlord or the tenant wants to cancel the agreement, it is assumed the tenancy continues as normal and the tenant pays on a periodic (monthly) basis. I felt then that my desire to pay rent on a monthly basis (incidentally, just like the rest of my flatmates in the house) was, therefore, entirely reasonable, legal and just. By contrast, Bristol Residential Lettings' threatening demands that I pay another six months' rent in advance seemed baffling – why did it matter how I paid the rent as long as I did pay? – and decidedly dubious from a legal perspective.

Initially, I couldn't wrap my head around why they were so insistent I pay in advance (that first email being chased by a flurry of half a dozen others, all couched in similarly aggressive, threatening language). Then, the penny dropped: it was greed. Pure and simple. In their eyes, I was good for the money and therefore they were determined to use every avenue available to them to ensure I paid again, including, apparently, the threat

3

of eviction. I was taken aback by their callous and utterly mercenary attitude: to them, I wasn't a paying customer who had purchased a service and was entitled to rights and respect. Instead, I appeared to be an entirely disposable source of income – a voiceless and nameless figure on a balance sheet. Call me naive, but I was shocked by this attitude at first, and then determined to fight it all the harder. But in the course of my researches to help me in this fight, I discovered my case was no exception. Far from it: in Britain today, thousands, if not hundreds of thousands, are being failed by a system that appears rotten to the core and swiftly crumpling under unprecedented pressure.

What I discovered was a rental system in crisis. A system that is broken and unable to cope with both changing societal expectations and the weight of profound demographic pressures. A system that needs fixing, fast. But to be fixed, the nature of the problem has to be understood. This isn't easy: the reasons for the failures of our rental system are long-standing, multifaceted and tangled. But fixed it must be, as, according to numerous studies, ever more of us will be forced to rent in the future. The estate agency Knight Frank has predicted that by 2021, one in four British households will be private renters; of that number, a quarter will be families with young children.*

---

* Julia Kollewe, 'Quarter of households in UK will rent privately by end of 2021, says report', *The Guardian*, 12 June 2017, available at https://www.theguardian.com/money/2017/jun/12/one-in-four-households-in-britain-will-rent-privately-by-end-of-2021-says-report

The insecure and often squalid reality of shared housing is not something confined to my generation though, the notorious 'Generation Rent'. It is something that the elderly must also frequently suffer through. Countrywide recently reported that around one in twelve renters is a pensioner, and that £1 in £14 paid by tenants across Britain comes from a pensioner's wallet.* Imagine the sheer grinding bleakness of renting on a pension: watching your savings dwindle away, month by month, as your rent climbs with inflation and you are faced with little opportunity to earn back your carefully accumulated pension pot.

I began to realise that these concerns are amongst the most pressing weighing on our society today. Housing is a fundamental need. In the pyramid of human motivation, devised by the psychologist Abraham Maslow, security – stability and shelter – is placed second only to health, food and air. It is thus, in Maslow's equation, almost as central to human development as the air we breathe. One needs a stable platform – a secure, comfortable, affordable home – from which to aspire, to dream, to struggle and to succeed. This security is important to my generation, who are just beginning adult life, but it is central at any age. The failure, then, to provide that platform, that security, must be considered a society-wide moral defeat. It is unconscionable, and cannot be allowed to

* Rosemary Bennett, 'More pensioners forced to rent as housing crisis grows', *The Times*, 12 June 2017, available at https://www.thetimes.co.uk/article/more-pensioners-forced-to-rent-as-housing-crisis-grows-xfbkqnm0g

continue. The question must be: do we give in to that defeat, or do we attempt to improve the situation, potentially making the lives of thousands of British citizens happier, more comfortable and more secure? One way or another, in the next few years, that question must be answered – the stakes are too high for it to be ignored.

In Britain today, renters are second-class citizens. There are many reasons for this, but a compelling one is that there is an ingrained cultural attitude which equates home ownership with adulthood and success. It is an assumption that has lingered in Britain for a very long time. Expressions like 'the landed gentry' and the 'propertied class' demonstrate that, linguistically, the equivalence of property ownership with power and prestige has persisted for many hundreds of years. After all, before the Great Reform Act of 1832, voting was a privilege reserved for men over the age of twenty-one – and only if they owned property over a certain value. Working-class men were denied the vote because they could not demonstrate they owned property and therefore prove a stake in society. This historic prejudice against those without property has left a bitter legacy, encoding a reciprocity between property ownership and full participation in society.

This is a narrative that prospered during the Thatcherite boom years. An observation often attributed to Margaret Thatcher was, 'A man who, beyond the age of twenty-six, finds himself on a bus can count himself as a failure.' This holds true for home ownership as well: anyone above the age of twenty-six who does not own a home is considered a failure. Though it has often been denied, this presumption has been a tenet of Conservative wisdom for the last forty years and has helped to shape Tory housing policy. It is a policy, however, that has proved a failure. The swing to Labour at the last election and, in particular, towards the hard left of Corbynism, was, amongst other factors, a generational protest by Britain's youth. Despite gaining higher qualifications than their parents (the proportion of degrees awarded firsts, and of postgraduate qualifications among the workforce, has increased exponentially), this is a generation that feels locked out of adult life.

Cultural attitudes to home ownership are only part of the problem, though. A significant contributing factor is the runaway property prices of our major cities. This issue is, of course, tangled in the inequalities of globalised capitalism that has made a tiny minority enormously wealthy but has left a vast and increasingly vocal minority poor, impotent and angry. However, only so much anger can be directed against faceless, implacable global forces. Britain's rental crisis is mostly homegrown, and its solutions are often most effective when they are similarly indigenous and rooted in local communities. This does not mean, though, the government can delegate responsibility for fixing Britain's housing problems to community action groups – that's a tactic that has been relied on for far too long. At root, new legislation is needed to curb our overheated and iniquitous property market and to enshrine the rights of renters.

Fortunately, lawmakers across the political spectrum are waking up to this reality. Usually this realisation is driven by a local recognition of the acuteness of the problem. In London, for instance, Sadiq Khan has joined calls from campaign groups for the government to penalise foreign investors who use its property market as a convenient bolthole for (ill-gotten) gains. Earlier this year, he commented that, 'Londoners deserve to know the identity of those that own property in their city, and we have waited long enough for Government to fulfil its commitments.' Research by King's College London substantiates these claims. Academics found that while average house prices in England and Wales climbed steeply from £70,000 in 1999 to £215,000 in 2015, they would have risen to only £174,000 without the influx of foreign cash.* This means that potentially 28 per cent of house price growth is attributable to foreign investment. The government has begun to take action against this injustice: since 2017, it has used the Criminal Finances Act to seize assets it considers 'suspicious'. It may be carried out under the guise of national security, but such a move is an effective step towards controlling and curtailing a property market that has, for many, become a fantasy – utterly unobtainable.

---

* Ben Chapman, 'UK housing crisis: Influx of foreign cash boosted average property prices by a quarter, research finds', *The Independent*, 26 March 2018, available at https://www.independent.co.uk/news/business/news/house-prices-increase-foreign-buyers-money-property-market-kings-college-london-a8274106.html

There is evidence as well that the Conservatives, shocked out of complacency by the bruising collapse of their vote in the 2016 elections, are keen to pass renter-protecting legislation of the kind Labour and others on the left have been advocating for years. Two bills in particular stand out: the Fitness for Human Habitation Bill, and the Tenant Fees Bill. Both bills aim to address glaring oversights in current legislation and bring England and Wales' rental rights more in line with countries like Scotland and Germany. The first enshrines the right of the tenant to live in a house that is 'fit for human habitation'. Incredibly, such a provision is not part of existing tenant law, so if the boiler explodes, or faulty electrics zap the cat, there is precious little recourse for tenants.

Meanwhile, the second, the Tenant Fees Bill, ostensibly serves to address a similarly outrageous oversight – that letting agents can, and do, charge extortionate fees to carry out the simplest of tasks, such as the notorious 'admin fee'. But rather more importantly, it will also be a blow to those landlords and letting agents who see tenants as disposable and interchangeable sources of income. Over the course of my own struggles with Bristol Residential Lettings, I realised that this perception must have been at the heart of their intractability and unwillingness to be reasonable in the face of all common (and legal) sense. Unsurprisingly, the lettings industry has been reluctant for new laws to erode its traditional sense of entitlement over tenants, and curtail its more outrageous powers and egregious abuses. Both bills have faced considerable industry pressure: trade bodies have complained that the proposed Tenant Fees Bill will put some letting agents out of business. But both pieces of legislation have made good progress through parliament and there is every indication they will become law. Alongside a vital legal framework in which to ground complaints, these bills will also give tenants a sense of legitimacy and entitlement.

These bills are so critical because Britain is increasingly a renter's nation. In itself, this is no disaster. In many European countries, lifelong renting is the norm. My cousins live in Germany, and when we have visited, I have often been struck by the orderly beauty of their street and home. The lawns and drives that sweep down to the road are masterpieces of geometric precision; the road itself is immaculate and pothole-free; and the houses that sit behind it are solid, square and stand a companionable distance from their neighbours. Inside it's a similar story: the rooms are double-height and well proportioned; the windows are triple-glazed, and having ample storage space in a proper cellar goes without saying. Surely, you might ask, this luxury must cost? Well it does, to a certain extent. But my aunt and uncle aren't rich. He is a retired Army officer and she is a counsellor. Their neighbours are the same: professional, comfortable, but far from wealthy. Coming from England, this is a shock. We assume that having such light, space and comfort in one's home is the preserve of inherited money, or doing something unconscionable in the City, or striving and grafting for many years. That it is achievable on two modest salaries and a career of careful saving appears a kind of miracle. That it also all comes without being saddled with a monstrous mortgage, as many British first-time buyers are, seems to be truly astounding. But most Germans rent, like my aunt and uncle, and the idea of buying your home seems like an entirely unnecessary difficulty.

Contrast this with the situation in England. Here, there is a strong narrative, long intrinsic to English culture and enshrined as creed in the Thatcherite years, that buying property is a tangible step towards adulthood and maturity. It is a crucial stage in the trajectory of job–marriage–house– kids–retirement–death. The trouble with this narrative, though, is twofold. First, it enacts a form of social shaming. Those who don't own homes by, say, their mid-thirties experience a creeping anxiety: 'Am I an adult? How can I afford to buy? I don't want a mortgage, but all my friends are settling down and getting one. Maybe I should as well?' If left unchecked, this anxiety is liable to develop into a roar, adding to existing burdens of stress, anxiety and depression which frequent studies have told us are endemic in our society.

Second, it is nonsense. Whilst it's true that most people would prefer to own their own home rather than rent – the 2010 British Social Attitudes survey found that 86 per cent would choose to buy, with the greatest preference unsurprisingly among eighteen- to thirty-four-year-olds – this survey reflected *preference*, not reality.* The difference is critical. The growing numbers renting year on year – thirty-year-olds are half as likely to own their own home as their grandparents were at the same age – suggest that these desires do not reflect real life. Combine these statistics with what the financial journalist Agnès Poirier describes as 'home ownership hysteria', and you capture the current fevered pitch of the housing debate. It's a perfect storm of stratospheric debt, acute social pressure, and a convenient smokescreen that deflects public anger around renting and allows the government to be *seen* to be doing a lot – by, for instance, promising new houses – but achieving very little.

Poirier, furthermore, detects conspiracy in this status quo: by encouraging private debt, including mortgages and credit cards, the government ensures the economy stays vigorous and GDP continues to climb. Yet this laissez-faire attitude damages private finances and public attitudes. The British are amongst the most indebted people in the world: the Office for Budgetary Responsibility forecasts household debt in 2019 to be at 182 per cent of disposable income. This indebtedness not only means that the average household is built on terrible financial precariousness, but also does incalculable social harm. By seeding the narrative that home ownership is a prerequisite of settling and maturity, irrespective of the appalling debt it involves,

---

* 'Homes, planning and changing policies', British Social Attitudes, available at http://www.bsa.natcen.ac.uk/media/38952/bsa28_8housing.pdf

a counter-narrative is established: that renters are immature, flighty, and disposable. It is this narrative that has infiltrated every aspect of the rental market. And it is this narrative that must be challenged, legislatively and culturally, if the rental system in Britain is to be improved.

To return briefly to Germany: contrast their existing renting legislation with our own. In Germany, fixed-term rents are commonly for two or three years, often longer; here, they are six months, on average. In Germany, after the fixed term has expired, the *minimum* notice period a landlord can give is three months, a figure which rises depending on length of stay in the property. Here, it is two months, regardless of how long the renter has considered the property their home. In Germany, landlords cannot evict without a valid reason. Here, the 'no fault' procedure, under Section 21 of the Housing Act 1988, allows landlords to evict without cause. It is this notorious 'no fault' procedure that threw my own situation into such sharp and panicked relief. I was apologetically informed by Shelter, the housing advice charity, that if I wanted to contest an eviction on the grounds that the letting agents were being unfair and stubborn, I could be liable to be taken to court simply for 'being a nuisance'. If I lost, I would also be liable for the agents' legal fees. They had seen similar cases all too often – an appalling indictment of how stacked the odds are against renters in England and Wales.

This is not to suggest that Germany's renting legislation is spotless – horror stories of tenants being served notice for failing to recycle correctly, shopped in by panoptic neighbours, are rife. But it is illustrative of what could reasonably be done to ensure that renting is not regarded as a social and financial burden but is considered simply as what it is: one of a number of ways of fulfilling the fundamental human need for shelter.

It is unlikely, though, that attitudes will alter unless economics and legislation change. For some, that is happening too slowly, so they are taking matters into their own hands, as I found during my investigations. I met Tony Crofts, founder of the campaign group Abolish Empty Office Buildings (AEOB). He told me, 'We're starting a people's revolution, providing housing where it's needed. The shrinking provision of social housing is a national disgrace. Local community organisations are the strength. They take up the slack where the government has failed. We put social good above profit.' When the Conservative-led coalition came to power in 2010 and began its austerity-driven hollowing out of social services, a multitude of community action groups sprang up to take up the slack. Research by Shelter found that provision of social housing completed in 2013/14 has shrunk by 23 per cent since 2011/12; in addition, the Child Poverty Action Group calculated that cumulative cuts to social welfare provision and child benefits have been £22 billion annually since 2010.* The effects of this welfare holocaust on communities have

---

* 'Families on the brink: welfare reform in London', Child Poverty Action Group, available at http://www.cpag.org.uk/sites/default/files/Families%20on%20the%20brink_welfare%20reform%20in%20London.pdf

been profound. However, it has meant that major cities like Bristol are now hotbeds of innovative, community-led solutions to critical issues like housing where the government cannot – or will not – take responsibility.

The AEOB illustrates this trend: founded by Tony Crofts, it sprang out of a meeting at a local church which had gathered to discuss the crisis of affordable housing in Bristol. One issue in particular resonated: the ranks upon ranks of empty office buildings that litter the Bristol skyline and yet contribute nothing to the local economy. They were purely retained as investments, precipitating a flurry of speculation. Bristol's situation is indicative of a national issue: it has 2.2 million square feet of empty office space, yet 13,000 people waiting for social housing.* For Tony and others at AEOB, this model is not just unsustainable, it is deeply unjust: 'Developers with lots of resources can sit on empty buildings for years, purely to make the highest profit. We feel this is immoral when there is a real need for affordable housing.'

AEOB decided to tackle the issue themselves. In 2014, they raised funds to buy an office block and began converting it into affordable housing. They financed this purchase by selling investor shares, and through a mortgage from a local bank, Triodos – one of a growing number of providers who specialise

---

* 'Bristol's Housing Festival aims to showcase potential housing solutions – and it is just one of a growing number of local innovators', Bristol Property Live, available at https://bristolpropertylive.co.uk/innovative-solutions-to-the-housing-crisis/

in ethical and environmental lending. The project continued apace and opened in 2016. It now houses six affordable flats alongside a laundry, community space and a workshop that is rented to local artists and artisans, providing a space for them to craft and showcase their wares. Even though rents were maintained at local housing authority rates (something AEOB hopes to change), demand far outstripped supply: over a hundred potential tenants were interviewed, and places were allocated on 'genuine housing need'. Such a system is vulnerable to prejudice and nepotism, cynics might complain. The AEOB, though, is bullish. As director Elinor Kershaw stated at the opening of the Battens Lane site, 'It pained us to see the reality of homeless people sleeping under "To Let" signs of vast unused office spaces. The injustice and inequality is just unnecessary.'

Nationwide, it seems many agree. Stung by palpable evidence of the failures of our housing market, communities feel forced to take action themselves. Alongside planning a second site, the AEOB are busy reaching out to other groups across the country, spreading ideas, funds, plans and coordinating political pressure. Tony's 'people's revolution' is moving at the speed of an email or a tweet, springing up around the country. This renaissance in community action is both encouraging and a stinging judgement on the inadequacies of our housing system. The AEOB are now working with the Bristol City Council and with other local groups like the Bristol Community Land Trust (BCLT) to meet the city's chronic need for affordable housing. But both community action groups and local councils are starved of funding and deeply vulnerable to the fickleness of the government, where policy appears to be dictated by the latest scandal as much as by the need to address slow-burning concerns like housing.

Progress, though, is being made. There is a gradual recognition that simply promising to build new houses is not enough: developers must be held accountable for their impacts on the local community. In particular, they need to invest in more affordable housing. Ingraining this requirement within our housing law is an effective first step. In fact, it is a hallmark policy of Bristol's Labour council, who have promised to deliver 2,000 new homes a year – including 800 affordable – by 2020. The grounds for affordability are, admittedly, not high. It means 80 per cent of the market rate, which in a city like Bristol, with a frenetic property market, still locks a significant proportion out. But it is a start. Certainly, it's an improvement on the efforts of the previous, independent, council. Darren Jones, MP for Bristol North West, told me that the previous mayor, George Ferguson, left a grand legacy of 'twelve new homes'.

At the last election, Labour put forward what it termed a 'New Deal' for housing. Borrowing its title from Roosevelt's plan to reinvigorate America's post-Depression economy, it promised to be a 'radical and credible plan' that would 'draw a line under the failings of the past seven years, and the shortcomings of the last forty years'. As Labour were not elected, that plan remains rhetoric. The New Deal for housing is promising, though. It would mean the biggest council house building programme in more than thirty years, new rights for renters (including an inflation cap on rent rises and making three-year minimum tenancies the norm), and the implementation of new 'build on it or lose it' injunctions, giving local authorities the power to compel developers to actually build on their land. These injunctions would be further enforced with compulsory purchase orders: councils could purchase brownfield land at close to market rate, provided that land is earmarked for affordable housing. All excellent, tangible steps to reversing the cruelty of shrinking social housing provision and the rental crisis it has engendered.

But, for now, they are only promises. Our civic duty, if we wish to see these policies become law, is to elect a government that prioritises them and then, critically, hold that government to account. In the meantime, organisations like AEOB and BCLT continue to serve a vital role and deserve our unconditional support. They need help in terms of time, money and experience. Their work is inestimably valuable in holding communities together and ensuring that none get left behind. As Darren Jones told me, 'Community is central. It's heartbreaking to see these out-of-town developments being built – we need local solutions to local problems.' When challenged, will the bonds of community clench tighter, or will they loosen, fray and come apart, leaving us stranded?

In today's climate, it is a malicious falsehood to suggest that renting is a lifestyle choice – and this myth has done terrible damage to our society. It has ensured that the poorest among us live a perilous hand-to-mouth existence. It has also engendered a silent split in our communities between those who, through family wealth or savings, can afford to get onto the property ladder at an early age, and those who cannot. Lifelong renters are condemned to meeting the expectations of adult life – a stable job, a partner, family – while being bound to the insecurity of fickle landlords and greedy letting agents. Shattering this apartheid is not going to be easy or quick. Its causes are, as we have seen, deep-rooted, and are caught up in inherited cultural assumptions as much as market economics. Legislation, such as that which is currently going through parliament, will do much to break these assumptions, giving tenants greater agency, exposure and validity. However, they cannot do the work alone. That is why community action groups like AEOB and BCLT are so critical.

As for my own struggles with Bristol Residential Lettings: eventually, they caved. After numerous letters back and forth, frequent trips to seek legal advice and even more frequent sleepless nights, they gave up and allowed me to pay my rent monthly. It hasn't altered the iniquitous power dynamic of our relationship, nor done much to rewrite the wider narrative around renting. Alongside making me a little cynical and jaded, it has convinced me of an important fact: the failures of Britain's rental crisis, though firmly embedded and complex, have, at their heart, a single cause – a failure of compassion and imagination.

It is this failure of compassion and imagination that has allowed politicians to neglect the fact that renting might not be a choice. Or that for many, homelessness is a cold, ever-present fear. It is a failure that has allowed unscrupulous letting agents and landlords to emphasise profit above all, forgetting that their properties are homes for individuals and families eager to settle down and live their lives in peace. And it is these failures, these cultural blind spots that, taken together, have done incalculable harm. Empathy should be pre-eminent in the construction of a modern, caring twenty-first-century society. But Britain's housing crisis demonstrates that, at least historically, this has manifestly not been the case. For too long, we have lived with a narrative that has disenfranchised and demonised renters. As a result, we have some of the most woefully inadequate tenant-protection rights in Europe. If we wish to combat this narrative – and we must, as it seems that ever more of us will be lifelong renters – then, above all, our politics and policy must be rooted in empathy. Acts of imagination are therefore as important as Acts of Parliament. Until we can imagine ourselves in the shoes of another, we cannot begin to walk the path that we, as a society, should aspire to.

RUSH

Liv Little and Charlie Brinkhurst-Cuff

Content warning: mental health, racism

We've communicated in a rush of text messages since we first met in the summer of 2015. We were still at university and eager to start the life we knew was waiting for us. This was the summer that *gal-dem* was born; a sweaty meeting on a hot day in Brixton Village, south-west London, a cluster of young women of colour (WoC) drawn together by an absence we'd all felt, whether that be in our personal lives, in our studies, or in the media. We weren't just seeking out representation, we were seeking a community of WoC who operated in the same busy way that we did.

Since then, *gal-dem* has blossomed into a magazine and creative collective exclusively run and produced by WoC, and while it's brought many triumphs, it's also revealed a new truth: the existence of Rushing Women of Colour Syndrome. In our minds, a rushing woman of colour is someone working in the creative industries who has at least two Instagram accounts and several email inboxes with notifications popping up on her phone – rarely with an interval. She's trying to maintain good relationships with her friends (who probably haven't seen her in a while), appear relaxed, but with a suitable amount of concern, upkeep a burgeoning social life and attend the most important cultural events, chase up the brands and businesses who still haven't paid her for that job she completed what feels like an age ago, see her family, find and maintain a great sex life, secure somewhere affordable to live in an overpriced city and remain (just about) sane. She might be constantly stressed, or struggling with anxiety issues, but attempting to keep it all together.

To be clear, much like imposter syndrome – also common in WoC, who negate any external evidence that contradicts the belief that they are unintelligent or unworthy of their achievements – Rushing Women of Colour Syndrome is not a clinically recognised psychological condition. But it is an incredibly useful term that can be used to encapsulate just how tough it can be for busy young WoC like ourselves. We're surrounded by women who move at a hundred miles an hour, rarely taking time to breathe and check in on themselves. Don't get us wrong, we're thriving career-wise because of it, but even when we love what we do, the burden of expectation to prove our worth above that of our white counterparts is only exacerbated by the intersections of race, gender, class and sexuality.

This is also why it must be viewed as a separate entity from 'Rushing Woman's Syndrome', the original incarnation of this theory, which was coined in 2012 by Dr Libby Weaver, a nutritional biologist (someone who investigates how the body responds to food, essentially). Her argument was that constantly being in a rush has biochemical and emotional effects, including hormone-based health challenges such as infertility, endometriosis, polycystic ovarian syndrome and debilitating periods or menopause, and that overall, women's mental and physical health are deteriorating due to them taking on domestic duties, employment and emotional burdens all at once.

And the stress is real. As women of colour, we often place unrealistic expectations upon ourselves; if we aren't killing ourselves for the job, imposter syndrome kicks in and we are left questioning how we've gained a seat at the table which we've worked hard to acquire. Personally, we've suffered from various stress- and work-induced ailments, from anxiety, alopecia and week-long migraines to repetitive strain injury from too much typing and texting. Emma Dabiri, a social historian, BBC presenter and writer, reflects on a recent conversation she had with a busy black woman. 'She said: "Babylon has a way of always keeping you busy," and I was like, "Rah, that's it you know." But it's kind of a paradox. The constant grind distracts you, and in many ways prevents you from enjoying this thing called life, but what's the alternative? Babylon is one big old trap.'

We've heard horror stories about young WoC on diversity schemes who've had to sit in meetings as a token brown body so that their company can appear diverse. Charlie was once asked to be in a semi-nude photoshoot while on an internship at a media company and almost agreed out of awkwardness;

when she eventually refused, they hired in a black model. Liv's seen *gal-dem*'s name put on £64k funding bids without permission. Women of colour are told that they aren't looking cheery enough, or that their hairstyles aren't appropriate. People rake their fingers through our afros, or comment inappropriately on our traditional dress in office environments. These racial microaggressions build up into something even more toxic when combined with our incredibly busy schedules. As revealed by Marcel Vige, head of equality improvement for mental health charity Mind, black women face an increased risk in terms of their mental health. This is the crux of our argument: that our Rushing Woman's Syndrome is exacerbated so much by our race that it is worthy of its own terminology.

We do appreciate that within some strands of the commentariat our proposed syndrome might look like a divisive method of identification. 'Oppression Olympics,' they might cry, or, 'I'm a man, and I feel constantly rushed too.' In austerity Britain, WoC suffer due to cuts more than any other demographic. New analysis tells us that by 2020, the effect of all the tax, public services and benefit cuts since 2010 will continue to hit black and Asian women the hardest, and will ultimately mean that their average individual income will be lower than it would have been if these changes hadn't been made.*

---

* Maya Goodfellow, 'A toxic concoction means women of colour are hit hardest by austerity', *The Guardian*, 28 November 2016, available at https://www.theguardian.com/commentisfree/2016/nov/28/toxic-concoction-women-colour-pay-highest-price-austerity

At university, we might be slightly overrepresented, but anecdotal evidence and news reports suggest that black and Asian women are being left open to systemic racism in the form of Prevent and having 'monkey' and 'nigga' written on their bananas. In the criminal justice system, twice the number of black women are imprisoned for drug offences than comparative white women.

And not only are we battling against the very real impacts of the Conservatives' rambunctious determination to destroy public services and reduce benefits, we younger WoC are growing up in the internet age. Instagram has become a way of life – in some areas of the creative industries, a necessity in getting a job. It's no coincidence that every time Liv deletes Instagram while suffering from a severe spell of chronic, stress-induced migraines, her headaches disappear along with her neurotic need to check likes and notifications.

The most frightening part about all of this is that our generation is not the one who will be most impacted by the pitfalls that come with social media. Our younger sisters, nieces and cousins will have these tools and platforms throughout their angsty teenage years – telling them that they are too thick, too thin, too dark or altogether too real. Whereas age might enable us to cut through the bullshit and decipher what is (semi) real versus what has been carefully constructed, the eleven-, twelve- and thirteen-year-olds growing up on Instagram, Facebook and Twitter may not be so selective.

This isn't to say that social media isn't without its benefits. Alongside our own platform of *gal-dem*, we've noticed a burgeoning community of young women who actively use their social media to discuss the painful realities of life. Women who use their online platforms to speak up and say: 'I'm not OK today, sis, how are you?' But again, the internet forces you to always be *on*, and rushing. To send that next DM, email, post that picture. And when you need to use it, as we definitely have done, to find a community of people like you, the pressure to remain rushing doesn't cease.

You may have noticed that it's difficult to find research on people of colour, let alone WoC as a group. Whilst intersectionality has become the word on everybody's lips over the last few years, this remains largely unreflected in political and academic discourse. For example, in her book *Why I'm No Longer Talking to White People About Race*, Reni Eddo-Lodge references the fact that she can only find research on the prospects for black men within higher education, due to the limited study on the experiences of black women. At university Liv encountered a similar difficulty in researching Conservative MPs who were also WoC. Statistics on people of colour and women were continuously classified as two distinct categories.

As said by Tharni Vasavan, writing for women's health organisation Global Women Connected: 'Treating women as a single cohort or voting group is erroneous. Women's lived experiences, opportunities and pathways to employment are very different depending on geography, socio-economic status, ethnicity and age. And those issues of intersectionality are largely overlooked.' Just as imposter syndrome has entered our regular lexicon, identifying Rushing Women of Colour Syndrome could be a necessary tool which will enable us to continue a vital conversation around an under-researched and little understood demographic.

Despite the unrelenting cries of 'divisive behaviour' that emerge when attempting to render the separation of BAME (Black, Asian and minority ethnic) and women from major political analysis, the most effective way to better understand how economic, social and cultural factors specifically impact WoC is to create a frame of language in which to do so. If the majority of statistical analyses fail to adopt the language which we, as WoC, use to explain the very layered and complex processes that define our existence within Britain today, mainstream discourse will continue to follow.

So how do we stop rushing, and do we even want to? With the explosion of self-representation happening on social media and beyond, it's no wonder that in recent years a dialogue has opened up amongst WoC on the impact of balancing multiple tasks and jobs. Sometimes these conversations are remarkably positive. We'll speak about all the things we've stuffed into one day, and laugh about the fact that we're using our toilet breaks to respond to emails, which leaves us wondering whether our bosses know what we are up to, or just assume that we are suffering from an overactive bladder. Neela Choudhury-Reid, a social media strategist for Young Turks, manager and video director, tells us about how she never wastes time. 'I often find people ask me how I find the time to do so many things, but I think we have a lot of time we don't use,' she says. 'I've written pitches on the Tube using the free WiFi, sent off strategies I've written in the bath, and closed deals with clients while on the loo.'

And Nicole Crentsil, who founded Unmasked Women (a platform which brings black women together to discuss mental health), informs us that despite having multiple projects on the go at once, she's rejected the 'struggling creative narrative', which justifies remaining forever burnt out. This is an incredibly important and pertinent point which we often utter when justifying our constant fatigue – we're young and full of energy, so it doesn't matter, right? For Nicole, despite initially adopting the narrative that she is always busy and burning the candle at both ends, she's moved towards an acceptance that her wellbeing should be prioritised. It's easy to speak about self-care, but how do we go about practising it? She says: 'I've openly discussed my burnout and vowed not to have another because it's crap. Feeling burnt out is beyond "being tired"; your body totally shuts down. Computer actually says, "No, babes." Imagine rebooting Windows 95, it just takes ages. That's exactly the process.'

As the months have ticked on by, and our schedules have seemingly only got busier, we do encourage each other to take a break every now and then, especially when one of us has fallen ill or is having a tough time at work. But there is another manic side to us that relishes the hard work. Although we wouldn't want to encourage people to live like we do, it is really fucking exciting to always have something on the go. To be creating and communicating things nonstop. In an ideal world, both of us would keep on rushing until we get too old to stagger around. But with things as they are, I think it's likely that at some point we'll need to take a real break.

Because, you know, it's hard out here for a woman of colour.

GENDER DIVIDES
Kaja Brown

Content warning: gender dysphoria, sexism, transphobia

Sebastian stretched, showing off his height and muscles, before leaning against the wall. He stared at the back of Moriarty's head. 'So how are we going to get out of this one?' he asked causally, folding his arms.

Moriarty clicked his neck and looked back. 'Don't worry, I have a few tricks up my sleeve.'

Sebastian grinned, pushing his sunglasses into his hair before—

'Anyone home?'

With the slam of the front door and Mum's familiar shout, I was dragged back to reality. I looked away from my phone and into the huge mirror which sat across from me, against the dining room wall.

'Just me,' I said, reflecting on just how true this was.

Because I could never be Sebastian Moran. It's not that I wanted to be him, specifically, but I liked the idea of being brave, strong, respected, rugged and manly – the things I felt as a male character, which aren't attributed to the female gender I've been assigned. As much as I enjoyed role-playing as Sebastian Moran on Wattpad, the accompanying feeling of loss when I logged out was painful. The sanctuary of the online world was too much to resist.

What is online role-play? There are different forms, but the one I'm most familiar with is creating a fictional profile on alternative social networks, such as Wattpad or Tumblr, and interacting with other players through online conversations. Often you create storylines and bounce off one another. Situations develop just as they do in real life, including dialogue and actions. It can be a lot of fun. It's a bit like an interactive book you're writing; a world you can create and live in.

It's also one of the only socially accepted ways I know for young people exploring their identity to step into the shoes of the opposite gender.

This isn't the reason everyone does it – a lot of people are there purely for the fun of it. But for some online role-players, it can mean a lot more. I used to participate almost every day with my friends on Wattpad. I had a fictional character called Sebastian Moran, inspired by fan fiction and the Sherlock Holmes books, and I absolutely loved role-playing as him. As Sebastian, a strong man, I interacted with other role-players, handled all sorts of challenges and adventures, and explored the realms of everyday adult life (such as buying a pet tiger, or going to see a play with your, er, eccentric partner).

This hobby was born of my love for the *Sherlock* fandom. This fandom is a large group of people dedicated to expressing their love of Sherlock Holmes. Having been given a sparing number of BBC episodes to watch, the fandom often finds its kicks elsewhere. They use fan fiction, fan art and role-play as ways to expand the world in which we have been so absorbed. It was a fun world to be a part of, but when I first got into it, I didn't know how much it would make me re-evaluate my life.

It fascinates me how the experience of role-playing can give the participant a window into a different gender, and that this can provide a space for role-players to explore questions society hasn't previously let us consider.

I had always experienced gender differently to some people, and until recently I didn't understand why. When I was little I used to daydream about living in fantasy worlds. In these daydreams I would be a pirate going on adventures, or a supernatural being living in a world of magic.

In all of these I was male.

My family challenged me on why I didn't imagine myself as female. That's when I realised this wasn't the norm. I used to play imagination games with my friends too. When we made up scenarios and acted them out, I almost always favoured a male role. I used to think gender was something that happened to other people, a weird conspiracy adults had going on which I didn't really want to be a part of. I wasn't girly, or a tomboy, or anything else people tried to tag me with. I was me. Kaja. It got harder as I got older.

'Why don't you ever fantasise about being a girl?' they would ask.

Because in my fantasies I was strong. I was brave, bold, powerful and respected, and these weren't things I associated with being a girl. Why is this? What is this divide I could sense so early on? I didn't know, but I knew it was the reason I enjoyed role-playing as Sebastian so much.

Suddenly, as a man, I was allowed to be all the things I felt inside – although this was also limited. I used to wonder if I was transgender, but sometimes I love being feminine and wearing dresses and make-up. I realised being male would have its own limitations. Being a man, it's not socially acceptable to wear make-up or dresses or to feel beautiful and pretty. You're expected to be tough, noble and emotionally boarded-up. So I didn't want to become a man. But I didn't want to be limited by the term 'woman'.

In the UK, women and men are far more equal than they were, say, fifty years ago. But that doesn't mean there aren't still divisions. Although women can now wear trousers to work and aren't seen as quite so 'weak' or 'feeble' as they once were, they're still expected to care a lot about how they look and to not apply for physical jobs or be muscly and strong. Men still can't wear dresses or skirts without the threat of being laughed at in public, and although it's more acceptable for men to cook and clean and take on roles assigned to women in the past, they are limited by how they feel they should act. These expectations and limitations are harmful to everyone.

So why are men and women treated differently? Why do we have different expectations of ourselves? A lot of people think there are intrinsic differences, yet studies show we're more similar than we think, and that these divides are sociologically enforced.

'Of the many influences on how we view men and women, media are the most pervasive and one of the most powerful,' Dr Julia T. Wood states in her book *Gendered Lives: Communication, Gender, and Culture.* She argues that the way in which men and women are presented in the media harmfully affects our daily lives. Wood points out: 'Typically men are portrayed as active, adventurous, powerful, sexually aggressive and largely uninvolved in human relationships,' while on the other hand, women are depicted as 'sex objects who are usually young, thin, beautiful, passive, dependent, and often incompetent and dumb'.

This is, of course, a pattern that is endlessly projected on our screens, most prominently in the kind of big budget action movies that attract the largest audiences. Almost always, men are seen as independent, strong and admirable characters with their own purposes, whereas women are used as romantic partners and are not remotely as complex as the men. Action movies are especially worth noting in this, as they are primarily directed at teenagers vulnerable to influence, and so should really be careful about how they are portraying their characters. Instead, they often hyper-feminise or hyper-masculinise their characters to a ridiculous degree.

Take Harley Quinn in *Suicide Squad*. She was completely dependent on the Joker, and sexualised enormously in the outfit she was wearing. I think it is fine for women to wear whatever they want, but the jailer's reaction to her putting on said outfit shows how the movie wanted the audience to find it sexy. Furthermore, the whole idea in that film that she was a smart psychologist who was then somehow liberated by an abusive man, the Joker, to become his brainwashed, devoted minion is problematic. Or let's look at Black Widow in *Avengers Assemble* – she spends a lot of her airtime flirting with the other Avengers and is used more as a sex symbol than a person.

The ironic thing is that these are meant to be strong female characters, for women to feel empowered by – whereas many of my friends and I have simply felt disappointed by how they've been portrayed. In a lot of these movies women also have to seduce men to get what they want, whereas men use their strength rather than their appearance. What message is this sending out to growing teenagers?

Wood, meanwhile, also points out that women are underrepresented in the media, which 'falsely implies that men are the cultural standard and women are unimportant or invisible'. This is a clear problem. If you watch any TV quiz show, you'll almost always find there is one token woman sat next to five or so men. In action films, again, Marvel has failed to make any solely about a female character, and DC have only provided two. I spend a lot of time watching TV. I've watched hundreds of movies. If we are constantly seeing men presented in only 'male' clothing acting typically 'manly' and women in only 'feminine' clothing acting 'womanly', then we will accept that this is the norm. For a child growing up wanting to be strong and independent, you can see why such depictions of women put me off. This can have a negative impact on men too, as this portrayal of hyper-masculinity is unrealistic and restrictive.

Neuroscientist Cordelia Fine explains how watching these representations of men and women can be harmful. As she writes in her book *Delusions of Gender*, 'The principle behind learning in associative memory is simple: as its name suggests, what is picked up are associations in the environment.' We have a type of memory which accepts things to be true that are associated with each other. If you repeatedly see women hoovering in adverts, then this part of your memory accepts that this is what women do. 'Most likely, it picks up and responds to cultural patterns in society, media and advertising, which may well be reinforcing implicit associations you don't consciously endorse,' says Fine. So even if you believe in gender equality and deconstructing gender stereotypes, you could still be subconsciously endorsing traditional, ingrained gender roles based on what you see around you.

Fine goes on to discuss how stereotypes about men and women secured by 'associative memory' can then impact negatively on us as we try to fit into the cultural norm. Associative memory also means we expect different stereotypes of others. This can be harmful if those expectations turn into judgements we then voice.

The media is more harmful than we think. But of course, not all our societal expectations come from it. Some are enforced by one another in day-to-day life, and they start young. Children are taught there is a different way for girls and boys to behave by the clothes they're put in and the toys they're given. This can be restrictive and affect how they behave in later life. For instance, girls are often given 'girl toys' such as dolls, whereas boys are given 'boy toys' such as trucks. Segregating toys this way actually delays their development, since different toys teach them important skills. These toy differences also teach them from an early age that girls and boys should like different things, which is harmful for children who don't fit in with this rule.

This reminds me of a video the BBC produced in 2017 called *No More Boys and Girls: Can Our Kids Go Gender Free?* The video showed how babies were treated differently by adults depending on what gender the adults thought they were. Girl babies were put in male clothes and taken care of by an adult who thought they were male. The adult proceeded to give them toys that are typically thought of as boy toys, which are toys that increase spatial awareness and physical confidence, but not the dolls which are better for learning care skills. The boys that were dressed as girls were given typically girl toys, which also limits their learning through play. When asked about it after, the adults hadn't even realised they were giving the toys to the babies based on stereotypes, which shows just how deeply ingrained in society this behaviour is, and just how much adults treat children differently from an early age depending on their gender. This is bound to influence how they see themselves and how they grow in life.

So why do we give children different toys based on gender? You could argue that children have natural preferences for different toys. However, Christia Spears Brown, author of *Parenting Beyond Pink and Blue* and associate professor at the University of Kentucky, disagrees. 'Gender preferences for toys only show up after children learn about their gender. Babies show no preference,' she writes. In fact, Brown argues that in experiments, if you gave a girl a truck and showed her other girls playing with it, she would see it as a 'girl toy' and play with it herself. But it's because of social pressures that children find these divides early on. Children are also given superheroes and princesses to play with, which are arguably symbols of hyper-femininity and hyper-masculinity. If children see these figures and imagine being them, then they're being told that they should look different too.

We're told that boys naturally like cars and girls don't. But if girls are never given cars to play with, how do we know if they like them or not? I remember as a child I liked to play with cars, but I could only have fun with them at playgroup, since no one at home had thought to give me one. I loved racing them and enjoyed it just as much as playing with a doll's house, if not more. I'm lucky no one decided I was acting abnormally and took this away from me. However, often this is the case. My grandmother talks of when she ran a playgroup, and how a little boy liked to play with the dolls, but his father forbade him. This kind of negative reaction from adults changes the way we think and resonates with us later in life.

It seems that a lot of the differences between males and females are socially enforced and not hardwired into our DNA. But are there biological differences that translate into a 'male' or 'female' brain? Are they so distinct as to bring about the gender divide we see in our society?

The human brain is a complex organ we still know little about. The relationship between consciousness, brain synapses and behaviour is still debated today and neuroscientists, although they have made progress, are a long way off from completely understanding exactly how it all works. One of the reasons for this is that every brain is unique. This diversity is why we shouldn't gender brains, according to neuroscientist Professor Daphna Joel.

Professor Joel's interest in the gendered brain was sparked by a study that suggested different levels of stress can change the gender of the brain. There are systems in the hippocampus (the part of the brain that's associated with stress) which were thought to look one way for women and one way for men. However, it was found that after fifteen minutes of stress, the structure of this pattern changed from typically 'male' to 'female', or vice versa. So why is it called male or female if it regularly alternates? Professor Joel argues it shouldn't be, and that language around the brain should be gender-neutral. Or, if it has to be gendered, then it should be described as intersex.

Professor Joel goes on to argue that all babies are born with 'intersex' brains: a mosaic of male and female qualities that change throughout life. Not only does the stress a pregnant mother feels impact on the gender of parts of an unborn baby's brain, but Joel also found that few brains have overtly female or male characteristics. Professor Joel conducted a study in which more than 1,400 MRIs were analysed, and it was concluded that there was extensive overlap between female and male attributes.

So, if our brains are demonstrating both 'female' and 'male' parts, which also change throughout life, why should we have to behave in a distinctly male or female way? Why can't we behave as a unique mosaic which reflects our kaleidoscope brains?

That's why online role-play can be such a haven. It's a space where young people can finally (figuratively) play with both dolls and trucks, or be both beautiful and handsome, strong and feminine in different characters.

Sebastian looked at his reflection, brushing a hand through his long hair before applying some eyeliner. Moriarty came clicking into the bathroom in five-inch heels and Sebastian smirked at him in the mirror. Jim put his hands on his hips.

'Now I'm as tall as you.'

Sebastian puckered his lips and applied some scarlet lipstick. 'And nearly as beautiful.' He winked, knowing full well he'd have to pay for that.

My portrayal of Sebastian cried, wrestled with his enemies, sometimes wore make-up, did push-ups every morning and had long hair. I didn't allow the societal rules which dictate our lives into my online world. I was making up my own rules, and that's why I, and a lot of others I think, loved it. But eventually I felt I'd got too old for online role-play and fell out of the Sherlock fandom.

Then I saw just how cold the real world is.

Recently, I watched a YouTuber who spoke of how one man flirted with her, then thought she might be a man. He got very aggressive, throwing things at her, trying to find out which gender she was. He cared so much about our societal divides and his own masculinity being challenged that he was willing to hurt her. In *Boys Don't Cry*, a film based on a true story, a transgender man is beaten, raped and killed when another man finds out he was born with a female body. Presenting as a different gender to the one you've been assigned isn't accepted by everyone yet.

All because we expect people born of one gender to look a certain way, and of another to look different.

All because the world is still divided, even if our brains and feelings are not.

Why can't we change these expectations like young

people are in the online fanfic world? Maybe we should bring some of these qualities into our lives. We need to seriously consider how to make it safer for people to present however they want to in public without fear. And that starts with accepting, understanding and supporting them. Some teenagers have been doing it online anyway for a long time, so why not accept it in real life?

Schools also need to be a safe space, because it's important for children that if they are to develop equally, then they need to be able to play with whatever toys they want and dress however they want. However, even young children who want to explore different aspects of gender are often victimised and bullied, by adults as well as their peers. Just last year there was a case where a couple wanted to sue a school for letting a boy wear a dress. This sort of thing makes me upset; why can't they just let this child be? Schools should allow children to be whoever they want; to learn, explore and grow.

I have a very strong philosophy, which is this: as long as you are not harming anyone, do whatever you like.

If a boy is wearing make-up, or has cried after something happened, or a woman is wearing men's clothes and just held the door open for you – so what? If they want to identify as genderqueer, non-binary, trans, or something different, what is the problem? Who are they harming? Why can't we just let people be people instead of making everyone fit into being a girl or boy?

★

Sebastian reached up and rubbed the last of the tears from his eyes, getting mud and blood on his face. Moriarty squeezed his hand beside him.

'You alright now, love?'

The wind played with Sebastian's tangled hair and he smirked up at the stars. It was all a game, he knew, and lying on the rooftop he felt a lot more alive than he had in a while. Finally, he was with someone who understood.

'I feel free,' he said, wincing slightly at the cliché. He cracked his dirt-speckled knuckles before laying them behind his head. That's all anyone wanted. To be understood. After all, Sebastian thought, we're only human.

Ultimately, I am Kaja. I am a beautifully complex person just like each and every one of us. I am strong, girly, muscled, pretty, brave. Sometimes I cry and sometimes I lift weights, sometimes I wear make-up and sometimes I let my armpit hair grow. I would be as happy doing a physical job like being a builder as I would washing up and cooking. I am a person with many sides to me that reflect my mosaic brain. Gender doesn't have to divide me. Nor anyone else.

★

Dedicated to my grandad, Martin Brown. Without him, who knows if I'd be writing.

THE MODERN FAIRY TALE OF MENTAL HEALTH AND 'JUST ASKING FOR HELP'

Ailsa Fineron

Content warning: suicide, drug overdose, mental health

Back home. Back in Scotland. Back with my mum in the GP surgery where I got my jabs when I was three, all chubby cheeks, box fringe and black teardrop eyes. The seating is the same clinical green, cushioned plastic bench. It lines three of the four walls of the waiting room. The toys I played with fifteen years before still in a box in the corner. And it all smells the same.

The GP who sees me is the one I lied to about my eating habits when I was fourteen and my period stopped for more than a year. I didn't trust her back then. Back then I didn't trust anyone, least of all myself. Silence has caught up with me though. It has been broken by desperation – by what I found out a month ago is severe depression. I'm ready to be more open.

We explain that I have been feeling like this since January.

It is now March. 'This' is low self-esteem, sobbing, lack of energy, sleeping more, doing less, loss of focus, hating myself, walking out into the road without looking in the hope that someone will be a little more careless this time. 'This' is calculating the good I've done minus the bad and the answer always being negative. 'This' is being so convinced that I am not worthy of a place in this world anymore that I tell my parents over the phone that I should die because to me it is obvious, inarguable.

I'm back home because my best friend and parents teamed up and got me to the university GP. My friend didn't quite know what was going on, but he knew I shouldn't be crying this much, shouldn't be struggling this much to get to lectures, shouldn't be thinking the thoughts I was. He knew I wasn't the person he'd decorated his room with Oscar Wilde quotes with last term. He encouraged me to book an appointment and offered to come with me. I declined, but he still checked in to make sure I'd gone along with my parents. This doctor was kind and she smiled – but not too much – and added up all my scores in the depression questionnaire efficiently. The numbers gave the result 'severe depression'. She referred me straight upstairs for counselling.

Upstairs was an artificial lilac cloud of constructed calm. A human interpretation of heaven that felt like purgatory. This waiting room ticked all the boxes in pastel colours, and overcompensated for its lack of personality with ambient music. An institution trying to care. The fucking water feature was overkill.

My counselling assessment fulfilled all suspected clichés: soft voice, furrowed brows, warm lighting, more fucking lilac, tell me about your childhood. The only thing that got me through was the lurid orange box of Sainsbury's basics tissues on the low table between us: a flash of practicality in a faux-feeling world.

At the second counselling session I didn't talk at all apart from to say that I felt guilty for not talking. She said it was fine not to talk. *But I spend the rest of my life not talking.* We sat in silence for thirty minutes before I left and didn't come back.

It took another month of covering my arm in biro scales of armour each lecture, knitting obsessively, and thoroughly researching potential methods of suicide before I decided – with the help of phone calls from my parents and friends – to take suspended study for health reasons and come back home. Those phone calls were reassurances that I was ill. *You don't have to spend the rest of your life feeling this way, Ailsa.* That I didn't have to persevere for the sake of it. *You are more than your grades. You are good and kind and we care about you.* That I deserved rest. Most of all they were reassurances that these people loved me. That they would still love me whether or not I had a master's degree in maths and physics from the University of Bristol. The most important thing was that I was well. That was their priority. And I needed that, because it sure as hell wasn't mine.

Me being well wasn't only not a priority for me: it was a long-forgotten myth. That myth had been undermined, corroded and then erased by the ceaseless 'logic' of my depression.

I will never be able to fully convey how the cold creeping fog of depression slips into every hairline fracture and fissure of your psyche and saps warmth and feeling, turning them from experiences to abstract ideas harder to comprehend than any mathematical proof. Depression is pervasive and persuasive. For me, it took my mind, which loved logic and numbers, and it twisted truths that were never meant to be counted or quantified into proofs that all led to the same conclusion: I was not good enough. Depression was rooting with long, grasping fingers into any cracks it could find. It burrowed deeper and deeper, leaving no space for argument. Any resistance was redirected by those fingers into thickening the tangled tightening net of *I am not good enough*.

But my friends like me. They say they like me. They're just saying that because you're sad at the moment. Who could like you like this? You're a mess. And what have you ever done for them to like you? You talk too much. You're not kind enough. You're definitely not fun to be around, especially now. They don't need you. They don't want you. But they say they want to spend time with me still. So what? You can cry on them? No one wants that. You're just dragging them down. But— You're a burden. You should stay here. Out of everyone's way.

When you can't believe in your own worth you need other people to. My loved ones provided that. Even though

I couldn't believe it at the time, it was enough to get me through to a new place where I could.

My friends wrote me a song and serenaded me the day before I left. My energy was so low that I – the girl who'd earned the nickname Mary Poppins for being so organised and ready for anything – didn't even pack properly before my dad came to pick me up. He helped me shove my belongings in bin bags and stuff them in the boot and back seats of the car before I waved my friends goodbye and climbed in after him. I felt even less animated than my stuffed toy penguin, Percy, whose softness I was clinging to, trying to feel something that wasn't that cold, grey fog.

So now my mum and I are sitting across from Dr de Burgh back in the GP's office and she's kinder than I remember. After some talking, head nodding, brows drawing concern across her forehead, she says she is going to refer me to a psychiatrist. She doesn't think this is just depression. *Just depression* is bad phrasing though: what she means is that she doesn't think I am subject to only extreme lows. She's uncertain and she's willing to admit she's uncertain, and she's willing to pass my case over to a specialist.

Now I know how lucky I was to see a GP who took the time to listen. She didn't immediately jump to a diagnosis of unipolar depression (experiencing low moods only, as opposed to high *and* low) and then onto the next inevitable stepping-stone of prescribing antidepressants. Over the past decade, prescriptions of antidepressants in England have doubled. This might be due to the increased number of people seeking help, but a number of professionals also point to a lack of other services such as talking therapies, meaning that often the only aid a GP can offer someone struggling is a prescription. Antidepressants are often a huge help for a variety of mental health issues, and I wholeheartedly support anyone taking them if that is what helps. But they do not work in all cases, and can sometimes make things worse before they start to make things better. I believe that the most effective treatment is multifaceted and not only includes medical interventions like meds and talking therapies, but also addresses the other basic elements of wellbeing, such as financial, housing and food security.

Five years have passed since then and I have now seen four different psychiatrists – one in Scotland, and three in Bristol, where I still live despite not returning to university. I'm still unclear on my diagnosis. I've definitely got 'mood disorder' on my notes, but not a definitive 'bipolar II' – just suspected. What I do know is that I experience extreme highs and lows of mood: sometimes only for a day or two at a time, at other times for weeks or months. I say I'm lucky to not have been put on antidepressants because, as someone with a mood disorder, they were likely to have made my illness worse by taking me from depression to intoxicating hypomania.

My 'luck' has been more than just a savvy GP though: unlike many others, I have had supportive and understanding parents and friends. Thanks to them I didn't feel I had to push myself through my maths and physics degree in order to get a well-paid nine-to-five job. Now I am much more stable mood-wise, I can support myself through freelance writing and photography, and by working at a local café part-time. And as I've learned more about myself and my mood disorder, it's become increasingly clear that trying to suppress my highs and lows in order to push on with my current plans only exacerbates them. Like some kind of horror movie jack-in-the-box, if I try to contain them, they only spring back harder, faster and more violently. I will never know, but I believe that it is very possible that, had I not had the supportive safety net and the option to take a different path from the one I chose at seventeen, I wouldn't be alive now.

Now, when my mood gets a little more extreme, I can go with it instead of having to fight against it. This usually means taking a day off, resting, watching trashy TV and distracting myself from the familiar fog beginning to cloud my vision, or letting myself have some fun if I'm getting a bit high again. It doesn't mean indulging these moods, but rather giving myself the space and time to acknowledge them, to let myself experience the feel of them.

Most often they don't come completely from nowhere but are sparked by other things going on in my life. Taking the time to rest and be kinder to myself when down or not immediately restraining myself when I feel my mood rising is very helpful in steadying my moods in the long run. Having a good grasp on the warning signs of a big mood swing, being able to spot potential triggers and stressors, and put self-care strategies that I've tried and tested into place all contribute to keeping those more extreme episodes at bay. I haven't had a depressive spell last longer than two weeks for over eighteen months now. I largely put that down to now having the flexibility in my life to ride the waves and ripples instead of having to plunge through them, alongside having a self-awareness that has taken years to cultivate.

Three years after that initial depressive episode, with another two lows and one more hypomanic episode fading into my personal history, I found myself exhausted, often anxious and indescribably weary after a few months of glorious hypomania in late summer. I'd broken up with my boyfriend of three years, spent too much money, slept and ate too little, had taken up smoking, experimented with new drugs, new people and new sensations: all products of the reduced inhibitions, god-like confidence and impaired judgement of a high episode. But that amount of energy with so little food and rest is an unsustainable formula. The extreme energy and extroversion left me empty and nothing could fill me up again.

Though it manifests in different people in a variety of ways, most people now have some idea of what depression can look like: low mood, low energy, low self-esteem, isolating oneself, destructive behaviours and coping mechanisms, suicidal thoughts. But as I've learned more about my own moods and talked more, I've found that relatively few people know what hypomania constitutes. I usually describe mania first: high energy, inability to sleep, reduced appetite, talking faster, mind racing, impulsive decision making, overspending, increased libido, dressing more provocatively, increased irritability, grandiose beliefs and huge energy. Hypomania is a less extreme version, but often harder to spot because of it. As with any moods though, it varies from person to person and no one can tick all the boxes neatly.

The weariness was not something sleep or food or any amount of trashy TV could fix. It felt like my soul had been hollowed out and handed to everyone I'd climbed hills with at dawn, everyone I'd fooled with an inebriating bubbling golden elixir advert of who I was. Like I'd burned through all of me and then borrowed recklessly from my future self, and now that future self was my present self whose energy had been dragged into negative numbers. Now I was at the bottom of the well with only the ability to look up at the ladder leading to the light. No amount of will could lift my limbs to climb.

I knew I didn't want to kill myself – I just wanted to be asleep for a very, *very* long time, or just have a break, or just have someone know and understand how bad everything was and how scared I was and how much I was struggling.

I overdosed in November. I'd been having the urge all day and had done all the right things: called friends, called parents, called the crisis line. (Though the latter made me feel worse by coming across as patronising overall, and responding to my telling them I was having very strong urges to overdose by suggesting I have a cup of tea.) I did all the right things but I still OD'ed. That doesn't mean I wasn't 'strong enough', or that my loved ones failed me. It means that we tried and tried damn hard, but this is a hard thing to fight. There's only so much control you have. You just have to do your best to be kind to yourself and others.

The conversation around mental health issues has opened up hugely in the past few years, but it remains focused around depression and anxiety, leaving 'scarier' illnesses like borderline personality disorder, schizophrenia and bipolar still relatively un-talked about and still steeped in stigma. The discussion is still also very white and individualistic. This leaves little room for acknowledgement of how your experience of race, class, sexuality, disabilities and/or gender can affect your mental health. For example, in the UK, people from a BAME background are more likely to be diagnosed with mental health problems, but also more likely to experience a poor outcome from treatment, and rates of suicide amongst men and trans folks are far higher than the overall population's average.

The opening up of the conversation around mental health has led to the sharing of many different stories with the same narrative: person gets sick (usually with anxiety or depression or both), person goes to see doctor, doctor diagnoses and assigns treatment, then, after enough of a struggle to imbue the tale with a sense of romance, the person gets better. I understand why this narrative is pushed – no one wants a story about someone struggling for the rest of their life, or the rest of their life never happening – but to me this story is purely a fairy tale. I have had too many friends struggle too much to be able to get on board with the 'if we just talk about it everything will be fine in the end' attitude.

I know that my own path so far can, with relative ease, be pushed into a nice inspiring story about mental health issues, but that tale is always missing something. It's been five years now since I dropped out of university, and I'm in the best place mental health-wise I've ever been. I still struggle, but am managing my moods a lot better, and I was signed off mental health services in January.

Other friends have not been so lucky.

Again we are sat around a hospital bed. Her body is going to be fine. Her brain remains the same. The recovery team arrive: a man with a leather necklace in sandals and hiking trousers, a woman with perfect hair and a perfect smile of sympathy. Every time she nods her head her eyebrows sketch out concern and her hair bobs up and down, up and down – perfect pointless synchrony. We sit there, three friends, as they say they have no beds, they don't think she'd do well in a psychiatric ward anyway, has she tried calling the crisis service, yes, she has a whole list of lines to call. We switch roles briefly so she can tell these passive actors with their ghost concern about services they haven't heard of. They say, *You seem to be coping; we're going to discharge you.* She's already said she's going to try again.

It's not their fault: they're working in a system that doesn't have the resources. Still, I want to scream into their eyes. Make a doll from her perfect hair and hang it from the ceiling with his leather necklace. I don't do this. I sit still, I smile, I ask if they will help her get home. *No, she has you,* they say. *What follow-up support will there be?* we ask. *Our colleagues will be in touch in a week.*

Thank you.

And it's been a year now since he killed himself. Since he took the fact *suicide is the biggest killer of men under forty-five* out of the abstract and etched it into reality across the inside of my skull. He will remain forever twenty-four. Forever the sweet friend who ate ice cream with me and held me whilst I cried and offered me some of the best advice at the worst times of my life. Forever the sweet friend who didn't get the help he needed for too many reasons. Forever the sweet friend whose memory will be manacled by the way of his passing. A reminder that this fight is a fight for lives and futures.

Our stories are never simple. I'm now twenty-three and my notes are interpretations from four psychiatrists and one psychological formulation: self-harm, a past eating disorder, two trials on mood stabilisers, one overdose, two more several-month-long hypomanic episodes with subsequent depression to match, a care coordinator for fourteen months and an as-yet-unfinished degree. But I still count myself amongst the lucky ones. Over the past few years I have watched several friends be begrudgingly handed from one mental health service to another. They are told that they're 'not depressed enough' for treatment. They are put on antidepressants without any other support, options or follow-up. They are weighed and told they're not underweight enough for diagnosis and treatment of an eating disorder. They get six sessions of counselling and then are discharged only to deteriorate again. They attempt suicide and they are not offered help. As appalling as it sounds, I'm surprised that mental illness has only claimed one of my friends' lives so far.

That mental health provisions in the UK are insufficient is not news to many people. And yet that fact is far too often neglected in the advice given to the loved ones of those struggling. Regaining and maintaining your mental health is never as simple as making it to your GP. In their 2017 manifesto, the Tories promised to 'address the need for better treatments across the whole spectrum of mental health conditions', alongside making 'the UK the leading research and technology economy in the world for mental health' without pledging to increase funding. In April 2017, cuts to spending on mental health services in five regions of England were revealed, despite the number of young people arriving in A&E with psychiatric problems doubling since 2009.

This lack of funding shows the magical fairy-tale path

from illness to wellness to be just that – a naive story. Reality, as always, remains messier, darker and with too many endings that are far from happy. When medical intervention fails, or never even gets the chance to, it is untrained but loving people who are left trying to prevent friends and family from spiralling. People who have their own lives to manage and their own wellbeing to look after too.

Supporting someone with mental health issues is not easy, but such support from families and friends is needed now more than ever, because, with continuing cuts to the welfare state, 2013 saw the highest suicide rates since 2000 alongside many news stories about deaths being linked to austerity.[*] The Samaritans' 2017 Suicide Statistics Report tells us that the rate of suicide in the UK has risen by 3.8 per cent and that female suicides are at their highest in a decade.[†] At a time when we are talking more about mental health than ever, when all of the main parties addressed the issue in their manifestos, and more people are seeking help, it's important to interrogate why suicide rates are climbing too. To me, as someone who talks openly about their own struggles with mental health, and hears many others' stories as a result, a lack of provisions and care is the obvious answer. As funding

---

[*] 'Suicides linked to austerity: from a psychocentric to a psychopolitical autopsy', *Discover Society*, 1 February 2017, available at https://discoversociety. org/2017/02/01/suicides-linked-to-austerity-from-a-psychocentric-to-a-psychopolitical-autopsy/

[†] 'Suicide facts and figures', Samaritans, available at https://www.samaritans.org/about-samaritans/research-policy/suicide-facts-and-figures/#

is cut further, waiting lists get longer and the bar of severity necessary to be able to access medical intervention is hiked still higher, meaning that many don't get the help they need until they are at their worst, or never get it at all.

In this climate of overstretched services, it is not mental health professionals over the years who have kept me alive, but my friends and family. They are the ones who, between them, have checked in daily, sent texts to remind me I am loved when I cannot tell myself that, who've shared dinners with me when my moods are too unstable to be able to juggle a job and feeding myself, who've looked after my medications when I've felt too unsafe around them. It is people who love me who have helped me to hold onto who I am both in spite of and because of my mood disorder. It is they who have looked after me during all those times when I've been standing perilously close to the edge of the many cracks in the system. Who've caught me when I've begun falling and the services that should have been there failed to appear.

Being there for someone who is struggling is not saving them. No one person can save another, at least not sustainably. It is not grand gestures but most often a series of small, routine and unromantic acts for which there is little reward. It is cumulative hours of listening to crying on the phone. Remembering to send a text to let someone know you're thinking of them. Checking social media to see if your friend has posted another cat video because you haven't heard from them for a week but now you know they're still functioning at some level. It's offering to do laundry or make food when they can't. It's still making plans and not taking it personally when they cancel, and still asking if they want to hang out and making more plans after that. It can be tough at points but well worth it – for the lessons learned, the laughter and the strength of relationships. I have found that my friendships with others who struggle with their mental health are the most loving and understanding I have.

Sometimes it's bigger things – having someone to stay because they can't be alone, or leaving a gig because they need someone. But what it never is is fixing someone. Fixing implies something is broken. It implies a before and after. Recovery is rarely that simple. My mood disorder does not define me, nor is it separate from me, and it never will be. I'm OK with that. It has been the biggest struggle in my life, but I would argue that it has shown me a wider spectrum of emotion than many others have experienced. It has left me bruised and wearier than you would think anyone still alive could feel but it has taught me empathy through darkness and confidence through dazzling my brain with light. It has made me a plethora of friends in the months of extroversion and proved those friends real when the golden energy leaves my body and I feel far less than mortal. And it is those friends who throughout all of it have, between them, shown me love continuously, in so many small and big ways, and given me the confidence and will to save myself.

Millennials are often demeaned by older generations,

criticised for being 'over-sensitive' or 'snowflakes'. From my experience, though, this 'over-sensitivity' is instead a recognition that we and others deserve kindness and consideration, whether that's over microaggressions, trigger warnings or mental health issues. My generation's openness around mental health has played a vital role in the improvement of many people's wellbeing. It's something I've seen and benefited from firsthand. It's something I'm proud of contributing to. The way we voice our struggles is often talked of derisively, as if it's a weakness. On the contrary, I believe it is a strength, and the path to growing that strength is through understanding and kindness.

UNIVERSITY AIN'T FOR THE LIKES OF US

Olivia Fletcher

Content warning: classism

I reached a point where I was begging someone, anyone, to please just get me out of the shithole I grew up in. I couldn't do it anymore.

There wasn't a specific event. It was just a build-up of many things. Where I'm from is a place where parents – and even, in some cases, grandparents – went to the same school as their children. Only just over half of my year group got a GCSE in English or maths. The father of one of my best friends was born in one house, lived in the house next to it and is now raising his family in the one adjacent to that. We're sort of like the people of Maycomb County described by Harper Lee – poor, socially immobile and unaware of what lies beyond the town's borders. We all know, for instance, about the bus fire outside Shoe Zone, and about the homeless woman who wears her mother's clothes but refuses to accept housing offers. These, like many others, have become folk stories – the sort of tales that get passed through generations. It seems like everyone knows the next person, and even if you don't, there's an unspoken affinity between you and them.

For me and my friends, the metanarrative we were raised on by our parents, and sometimes even teachers, was: A) leave secondary school with the bog-standard five A*–C grade GCSEs, B) get a job, one that you'll keep for life, and C) do as you're bloody well told. This message was probably similar to the one the teachers themselves received when growing up, but fortunately for them, they were entering a more stable job market. Today, young people – that's those of us between sixteen and twenty-four – are three times more likely to be unemployed than the rest of the population.* Our parents and teachers, too, could leave school as soon as they were sixteen, which today is not the case in England. You either go into further study of some sort, or an apprenticeship.

My mum and stepdad were adamant that I leave school at sixteen and get a finance or office-based apprenticeship, like in a local travel or housing agency, because it would guarantee me a living and set me up with a career. It was what they had done, and what most of my other family members had done too. In 1989, the year before my mum would have applied to university, the poll tax was introduced and students had to pay this while studying. This in itself would have deterred

---

* 'World Employment Social Outlook', International Labour Organization, available at http://www.ilo.org/wcmsp5/groups/public/---dgreports/---dcomm/---publ/documents/publication/wcms_337070.pdf

working-class students from further education, but even more so for people like my mum, who had the option to go straight into work instead. She didn't enjoy studying much anyway, and had been educated at a comprehensive school where there was no particular emphasis on university unless A) you could afford it, or B) you had parents who had been, and could give you guidance. Neither A nor B applied to my mum. Doing the same should have been an unquestionable choice for me. Although I couldn't go straight into work, I could do an apprenticeship, which was the next closest thing. University was never the obvious option. I lived in a low-participation area, had no immediate family who had been and it was rarely, if ever, promoted at my secondary school. But at the same time, whilst applying for an apprenticeship in something office-based would have been the most straightforward option, it wasn't what I *wanted*.

I still didn't know what I wanted to do – 'Just marry rich,' one of my friends joked – but I knew one thing for certain: I didn't want to stay in my hometown in a career that I didn't actually want. A top university was a ticket out of this place. It was a chance to meet different people, live independently and increase my employment prospects in jobs that I previously couldn't have dreamed of.

As we sat on the AstroTurf during lunch watching boys play football, my friend joked, 'Why not Cambridge?'

I laughed, because I knew it was as unrealistic as marrying rich. Going to university was considerably uncommon for students at my school. Going to Cambridge, or marrying rich for that matter, was even rarer. At this point, I hadn't given much thought to what I'd do post-GCSEs. I had only just started considering going to university, but Cambridge University had never entered this thought process.

I was shit at maths, which ruled out an accounting-based apprenticeship. I wasn't a diligent or pragmatic person, so I couldn't go into business either. Being a girl meant that childcare, hair and beauty, or air hostessing would have been the next most likely prospects. If it wasn't finance, or one of the above careers, it would have been something construction- or joinery-based, where only 2 per cent of apprentices were female. I knew that these were equally legitimate and honourable career paths, but they were ones that I was neither interested nor welcome in.

Even more importantly, I assumed I'd stay in the same occupation for life with an unchanging salary and a high-rising glass ceiling, which was something that terrified me. So, like a dork on *Dragons' Den*, I began reciting what I was going to tell my mum about my alternative plan.

I could see that the door to the front room was ajar. It was late evening, about half nine, and through the gap in the door I could see that the coffee table had been moved from the corner of the room to the middle. The sizzle of the steaks being grilled and the smell of thick-cut chips being deep fried in a pan of oil from the kitchen meant that they were soon to be serving up. I knew that interrupting their dinner time was a stupid thing to do; it usually ended with me being shouted at. They had both had a busy day at work, and this was the only time they got to relax. But I didn't want to leave my proposal tossing about in my head like a game of pinball any longer. Besides, I reassured myself, it would only take a minute.

I took a breath and stepped into the room.

'I implore you to let me study A levels. There is nothing else I can offer to this society besides my devoted hours of studying, my thirst for knowledge and my inquisitive mind. I apologise for my lack of practical skill, but I would be of no use in the workforce. Now, if you would be so kind as to listen, I've got a proposal that you can't refuse.

'I want to go to university, and in order to do so, I need A levels. Yes, before you ask, I know that only 20.8 per cent of undergraduate students at Russell Group universities are from working-class backgrounds, but with a degree, people are more likely to hire me in a job that I *enjoy*. And that, Dragons, is why I would like you to invest.'

Actually, I can't remember exactly what I said, but with a dry throat devoid of grammatical coherency, it probably wasn't that. Whatever I said, it lolloped haphazardly from my tongue, like when Boris Johnson tries to talk about racial equality policy, or when Piers Morgan blunders his lines discussing women's rights. Listening to me confessing my desire to study A levels and go on to university, my mum laughed.

'Nobody enjoys their jobs,' she said.

'You might as well get a job now like we did, and save the nine grand it takes to realise this,' my stepdad added.

To go to university – especially a research-intensive Russell Group one – would be subversive. It would be a deliberate infringement of the values that had been instilled in me by my mum and stepdad. Their reluctance to see beyond the cost, and their own experiences of being deterred from university, had distorted their vision. If university was made more financially accessible for me, and had been more of a legitimate option for my parents growing up, then perhaps they would have been more eager. The institutional barriers that they faced were deeply linked to their rejection of higher education. It disparaged them, so they dismissed it in return. I was allowed to study towards A levels, but in doing so, I was flouting what it meant to be part of my family. University would mean leaving home, rejecting not only my responsibilities but also plenty of respectable apprenticeships. I was being selfish.

During my A levels I was always divided between my aspirations and my roots. I was going to college every weekday until four, and tried to study for at least the recommended additional four hours per night. Yet at the same time, I had a part-time job as well as family commitments that needed to be met. Often, I'd study into the early hours of the morning to meet all of these obligations. I constantly felt guilty.

Why should *I* apologise for wanting to go to university?

Why should *I* – a working-class alumnus of a closed-down

comprehensive school living in an economically depressed, low participation area – be less deserving of an education because I'm *poor*?

The answer is simple: I shouldn't.

And it was with that conviction that I decided to apply to Britain's – heck, the world's – most prestigious university, Cambridge, because *ha, suckers! Me? Bound by class barriers and tied to social structures? Think again, losers. I'm fucking invincible!*

That's right. If I could make it down my local high street without being wolf-whistled at by a sixty-something-year-old man or passing by another closed shopfront, then I could make it anywhere.

I'd like to think it was the sort of experiences described above that gave me the self-assurance to be able to apply. In actuality, though, I was just angry about being sentenced for life in the prison of social immobility, and wanted to prove to a lot of people – my family, friends, teachers and anyone else who was interested enough to care – that anyone, regardless of background, had a fair shot. If I had the opportunity to apply to Cambridge University, then I should seize it. I was scraping the same grades that other candidates were acing, but a place there would surely bail me out of my life sentence.

In the library of my sixth-form college, I had found a leaflet strewn across a table. It said something that made the idea of applying sound colloquial and welcoming, like, 'Is Oxbridge the place for you?' or 'Want to make Oxbridge a reality?'

I opened up the leaflet in a Charlie Bucket-esque manner, hoping that I'd find my golden ticket – my 'get out of jail free' card – to see if Oxbridge was indeed the place for me, or if I wanted to make it my reality. So, I went for it. It was going to be easy. Simply apply, go to the interview, get the offer and then get the grades. Either they were trying to save printer ink, or just forgot to mention, for instance, that the average offer of a place requires three A-level grades at A*AA; that preparing for and sitting an admission assessment was now an entry requirement on all courses, and that you would have to pay for your own travel. I couldn't help but think that if my family was richer, or I was allowed to concentrate entirely on my studies, this would be less of a concern to me.

I knew it wasn't going to be easy, but around the same time, I had been on abundant widening participation schemes that inflated me with the idea that access to higher education was entirely meritocratic. On the schemes, I'd be serenaded with PowerPoints by current students from a similar background explaining how great university is, given workshops on student finance and be invited on a day trip to a university in London. More importantly, on these schemes, the coordinators of various Russell Group universities promised you an offer on the course you wanted – you just had to meet the grades in order to gain a place. It was, I suppose, a gesture that emphasised that, regardless of educational or parental background, a place at a research-intensive university was a real possibility. Cambridge didn't take part, but I thought that was because they were playing hard to get. They were flirting with me. I didn't want *them*, I thought. They needed *me*. They can't tick the 'working class' box to fill their quota if I'm not there.

And so on 6 December, I attended my interview at Cambridge, infatuated with the belief that I had just as much potential here as Prince Edward, Earl of Wessex, who got in despite having a C and two Ds in his A levels. To some extent, I thought that my lack of royal blood gave me edge: being working class at Cambridge was *cool*.

My regional accent and NHS glasses became my asset. Usually, these attributes made me common, but here they were somehow deviant from the norm. The gates of the college had just opened to the applicants and I could see all these smartly dressed, erudite-looking people making their way to the porter's lodge to collect room keys. I was sat on a bench, observing from across the street before making my own way through the gates, when a black taxi hummed past. As it drove away, a man sat in the back rolled down the tinted window and cried, 'Cambridge tossers!' A few people furtively ignored him, while some responded cordially with laddish chants of, 'WAHEY.' I laughed because, even in spite of my fellow applicants, it was me who looked and felt like the biggest tosser there.

I swaggered through the gates like I was in a nineties Britpop video. I was a Bristolian Liam Gallagher. His tambourine was my suitcase of books, and the other candidates arriving alongside me were Liam's estranged brother: ultimately more intelligent than me, and better at mingling with the elite.

It was at this point that my worst suspicions, the ones I had strived so hard to ignore, were confirmed. Most of the other Oxbridge applicants I had met had been educated in something other than a comprehensive school. Even though on paper the university had a higher intake of 'maintained' school students than 'independent' school students, what this actually meant was questionable. This, it seems, is the case for most Russell Group universities.

During the application process, I looked at other universities too. Even at other research-intensive ones, the talk was always of Oxbridge. Like me, many prospective Russell Group students were also Oxbridge applicants. At a UCL open day, I had planned to visit one of the lecture blocks to hear a presentation about my chosen subject. When I arrived at the building, I was pointed to a lift. Two other prospective students – I could tell from the numerous pamphlets and freebies they were clutching – were waiting for the lift too, in mid-conversation. They were talking about Cambridge.

'If I got an offer from there, I'd put that as my firm, and probably here as my insurance,' one contemplated idly.

'Oh, so what college are you going to apply for?' the other asked, stepping into the lift.

I followed after, and couldn't help but ask, 'Are you guys talking about Cambridge?'

They said that they were, and we chatted about this on the way to the lecture room, not caring that we were late. It was because of this that I was taken aback when one asked, 'So, what schools are you guys from?'

This sounded pretty dumb, I thought. How would they know what school I went to when there are *thousands* across the country? The other replied with some polysyllabic noun, which I was unfamiliar with and immediately alienated by. When I got home I looked it up. It was an independent boarding school, founded in the seventeenth century, with fees starting from £31,000 per annum.

'Oh, I go to a small Catholic college in Bristol,' I lied. My sixth form has 2,000 students, only a handful of whom are actually Catholics.

'Maintained' refers ambiguously to any school with state influence, which could therefore be any number of institutions: comprehensives, academies, free schools, grammar schools, or faith schools, for instance. Although said schools are theoretically non-selective, that does not mean that certain schools will not attract a certain type of pupil. At Bristol Free School, only 8.8 per cent of its students are eligible for free school meals, as opposed to 22.5 per cent of pupils across the city on average.* Similarly, the Sutton Trust – a charity interested in improving social

---

* Jessica Shepherd, 'Most free schools take fewer deprived pupils than local average, figures show', *The Guardian,* 23 April 2012, available at https://www.theguardian.com/education/2012/apr/23/free-schools-deprived-pupils-average

mobility – found that in 2016 less than 3 per cent of pupils at grammar schools were entitled to free school meals. These schools are inherently middle class: they're more likely to be in economically affluent areas, and tend to rely on the parents' knowledge of how the education system works. Even though, therefore, less than half of the pupils at Cambridge have been privately educated, it does not mean that those who have come from the state sector are *always* disadvantaged in comparison.

When applying, I didn't know or care much about what a maintained school was, because I didn't want to play by the statistics. I wanted to, as the Cambridge website says, be judged on academic merit alone. 'Ultimately,' it claims, 'all admissions decisions are based on academic criteria – ability and potential – and excellence in an extracurricular activity will never "compensate" for lower academic potential' – which I thought was entirely fair. To me, this was not an interview. This was an opportunity to discuss a subject that I loved and had read as much about as I could in the time I had, with arguably some of the best academics in the field.

This wasn't about who I was. This wasn't about how I'd grown up surrounded not just by financial poverty but the poverty of ambition that attends it. This wasn't about my life at a failing school, or the ways I had coped with that. No. This was who I was *going* to be. My books were my holy scripture. I had studied the text well. I was ready to convert.

I waited for my interview on the top floor of a Georgian building, where I had a panoramic view of the gardens below. It looked serene. It was the iconic image of Cambridge University – the photo you see on all of the postcards littered about the tourist shops on every cobblestone street. Below, people were stopping to take photos from beneath the chapel's immense shadow, cast by the morning light. Even though it was December, the sun had risen, and it sat just above the horizon, nourishing the mown lawn and the flower beds with its rays. A thin layer of residue from yesterday's frost rested, crystalised, on the grass and reflected fragmented parts of the chapel's medieval windows. My presence in the picture felt wrong. I was an artist's mistake, in need of being blotted out by a different shade of paint.

My Britpop confidence was becoming more Radiohead by the minute. I had never actually had an in-depth discussion with anyone before about the subject I was applying for. Some of the candidates had been preparing for this since, let's face it, they were conceived. They had been prepped and given all the cultural capital they needed to be able to speak at length and with ease to important people. Some could afford to take part in Oxbridge preparation days, or attend mock interviews and assessments. Others, from the vague 'maintained schools' category, were, as discussed, closet posh people anyway.

In the weeks prior to my interview, I had not been nervous. But in spite of the cream-coloured ceiling, the walls lined with books, the wide-panelled windows that lit the room with soothing winter light and the cushioned armchair I had sunk into, I suddenly felt all the nerves I needed to compensate for the weeks that I hadn't.

'I don't agree with you. Why do you think that?' was asked a lot. My voice box – like when I had asked for my mum's permission to apply in the first place – swelled up. Almost every response I had from my interviewer was fronted with a challenging 'hmmmm' or a 'no'. Whatever I said could have been contradicted. I knew this was a part of academia, and I was trying to fight my corner, but I was unfamiliar with this kind of interaction. I'd had a practice interview with a teacher, and I had been to an Oxbridge conference with my college, and this filled me with confidence. Even so, I'd had much less practice than other applicants.

Usually, if I had been told 'no' by a parent or a teacher, it meant no. End of discussion. I knew now what my mum had meant when she discouraged me from taking my A levels and applying to university. Although the application may truly be based on academic achievement alone, it's undeniable that you're more likely to be a high achiever if you've been given the cultural and economic capital to be so from your parents, and the universities themselves are more accommodating to those who have that. I had made it here, but it didn't mean that I had as much of a chance to succeed as other applicants did.

Wanting a first-class education shouldn't be based on having the economic capital to do so, having a quiet place to study for as long as you please, or how eloquently you've been taught to communicate. But it is.

The intimidation and exclusion I experienced – even if not overtly – is not uncommon. There is a reason why young people from low-income families tend to get lower grades, and it's not because they were born academically low-achievers. It was because they were born poor. And being born poor comes with a whole bunch of strings attached. You learn to internalise your fate until you see no monetarily successful future. You seek instant gratification instead of planning for long-term rewards, so going to a university like Cambridge becomes an impossibility. If you ever got anywhere near to completing an application, you'd be an imposter, and somehow less deserving of a place.

Young people in Britain today are swindled by the claim that society is meritocratic. If it was, then more working-class students would be at university, and fewer middle-class students would feel the need to go. If it was, then Oxbridge would be genuinely accessible to poorer students, rather than simply appearing to promote widening participation. There would be less stigma surrounding who went, and who didn't. University would simply be an institution for learning, regardless of who the learner might be. If society was meritocratic then a quarter of our doctors wouldn't have been privately educated, 71 per cent of our senior judges would not have attended independent schools, and nineteen of our prime ministers wouldn't have gone to the same school, Eton.* Until Oxbridge becomes more open to and inclusive of *all* young people, the social class division in these two institutions will remain.

University isn't what everyone wants, but working-class youth shouldn't be deterred before even considering it. Ideally, any teen finishing school should have the right to make this decision, regardless of class barriers. In reality, however, the risks of going to university are higher than the benefits. We are given compensatory education – such as the numerous widening participation schemes I had attended – but they are mere tokenism and not available in all schools. And although they fix surface problems, like lowering grade offers, they do not tackle the structural causes that prevent many working-class teens from entering higher education. Most of the university representatives in the schemes I attended seemed like they had been hired to pitch to some poor kids about how good their university was, and why we should choose it, just so we'd fulfil their 'working-class' quota. I, and many other students I spoke to, felt patronised by numerous instances of being shown – literally in step-by-step guides – about why eating breakfast is important, and why mind-maps get you good grades, for example.

Instead of compensating for educational deprivation, why not seek to remove the inequality that causes it? We should be

---

* Owen Bowcott, 'Most senior judges and top QCs still privately educated, figures show', *The Guardian*, 23 November 2015, available at https://www.theguardian. com/law/2015/nov/23/most-senior-judges-top-qcs-still-privately-educated-figures-show

asking *why* the social classes are still so divided in education. We should be seeking to challenge and deconstruct these rigid social barriers, rather than merely reforming them. It will take time, effort and investment, and will not happen overnight, but its long-term effects will mean that social mobility becomes legitimate, and not just for a few who 'made it' in spite of their family background.

When I received my invitation to the Cambridge interview, I searched online for a coach ticket, only to find that it would cost me about fifty quid – fifty quid that I didn't have. I emailed the admissions office asking if there was any bursary available. I had the evidence and teachers' notes at hand, but the reply was no. Already, I was being pushed out of the application process because I couldn't afford travel expenses.

It is this kind of thing that deters poorer students from applying. It is these kinds of things that made me wish I had listened to my mum when she said that university wasn't for the likes of us. It is because of my social background that I was unlikely to get an offer from Cambridge anyway.

My secondary school, a comprehensive, was closed down in 2016, the year after I had completed my GCSEs. My year group was the collateral damage – the afterthought of a financial crisis in which our school was either to be reinvested in as a comprehensive, turned into an academy or closed down entirely. After increasing pressure to convert all comprehensives into academies, my school wasn't deemed worth the money it would cost to fund. I, along with a hundred other pupils, was not worth saving.

At a time when qualifications have become increasingly crucial in a competitive job market, we were shut down. As I mentioned previously, *just over half* of the students in my year got 5 A*-C, including English and maths. We were put on death row. Our teachers' jobs became unstable, so dozens of them left. The funding was slashed, and we lacked resources. There was no paper in the libraries. Half of our canteen became the art department. If we wanted to apply to sixth form, it was our own responsibility – assuming that our parents couldn't help – but by this point most students had felt so disparaged by and disengaged with the system they were in that they wanted to opt out of studying as soon as they could.

I just *know* – I have a burning, unremitting feeling – that if our school had been given the funding it needed, it wouldn't have turned into the pile of dying embers it became. If visiting and talking to parents – ones like mine and my friends' – to help them understand what options were available to their children and that university wasn't necessarily bad, or offering regular career services and advice sessions, or paying for university lecturers to come and speak to us, or giving every individual student a support programme is what it would have taken, then it should have been done. I can only speak on behalf of my school, but I suppose that the same ought to be done in other comprehensive schools on the verge of being closed.

Working-class children in Britain are being failed. I do not blame my fellow classmates for not being the *right* kind of achievers. I do not blame my parents for the institutional barriers that affected their own entry to higher education – I thank my mum for putting up with me. I blame the system in which the restrictions to achieve were imposed. We did not fail, but we were failed by an education system that refused to acknowledge the struggle of working-class students, so ignored us instead. They might as well have left us in the rubble when they knocked down the school.

Once upon a time, class divisions may have been unquestioned. The working class belonged here, and the middle class belonged there. But today, when British youth are promised something more than this – when we are told that anyone who puts their mind to it can be our next generation of doctors, lawyers, academics, politicians, dentists, journalists, teachers and scientists – we are being lied to. Our parents' educational background and behaviours are not considered at all. Our inability to study as much as some others is regarded as our own problem. Financially, parents are burdened, and students are faced with signing up for loans of unthinkable sums of money. How is someone like me supposed to get into Cambridge when my parents barely have GCSEs and I'm made to feel so completely unwelcome by the institution?

Social mobility is not, of course, impossible. Some of us are lucky. But most of the time, I cannot help thinking about the majority who *don't* make it – my classmates, my siblings, my best friends, and those who I will never meet but are faced with similar afflictions.

I worry for those who open their curtains every morning and see the same unchanging town in which opportunity no longer exists – a town in which the chances of leaving are slimmer than ever. I worry because I do not trust that we are being thought about enough. I worry that we are being forgotten.

★

After being rejected from Cambridge, I accepted my offer from another university. After studying there for two years, I took the personal decision to withdraw from my studies and have considered reapplying for university in 2019.

I AGREE WITH THATCHER

Ella Marshall

Content warning: sexism, racism, classism

'Why do you care so much?'

I was running on four hours of sleep, newsreels and graphs from the night before seared on my retinas.

At 3 a.m. I had succumbed to the reality of Donald Trump being elected as the 45th President of the United States of America. A caricature of capitalist excess was about to become leader of the 'free world' on the back of a campaign built on racial tension, misogyny and religious discrimination. I had stayed up to watch what I thought was going to be a historic victory for womankind. Instead, it felt as though I had watched the downfall of humankind – 62,979,636 Americans had been seduced by a form of political dogma that had (largely) been rejected by liberal democracies in previous decades: prejudice.

I had spent all seventeen years of my life being taught that discriminatory behaviour was strictly immoral. Classmates had been put in detention for making ignorant remarks with less malicious intent than those which had spewed from the mouth of Donald Trump and his campaign team. He had been elevated to presidential office despite labelling Muslims as terrorists, Mexicans as rapists and having been exposed as the kind of man that thinks it's OK to grab a woman by the pussy. Much of my educational career had been spent learning about the horrors of the Holocaust and the Second World War. Donald Trump's promise of economic prosperity aligned with xenophobic policy had clear and terrifying resemblances to Adolf Hitler's brand of nationalist right-wing populism. How had we let this happen? Again?

This election result was unfathomable but, with hindsight, perhaps predictable. And the Trump phenomenon, thanks to globalised media, would not be confined to the United States, I supposed. We had already witnessed a similar strain of conservatism gather momentum in the UK with Brexit and the rise of UKIP and its smaller, more extreme cousins, the English Defence League and Britain First. This was the second time in a year that a positive left-wing campaign had been defeated by silent majority conservatism, which seemed to only bare its teeth on polling day. All the activism that I had ever taken part in suddenly seemed futile. Perhaps those who had sneered and sniggered in response to my own political convictions were right. Maybe political apathy and thus injustice would always prevail.

The next day at sixth form, I was confronted by scorn: 'Why do you care so much?'

The conversation that ensued was predictable but nonetheless disheartening. Why would I bother to care about people who live 'across an ocean'? Surely their livelihoods are of no consequence to me? At first, this attitude startled me – as it might startle you. However, most of us subconsciously adopt this same attitude whenever we buy from high street clothing brands: the child labour used to make the garments is of no consequence to us. Whenever we unnecessarily leave electrical devices on: the future generations who will suffer most from climate change are of no consequence to us. Whenever we buy products from tax-dodging firms: the most vulnerable people in society who rely on the money available to the welfare state are of no consequence to us. And so on. We live in a world where living ethically is inconvenient. Being blind to the suffering of whole communities makes our lives easier. It is quite acceptable to be complicit in social, political or economic injustice under the auspices of convenience and status quo; living ethically seemingly requires a total upheaval of our (Western) lifestyle. Furthermore, engaging with social justice campaigns – whose outcomes often fall short of expectation – requires an emotional, physical and sometimes costly dedication that is beyond the ordinary person. Put simply, it is easier not to care at all.

Margaret Thatcher's neoliberal proposition was initially perceived as radical in a Britain that had spent the last forty years shrouded in 'post-war consensus': an agreement between the major parties to allow strong trade unions, maintain high taxes and facilitate a generous welfare state. By

1979, having endured the lengthy mid-seventies recession, Britain was hungry for change, and Thatcher's seemingly new ideas were welcomed. Her legacy? The primacy of the individual. Reagan caused a similar phenomenon across the pond. The Wolf of Wall Street that emerged snarling and ready to eat up the world in the boom years of the latter part of the twentieth century distracted and even discouraged us from caring for 'the other' because 'there is no such thing as society … people must look to themselves first'. It is well documented that capitalism cultivates selfishness. Sue Gerhardt's *The Selfish Society* proposes a rejection of divisive profit-centred capitalism and the embracing of a political-economic framework that fosters compassion in childhood through extended and better-paid maternity and paternity provision. 'Impractical at this point in the economic cycle,' sneered Liz Hunt of the *Telegraph*.

Hunt does, however, conclude that Gerdhardt makes a 'valuable contribution to fixing "Broken Britain"', echoing a term coined by David Cameron's Conservative Party and frequently used by tabloid newspapers to summarise a perceived state of social decay within the UK. 'Broken Britain' connotes gang crime, underage drinking and teenage pregnancy. In short, it is a device used to demonise young people. Speaking in 2011, after the London riots, Prime Minister David Cameron asked if we had the determination to 'confront the slow-motion moral collapse that [had] taken place in parts of our country these past few generations'. He was referring to Thatcher's children and grandchildren, quite unintentionally implicating an idol of his own Conservative Party in this perceived moral decline. Cameron inadvertently condemned Thatcher's legacy of individualism by promising to 'build a bigger, stronger society' in response to the riots, although in reality he extended her policy of privatisation and dismantling of the welfare state. He held 'children without fathers, schools without discipline', and thus, ultimately, troubled young people from deprived socio-economic backgrounds accountable for social unrest in the UK, rendering the revolving door establishment (political, media and corporate institutions) blameless.

Plan B's 2012 album *iLL Manors* deconstructed the notion of 'Broken Britain' and gave voice to a generation that had been so clearly marginalised by the establishment: 'We're just bloody broke in Britain. What needs changing is the system.' His social commentary echoes the sentiments of academics Richard Wilkinson and Kate Pickett, who argue that income inequality has led to this 'broken society'. They hold Thatcher accountable on the basis that 'in the 1980s the gulf between the top and bottom 20 per cent widened by a full 60 per cent'. Wilkinson and Pickett also reject the notion that broken families have led to moral decay, citing that a high rate of single parenthood itself does not seem to directly affect child wellbeing, but the overarching issue of 'poverty' does. They explain how inequality leads to 'status competition and consumerism', people feeling 'a greater sense of superiority or inferiority' and 'prejudices towards those lower on the social ladder' taking root. Neoliberal policy and subsequent wealth inequality breed self-absorption and bigotry. David Cameron was able to scapegoat young people as the perpetrators of Britain's socio-economic problems because the intolerance for others set in motion by Thatcher's capitalism enabled him to do so. Thatcher's grandchildren, or Blair's babies, have been found to 'hold more right-wing views than their predecessors', according to a paper published in the *British Journal of Political Science*. Social responsibility splintered under the fist of the Iron Lady, and continues to do so. After her death, David Cameron claimed that 'we're all Thatcherites now'. And he was right. The society that Thatcher so adamantly denied existed crumbles under her legacy of insularity as we willingly subscribe to the neoliberal measurement of success: material wealth.

Good grades. A good degree. A good job. A good house. A good spouse. A good car. Good kids. A good retirement plan. A good funeral. Our sense of agency and person is overshadowed by this societal prescription. It substitutes self-determination for pay cheques. The impact of our current grade- and career-focused education system on the mental health of students and teachers alike is well documented. In the first year of my A levels, I wrote an open letter to the then education secretary and head of OFSTED describing how I had watched 'many of my previously buoyant close friends sink into a pit of self-loathing and misery'. It does not surprise me, therefore, that a despondency and lack of interest in response to matters of injustice often prevails. When we are so preoccupied with narrow guidelines that supposedly determine the worthiness of our own lives and are continuously measured against these, it's quite natural to be blinded to the misfortune of others – or even to revel in it. The pursuit of conventional 'success' leaves little room for compassion. We are a people disempowered by our own design.

Without a sense of self and pretext for doing good, it is easy to believe that the bad guys – often backed by or part of the establishment – will always win. Far too often we use the excuse that suffering is inevitable to prevent our own efforts at intervention. What is the point in emotionally exhausting ourselves by caring and campaigning for justice that may never materialise in our lifetime? Even if we do care, what can we effectively do? Petition? Over 4 million people signed an e-petition for Parliament to call a second EU referendum. Lobby? There are hundreds of lobbying organisations that campaign tirelessly for the better treatment of asylum seekers, and yet Western countries still force them to camp in squalor at our doorstep or – worse – send them straight back to the dangerous situations they have fled from. Boycott or strike? Concessions have rarely been satisfactory since union power was eroded and dismissed by neoliberalism. Protest? One million people attended the march against the Iraq war. Political extremism or terrorism? Definitely counterproductive to the leftist agenda…

The attitude that injustice will always prevail has ensured that narratives about suffering are disposable. Twenty-four-seven, marketised, digitalised media churns out thirty-second clips of bombed hospitals and dead children's bodies being recovered from rubble as clickbait. Images and accounts of horrific adversity appear frequently on our social media feeds, our television screens and in newspapers. In the modern age, empathy for victims of oppression, war or disaster is expressed most often by a crying-face react. Clicking 'share' has replaced more tangible and consequential acts of solidarity. Whilst you may be exposed to the plight of Syrian refugees in the morning headlines, by lunch you will have read about the oppressed Rohingya Muslims, after dinner you can watch a documentary about the victims of gang violence in Mexico, interrupted by charity commercials showcasing the street orphans of Kenya, and by the time you go to bed, the campaign against police brutality in the US will be trending on Twitter. We are presented only with transient and incomplete accounts of injustice. Empathy is momentary. And yet it is clear to us all that the sheer scale of suffering on Earth is vast. So why is it so easy for us to do nothing about it? Desensitivity is the easiest way to absolve ourselves of anguish – and therefore responsibility – for human tragedy. I repeat: it is easiest not to care at all.

In fact, in some dark corners of the universe inhabited by the likes of Richard Spencer, Katie Hopkins and Roosh V, it's actually on trend to express contempt as opposed to compassion for others. Holding extreme, usually oppressive opinions guarantees access to an exclusive anti-liberal, anti-establishment crusade. The favourite activities of this regressive community include taunting left-wing 'snowflakes', criticising vegans and feminists, and denying that cyberbullying is real. All of this occurs (predominantly) online: it is an easily accessible cesspit of hate. Desensitivity to injustice has gone one step further by encouraging people to actually advocate for it – the 'meninist' movement being a prime example. Matters of objective gender inequality are debated as subjective opinion. The gender wage gap is a fabrication. Yeah, sexual assault is wrong, but some women ruin men's lives by falsely accusing them of rape. Catcalling and commenting on women's bodies is flattery, not sexism. There aren't as many female business leaders because women don't really want those kind of jobs. Why isn't there an International Men's Day? This new breed of Western misogynists describe themselves as 'equalists' rather than feminists because they can't accept a prefix that pays homage to thousands of years of female oppression. And if challenged? It's just banter. Don't you care about freedom of speech?

Calling out discriminatory views makes you part of the dreaded 'politically correct brigade'. Caring is not just inconvenient, it is sneered at.

All this can be seen as the inevitable resistance against the tide of Western liberal triumph that occurred in the twentieth century: women gained the vote, institutional racial segregation was largely dismantled, gay rights began to be solidified in legislation, anti-Semitism was no longer an acceptable political agenda, and quality of life for migrants generally improved. The old established order has, however much it seems to be making a resurgence in the Brexiteer-Trump-supporter-led dynasty, been eroded significantly. And now, the groups who traditionally benefited from an unjust societal order – largely, but not exclusively, wealthy white cis straight men – have been led to believe that their rights are revoked when others gain. Instead of progress, they perceive this as a symptom of the supposed moral decline that has 'broken Britain' and point to the erosion of nuclear familial roles to illustrate this point. Stigma, prejudices and injustice still exist, but the progress made in recent decades cannot be underestimated. It is unsurprising that those who have historically benefited from oppression and tradition are reluctant to relinquish their privilege in aid of equality. It is this insecurity that underpins the sentiment that we need to fix Britain and 'make America great again'. Thatcher's children are succeeded by something arguably more harmful: the spawn of Trump and Farage.

History teaches us that retaliation to liberal progression is to be expected. After the emancipation of Black slaves in America came Jim Crow, after progressive Weimar Germany came the Nazis, and after the blossoming left-wing social consciousness of the 1960s and 70s came Reagan and Thatcher. After Obama came Trump. Socio-political zeitgeist moves like a pendulum. But why? When discrimination takes precedence – in the form of government or civilian attacks on the rights of minorities – liberals mourn and retaliate in fury. Conservatives do just the same when their belief systems are challenged. Left or right, when our convictions about what we believe to be in humanity's best interests are threatened, we feel devalued, degraded, despondent and angry. The chasm between liberals and conservatives grows wider, deeper, more treacherous each time one side is victorious.

The left are guilty of 'othering' those with opposing political standpoints. Far too often, we engage in intellectual snobbery rather than intellectual debate. Calling someone a racist, a xenophobe, a sexist, a homophobe, an anti-Semite or simply a bad person is no way to achieve progress. Any response to intolerance must be one that regards the other as human, as flawed, and as explicable by societal factors. Hatred is often favoured because it is the simplest way to satisfy socio-economic anxieties and it is often incited by the establishment to distract from their culpability.

Responding to those with a discriminatory or apathetic political disposition with scorn is counterproductive. Equally, retreating into echo chambers only ensures we are shocked and disappointed when a resurgence of regressive views rears its ugly head (Brexit and Donald Trump's presidency being some recent, painful examples). We can't commend ourselves for the progress we make if we aren't taking everyone along for the ride with us.

In this age of desensitivity, humanity is often not tangible in the rolling stats, graphs and diagrams used to explain injustice. In quantifying catastrophe, we remove its many faces. Human narrative and an understanding of victims is lost, diluting our belief in our capacity and duty to help them. It is easy to not care about huge numbers of dead, dying, suffering when we have no real conception of what those numbers mean – and when it is more convenient to ignore their plight. Whilst scepticism is wise, distrust of the media and the prevalence of 'fake news' means that when we do hear of injustice, doubts arise about its sincerity. Supposedly charitable organisations have been implicated in investing in harmful industries, such as oil and tobacco. It is often hard to know who are the bad guys and who are the good guys. But what we can know is whether we are personally making an effort to aid social justice. Whilst not everything we do need be selfless or for the benefit of others, being conscious of how our decisions – where we shop, what we eat, who we vote for – impact other people is crucial.

Each and every one of us has the capacity to make the world a better place, and whether our impact is slight or huge, it matters. We just have to occasionally shun the easy route or reject what feels most comfortable. Choose not to buy from companies that exploit labour, challenge the throwaway bigoted comments and always head down to the polling station to vote for whoever will benefit society, and not just yourself. Why? Because it works. In 2016, the year of Brexit and Donald Trump's election:

- Volunteers in India planted 50 million trees in twenty-four hours.
- The global poverty rate decreased.
- The wild tiger population increased for the first time in a hundred years.
- The Paris Agreement on climate change came into force.
- World hunger reached its lowest point in twenty-five years.
- Norway became the first country in the world to commit to zero deforestation.
- A new report revealed that for the first time ever, the death penalty had become illegal in more than half of the world's countries.
- At the beginning of the year, we heard that global spending on aid and development increased by 7 per cent, and spending on refugees had doubled.
- Costa Rica ran solely on renewable energy for over a hundred days.
- Same-sex marriage was legalised in Colombia and the Isle of Man.

These triumphs were fought for by people who care.

The success of the Labour Party's 2017 general election campaign, although not enough to put Jeremy Corbyn in Number 10, was that it made people who had never engaged with the electoral system before believe that through it, they could make a difference. On 8 June 2017, people believed their vote mattered. Young people – an unprecedented 69 per cent of us – transferred caring about society into a definitive cross on a ballot. #Grime4Corbyn and other campaigns led by young people marked a rebellion against Thatcher's individualism as they clamoured: 'For the many, not the few.' Although arguably this sentiment has, and will, always exist in counterculture. The mood behind #Grime4Corbyn didn't start with the Labour leader, it started with the beginnings of hip-hop as the protest music of deprived communities of colour in America, travelling across decades to inspire people of similar urban environments in the UK. It grew with Dizzee Rascal's 'Imagine' in 2004, Skepta's 'It Ain't Safe' in 2013 and just surfaced in the mainstream with Stormzy's endorsement of the Labour Party and that infamous JME–Corbyn interview. As a pinnacle of political engagement, #Grime4Corbyn was just the tip of a very large iceberg that spans generations of young people, various countercultures, protest music and creative means for change. Perhaps it's only once in a while that this hunger for change will translate into votes reaching the ballot box, but it always exists. There is always a place for people who care.

Ultimately, the question is not why I care, but why we should all care. The answer: because we can (not necessarily because we should) all make a difference. In one respect, I agree with Thatcher: people must look to themselves first. Accepting our own ability to bring about positive change is the ultimate restoration of agency. We each have no less and no more potential to better humanity than the social justice leaders we are encouraged to admire in school: Nelson Mandela, Malala Yousafzai, Martin Luther King Jr.

Furthermore, all victories count. Translating compassion into action doesn't necessitate huge gestures or a lifetime dedicated to activism. You don't need to lead a million-man march or address the United Nations to impact this world positively. In his essay 'Famine, Affluence and Morality', Peter Singer illustrates injustice with the analogy of a drowning child. Apathy or passivity is the equivalent of standing at the edge of the shallow pond and watching that child drown. You may be incapable of retrieving them directly, but I don't think it's presumptive to say that you would not just shrug and walk the other way. You wouldn't refuse to care because it is somebody else's child, on the other side of the pond. It's possible to make a positive difference if you accept your ability to do so.

RITES OF PASSAGE

Rosalind Jana

Content warning: sexism

What's the story behind your first kiss? Was it a fizzy, knee-trembling explosion? Was it just fine – nothing awful, nothing special? Was it awkward? Underwhelming? Did it involve the clashing of two sets of braces, or more spit than expected? Was spin the bottle or something similarly inane to blame? Was it stolen, hidden, delicious? Can you even remember it?

What about the first time you had sex? What was that like? Special? Damaging? Expected? Nerve-wracking? Something that really shouldn't have happened? An encounter so mundane you hardly recall the details? Access to a new realm of possibility? An act providing sought-after entry into the smug club of people in the know? An experience you've since had to unlearn? One you're still working through? A moment of going, 'Oh, that's it? That's what all this fuss is about?'

What about your first proper boyfriend or girlfriend? (Or whatever other word works for you.) Was it love – truly, deeply, and probably a little insufferably? A level of intimacy you'd never had before? One set of mistakes after the other? Scary, in a good way? So inconsequential as to be a minor footnote in your life thus far? An experience you'd rather forget? One you learned a lot from? One you learned nothing from? Awful for reasons far beyond your control? Do you ever think about it now?

Are you scanning this exhaustive (though inevitably incomplete) list of questions and feeling increasingly frustrated with the assumption that everyone reading this already talks about first kisses and virginity loss and exes in the past tense?

I didn't kiss anyone until I was eighteen. For several years preceding that point, this felt like an acute personal failure – as though I'd somehow ducked under all the hoops labelled 'teenage rite of passage' rather than enthusiastically launching myself through them. Most of my peers were seemingly busy kissing and fumbling and doing 'other stuff' (always phrased like that at lunchtime as we huddled next to the radiators, trying not to burn the backs of our knees, the girl who'd got fingered or given her boyfriend a handjob on a quad bike talking in the conspiratorial tones of someone who knows that experience equals status). Then, one by one, they started having sex. This was even more valuable: news to be delivered with a thousand times more glee than a hushed announcement that you'd started your period, or got drunk and kissed someone called Rhys or Liam or Mattie at a Young Farmers' do over the weekend. This was something new, powerful, adult. Not only that, either. Some of my friends were wanted. They had older boyfriends or guys in other schools who'd decided to exclusively spend time with them, who valued their company – or at least thought they were attractive enough to seek out for a snog.

Well, that's how I saw it all at the time: convinced, in a tangle of melodrama and genuine worry, that I was one of the unlucky few who'd be forever stuck on the outside looking in. Alongside all the other supposed markers of adolescent rebellion, like parties (where I felt uncomfortable, out of place and disgruntled at being surrounded by drunk, messy teenagers) and illicit boundary-stretching (which scared me – I was the kind of anxiously rule-abiding girl who didn't get a single detention during my time at school), this exclusive realm of lips, hips and tortured analysis of text messages remained inaccessible. It was for the likes of other girls in my year. Girls who were confident in their allure, or at least their ability to flirt easily, kiss with impunity and play up to the kind of sexist jokes and inane behaviour from the boys that made me want to roll my eyes in despair (and then shrink away, stay invisible so they couldn't tease me further, hide in the library for five years' worth of lunchtimes). And yet in that complicated teenage way, despite not wanting to actually be them, I still deeply envied these girls; I was so incredibly jealous of their social power and visible desirability.

Of course, plenty of us go through this. At the time, perhaps, we mark ourselves out as the special unfortunates, the ones who hate our surroundings and crave the sweet release of accumulating extra years, getting away, living fuller lives beyond the expected order of secondary school. Maybe later we talk about how much we hated our teens. This becomes part of the mythology of how we grew up and came to situate ourselves in the world. Often we take a strange type of pleasure in thinking on the grim. We are glad we're beyond it. Occasionally, stupidly, some of us elevate ourselves above those girls – declaring our experiences as a dim badge of honour, rather than acknowledging how, yes, it's shit to feel alone and lonely, but also there's no superior way of being teenaged. We all make our way through those years differently. Very few of us are graceful about it. Very few emerge unscathed.

My unease continued into sixth form. There I grew ever more desperate for my prolonged state of singledom to change. Hell, a stop to the lack of lips on mine would've been nice. But I still hadn't met many people I'd wanted to kiss – and the few I had weren't interested in reciprocating. I fell for one boy partly because he was the first I'd met who liked poetry (ah, I was so sweet and young), but he decided to tumble head over heels for another friend. I spent a long time mooning over another whose mixed messages – dallying between intense rounds of late-night Facebook chats and long, personal conversations, and a sudden cold-shouldered distance, sometimes in person – left me confused as to whether this person had ever been interested, or if

I'd constructed it all in my head. In my most full-blown histrionic moments, I wondered if it would be like that forever. Those various firsts – still unfulfilled – loomed large. My thinking went that if they hadn't happened yet, perhaps they never would.

By this time, I was also increasingly stranded between various worlds. Professionally, I'd already been weaving in and out of adult realms, having begun modelling at thirteen, blogging at fourteen, and writing semi-professionally at fifteen. By sixteen, I already had friends in their thirties and beyond. By seventeen, I turned up to fashion shows and events by myself, and spent an increasing number of weekends scurrying off on the train to London. I loved the chance to escape, relishing any situation where I didn't have to be defined by my age. There was an inevitable mismatch though. There I was, acting like an adult, hanging out with adults, without some of the experiences I'd been told would help to define me as an adult. It remained a sore point. I loved being able to exist in these realms where I could dress as I pleased, go where I wanted, and have conversations that fired me up. But the inevitable corollary was that sixth form felt ever more limiting: just a holding pen where I had to bide my time until freedom called.

Here's the thing: I did recognise my own worth, and knew that, inevitably, as a very tall, very driven girl living in the middle of nowhere, a girl, moreover, who couldn't play games, didn't dress like her peers and would pretty much always prioritise blogging above drinking cider in a field (the joys of rural living), I was unlikely to have people clamouring for my attention. Older friends reassured me that my time would come. But that was easy for them to say. They'd been there, done that, moved on. I was still at the stage of struggling to imagine that anyone could ever, would ever find me attractive – that affirmation could come from anything linked to romance, rather than work.

When I got to university, I felt even more out of step. Whenever the drunken conversations began about who'd got up to what or which people had slept with each other during freshers' week, there was little I could add. I stayed glumly silent, nodding in the right places but keeping my mouth shut. There it was again. The lack. Didn't matter that I stayed busy cultivating new friendships and being ambitious and generally getting shit done. This thing, so seamless to others, was fraught for me.

Then, one night, I kissed someone. It was at a student night. I'd seen the guy around before, and drunkenly said 'hello' as though I knew him when he brushed past. We chatted, danced, and then he leaned in. That was it. First kiss done and dusted. Though easy on the eye, he was less appealing on the lips. I was underwhelmed, albeit secretly pleased that it had happened. This pattern would continue with the next few people I kissed: all largely lacklustre experiences, but still with some novelty attached. I quickly realised it was doable. That it wasn't some huge mystery. That

I should probably be more selective. And that it didn't change jack shit about me beyond my willingness to flirt more, and, eventually, to feel less brittle about my own desirability and instead start owning it.

What frustrated me then, and interests me now, are the very specific messages we absorb about the order we're meant to do things in. I was miles ahead in some areas, given that I'd turned up at uni with an imminent book deal in the wings and a blog that had seen me featured in publications around the world. But I'd still been swayed by this idea that I was incomplete until I'd ticked off everything else on the 'growing up' checklist.

I finally had sex in my second year at uni, when I was just on the cusp of twenty. The one thing I'd assumed in advance was that this would happen in the context of a relationship, probably with someone I'd trusted for a while. Instead it was with a person I hardly knew, but came to trust – and enjoy time with – hugely over the next five months. Everything about it confounded my previous expectations, and I was glad for it. It was casual, communicative, non-exclusive, and revelatory; my inexperience was negotiated with relative ease given how carefully this person made sure that everything was conducted on my terms – always at a pace I was comfortable with.

It was a heady near half-year, one peppered by new experiences: late-night cycle rides, the odd afternoon lying in bed with the windows open and a breeze rattling the leaves, conversations over tea as we both sat naked and cross-legged on my bedroom floor, wide-awake humid nights where I resented his ability to fall asleep so easily, and all the other little details that come from one body being in proximity to another. It wasn't perfect. These things rarely are. In fact, sometimes it was difficult, badly handled on both sides. But I still remain grateful for the experience, for the way it gave me an avenue into approaching sex as something that should be both practical and pleasurable. It took time, but the timing worked well.

I don't know if it was the 'right' way, given that much of it was down to circumstance (as well as temperament, and that irreducible coexistence of low self-esteem in some areas of my life and unnerving confidence in others). I do know that, much as it was exasperating beforehand, in the long term it gave me room to figure out my body and my boundaries. It offered space for making active choices. And it equipped me to view sex as something I should try to approach like any other type of interaction I enjoy: with thought, fun and a healthy dose of self-respect. For that alone, I feel weirdly lucky.

Of course, since that point I've had mediocre sex and made decisions I regretted afterwards. As with everything else in life, there's a lot left to learn and improve on. I know I am often unwilling to make the first move, much as I like to think of myself as upfront. I second-guess everything. I know my worth does not lie in the measure of my romantic or sexual relationships, but still, on my bad days, I end up irritated that my natural state of being often remains 'consistently single'. But I've learned to view this whole business of sex and dating and sense of self as an ongoing process. (One that's definitely proved more interesting for me since acknowledging – and acting on – the fact that a lot of my personal confusion was also down to me much preferring women.) Most importantly, I finally feel OK with where I am. It's comfortable here.

What I struggled with as a teenager wasn't just all the usual 'Will I ever be loved? Am I doing this wrong? What if I do actually die a virgin?' style stuff, but also the clashing cultural narratives one was expected to navigate. An absolute mire of them: each suggesting there were clear ways of getting things right and wrong. Of course, sex ed had been paltry, painting shagging as a largely mechanical act full of dire consequences. Sure, we all giggled when we had to write down every single word for 'vagina' and 'penis' that we knew (Ha ha! Foof! Trouser snake! How funny!). But we learned little about consent, or the pressure and expectations we might, and would, face. There was nothing on how to navigate the emotional implications of relationships and bodies and everything else – let alone the tiniest sniff of an acknowledgement that sex wasn't exclusively reserved for heterosexual couples. I still wonder whether I might have worked out an awful lot more about myself sooner, had that been different.

Some of this has changed since. MPs and students alike have pushed for better, more comprehensive and inclusive SRE. It's not there yet. But hopefully it's on its way (and in the meantime, at least there are online resources like Scarleteen and BISH). But my God, is it needed more than ever. Many of the messages I was confused by in my teens have only been amplified now, from the bullshit language of innocence and shame – a woman's worth equated with her, ugh, 'purity' – through to more complicated, and just as toxic, messages.

Summarising all the conflicting representations of sex and sexuality would take the time and length of a PhD, but there are two particular narratives I used to feel especially trapped by. Firstly, there was the way society and culture at large demonised female sexuality when it was anything other than decorative. Women's bodies were dissected piecemeal in the tabloids, but those who chose to use their bodies actively – who were vocal in owning their sexuality – were castigated. In films, the 'bad' girls slept around, while the 'good' ones usually waited. Those were the two choices. And as far as porn went... Well, I can still remember just how uncomfortable I felt when the boys waved around unsavoury clips on their crappy Motorola phones at break: enjoying the shock factor, the power they got from pushing them in our faces. These weren't depictions of women enjoying themselves, of equal fun being had by both parties, but rather a way of reminding us of our place.

See, sexiness, in this context, was an essentially passive quality, enacted for men's eyes and expectations, rather than one's own pleasure. It was riddled with double standards (that fun old 'slut'/'lad' chestnut) and contradictions (as a woman, having sex was good, but being too voracious or active about it was bad; in fact it was something provided rather than shared, and you were definitely at fault if you were too keen, or clear in your intent).

In response to this, however, there was a counter-narrative: one that lauded sex to the point that anyone who wasn't fucking around was doing it wrong. This was one I encountered less in real life – up until university, anyway – and more in the world of articles and social media that I was continually consuming. Here, the suggestion went, was the antidote to those crappy, gendered expectations. Bollocks to all standards! Bad one-night stands and cringe-inducing stories for all! Sex equals empowerment, regardless of nuance or context! How dare you say you don't want to be defined by your sex appeal – it obviously means you judge people who do! This one perplexed me too. But I wasn't sure how to articulate that feeling. Was I being judgemental? Slut-shaming? A prude? Then it crystallised one weekend when I sat down, opened the paper, and read an article from a female columnist who praised to high heavens being a young woman and having sex with everyone you could. She didn't paint it as an experience that had been great for her, but rather as one that was pretty much categorically great for all women. I remember feeling, once again, that maybe I'd got it wrong if that wasn't my approach – but finally, I also realised something. My problem wasn't her experience. Not in the slightest. It was the way she'd taken the personal and scaled it up to the universal, implying her perspective was the best lens through which to filter the world.

Of course, I've over-simplified some big, messy things here. I wholly understand why the counter-narrative exists. It needs to. From Eve and her leaf bikini onwards, women have been encouraged to feel uneasy about their sexuality. Reacting to that is important, as is proudly sticking up two fingers to anyone who thinks sex – especially casual sex – is shameful. But rarely did I find the more temperate acknowledgement that what works for one person doesn't work for another, that talking about young women and sexuality and sexiness is not only very personal, but also fucking complicated.

Now, I like having sex. I like writing about it. I spend too much time on WhatsApp with my best friend chatting about cunnilingus and bad dates and sex droughts and all the other stupid things you talk about in passing when you're not screenshotting ridiculous tweets or catching up on each other's days. A few years ago this would've been a mildly inconceivable future – but even knowing that, I can recognise how easy it would be for me to accidentally dismiss my younger self's anxieties as inconsequential. These days it'd be a little too simple for me to write something like that columnist did, to talk blithely about sex as this thing that has added lots to my life, from the big and brilliant to the strangely formative to the 'regrettable, but made a good story', while forgetting to emphasise that my experience is only that. Mine.

In fact, occasionally I pause, try to crawl back into that adolescent skin, and properly access the intense frustration and doubt I used to own. I remember those lunchtime confessionals, the conversations on the train at sixth form, the rounds of 'never have I ever' at university that, if I'd followed the rules properly, would have meant I was still entirely sober at the end; the way I felt so horribly inadequate and lonely for years. I nudge myself into acknowledging that, yes, it was temporary, but, no, it wasn't silly. I remember the things I could've done with being reassured about back then: like how you could be aware of your own sexuality without yet having had sex; or that just as there's no inherent value in virginity, there's also no inherent value in losing your virginity by a particular age; or that it takes some of us longer than others to figure out who we desire; and that, of course, you get to choose how and when you want to feel sexy, if you do at all.

Remember that book deal I mentioned above? It was a publication for teenagers, with chapters covering everything from mental health to body image to relationships. I wrote pretty much all the material on sex before having it. I talked about consent, double standards, wanking, sexting, porn and how idiotic a phrase 'losing your virginity' is (things you want to lose: ugly jumpers and incriminating photos of bad haircuts. Things you want to gain: the frisson and satisfaction of a good time with a good person). I approached the chapter with time, care, research and passion, but remained more anxious than necessary. I felt I lacked authority.

Then I had sex. Then I had to edit the book. Then I realised I still stood by everything I'd written beforehand, bar the odd detail. Of course I did. I'd already spent years reading about all of those topics and reflecting on how they affected me. I'd developed a set of principles to stick by. And I'd chatted with friends whose experiences were vastly disparate. We all had varied trajectories and very different levels of insight. Each was just as valid as the other.

This is the nub, really: the need for ever more plurality in the stories we tell, and the stories we are offered access to. It makes all of us feel less alone. Especially with young people, there's that ever-creeping tendency to generalise. Not just in how we label them (deeming teens difficult, or awkward, or magic en masse), but also in the way we unfurl the map of growing up. We peg out those rites of passage, those markers and milestones, as absolute. They become a string of qualifiers rather than various possibilities that should, when it feels right, make life more interesting.

Adolescence is a time of exploration – of working out everything from clothes choices to sexuality to where you fit in the world at any given point. And it can be painful.

And sometimes great. There are physical transformations to contend with, friendships to navigate, new things to try out, a sense of feathered independence to test, common points of reference, both culturally and socially, to share. There are also the messages – many of them toxic – to take in (and then hopefully expel again) about where worth lies, what gives you power. Talking about all of that is important. As is stressing that no one route is the same. And pointing out that the exploration never, ever stops.

Besides, it's not the firsts that have defined me. It's everything since that point: the charge of suggestive talk and knees touching under tables, the unexpected spontaneity of a good kiss with a gorgeous woman while everyone is dancing, the mornings of waking up with a warm body curled round mine and letting lips brush and fingers link, the encounters that have changed me, the ones I can hardly remember, the fact that there's so much left to discover. Those are the stories to focus on. The ones to carry on unfurling.

THE LATTE DRINKER THAT SPILLED THE TEA

Malakaï Sargeant

Content warning: classism, racism, violence

I remember a time not so long ago when the utterance of the place-name 'Hackney' drew looks of sympathetic concern, coinciding with a false smile that read, 'I'm so sorry you have to go through that,' as if living in the borough was synonymous with suffering from continuous traumatic stress. Largely, this was true. The Hackney I knew was enveloped in crime, violence, poverty and postcode wars, and growing up, the constant suspicious stares and blaring sounds of sirens increasingly became synonymous with home.

I lived on one of the few 'Murder Miles' in Hackney; it acted as a border, with one half of it being in north London and the other half in east. As you may be able to guess, the geographical location meant that this no man's land of a road was a catalyst for criminal activity, perpetuating the divisions between north and east London while simultaneously strengthening the alliances of troops on either side, ready to defend their territory. The damp-infested flat I shared with my mum was smack bang in the middle of the road, and thus became a fantastic viewing point for spectating and commenting on the hotbed of crime that plagued the area. In short: the block was always hot. Life was a lottery for those who were engulfed in this way of life, and the proliferating figures of knife and gun crimes in the borough as a whole at this time meant that many on my estate – including my childhood self – lived in constant fear. The road played host to a plethora of stabbings, drive-bys and shootouts throughout much of the 2000s, with many such instances going unreported and many innocent lives lost. My block was nestled in the jaws of the estate, barking at passers-by who looked at it the wrong way, nuzzled by the flimsy mesh wired gate, dividing me from all that I wanted to be. The estate itself was cornered by a railway line, sat shoulder to shoulder with a rival estate on the other side, and on the very edge was an abandoned warehouse, one that now houses middle-class dreams that've been trust-funded into fruition.

For a long time, the turmoil and chaos that Hackney played host to clouded the beauty that lay beneath it. There's no hiding the fact that throughout much of the 1950s onwards, Hackney was regarded as a slum, and in 2010 it was the most deprived borough in London, and overall the sixth most deprived local authority in the country. But, for many, economic deprivation wasn't the be-all and end-all of their existence. Despite differences in aspirations, culture and class, Hackney has long been a community. It completely encapsulates the positivity of multiculturalism – Hackney is diversity, and has been so long before that buzzword got thrown around by every corporate and creative organisation that needs more brown people in their offices. Even today, just by walking through a park such as Clissold or London Fields, you will see families and friends making use of facilities and interacting with one another in complete harmony, like every liberal's utopian fantasy. You can almost see it in a nostalgic, sepia hue: the clammy hand of one toddler in another's, bumbling with joy through the play park, zigzagging from the sandbox to the slide, both from completely different backgrounds but brought together simply by the innocence of youth and sharing the same borough. Hackney was no idyll, but in the era I grew up in, it almost was. The number of opportunities and facilities that were, and are still, available, if at a cost, were ample; from rowing and canoe clubs on the river Lea to the Boxing Academy to support young people's education outside of the traditional school setting, Hackney accommodated all kinds of people. And within that lay a sense of basic humanity and human decency, too. When our washing machine broke, we had neighbours who volunteered to do our washing, free of charge, because there was an underlying sense of community – we were all on low incomes together, and because of that we supported each other. Today, however, the polarisation between the wealthy and the poorer – and even among these groups – is widening violently, and within this increasing gap is the deterioration of Old Hackney's sense of community.

As with any place, particularly one in an urban area, there will be discrepancies between the wealthy and the less wealthy. However, growing up I saw all of the people that called Hackney home come together; not in a *High School Musical*, 'we're all in this together' sort of way, but in the sense that anyone could walk down Kingsland Road and go into any shop and be welcomed, instead of being greeted with 'Are you lost?' stares. Or be walking through the Narrow Way and being able to guarantee that they'd see somebody they knew and stop to chat, instead of having white women who clutch their purses tighter when you sit next to them. I won't lie and suggest that there is no longer a sense of community in Hackney, because there definitely is – among the white middle class who have infiltrated and colonised all of the places I grew to love.

The stark lack of integration between the old and new communities in Hackney hugely contributes to my feeling of no longer being at home walking down streets with memories and experiences ingrained in their pavements. Like the street where I grazed my knee after falling off my bike, where my uncle taught me how to cycle. That road has been resurfaced now, with the council filling in potholes as per their deals with housing developers after responding to complaints by the new residents. Or the street where my great granddad walked with me to take me to primary school, quickening his pace when going past the park. At any time of the day, that park would have been a shelter for the homeless and drug abusers; now, the climbing frame is actually used by children – but only children whose parents can afford to take them in the middle of the day instead of working a ten-hour shift. Children of all creeds, colours and classes would play for endless hours in the rotting mouths of rusty MUGAs, but now it plays host to the blinding Colgate white of 'regeneration'. It relentlessly bleaches over the crookedness and imperfections of the teeth of various estates that were resilient enough to stand firm throughout two world wars, but whose bite couldn't withstand the crunch of gentrification. Those teeth now are crushed tombstones, reminders of former lives, destroyed not by decay or wear and tear, but by the sweet appeal of luxury flats, gated communities and a socially cleansed borough that has replaced where these towers once stood. I know that Hackney wasn't perfect, but it was home. But now that everyone else wants to make it home (and with me having moved house four times since I left Hackney), I have no idea where else to call home in London. But as long as Sarah and Richard are happy and are contributing to the local economy by going to the weekly farmers' market and buying ethnic food from the independent café to relieve their conscience from the guilt manifested within it after chasing out the locals by agreeing to high house prices, that's all that matters, right?

A complete and exhaustive account of what the first wave of gentrification probably looked like, maybe.

'Look!' said Sarah excitedly, with one hand rubbing her growing stomach, the other clasping onto the arm of her fiancé, Richard. Together, they stared longingly at the Victorian three-bedroom house with the generously sized garden and potential for a loft conversion in the estate agent's window. 'The rooms are so big! It's practically the same as those houses we viewed near Angel, just cheaper,' she continued, naively choosing to ignore the article in the *Hackney Gazette* about the most recent stabbing in Clapton.

'I wonder what the schools are like around here,' proposed Richard, implicitly dressing up his fear about how densely populated the area was with brown people.

'I heard they're improving, and when baby grows up they'll make all sorts of multicultural friends – think of the play dates and the dinner parties we could—' Sarah looked over at Richard. He wasn't sold. Sarah was close to pleading now: 'I read in the *Guardian* that Hackney is really up-and-coming, you know... we could sell it in five, ten years and move.' She hesitated. 'We could make a lot of money out of this.' She looked into her fiancé's blue, capitalist eyes; he cracked a smile.

A week later, the house was off the market. Sarah and Richard sold it in 2011 for £850,000, making a £500,000 profit. They live somewhere near Dorset now, with their child and a pony or some shit.

Don't allow this hypothetical situation to go over your head; Sarah and Richard, and thousands like them, are the reason why I'll never be able to afford somewhere to live in the place I was born. And herein lies the greatest issue: as long as we continue seeing property as investments or assets instead of homes, we will never be able to halt skyrocketing rent and housing prices, making Hackney and other areas following suit (Tottenham, Walthamstow, Peckham) simply unaffordable for the ones who made these places homes to begin with. Places where people have spent their entire lives living and working are rapidly losing their identity, and are becoming replicas of other bougie-fied areas where the white middle class have Christopher Columbus-ed entire neighbourhoods by claiming them as cool, telling all their mates to come and forming their own communities within them, rather than engaging with the existing community who, more often than not, lose out economically and become displaced once their area begins to be infiltrated by self-interested 'young professionals'.

Of course, Hackney has always housed pockets of affluence and wealth, with the pressure for Hackney to become 'better' (read: more white, more wealthy) having existed for a long time – and in recent times the local authority has been dancing with the devil to appease the desire for a 'rejuvenated' Hackney. Prior to questionable collusion between the council, the Greater London Authority (GLA) and property developers, Hackney provided a great deal of social housing to some of the poorest individuals and families in the UK. For a long while, its name grew in notoriety, and it was infamous for being grimy, unwelcoming and dangerous. So of course, with the poor being, well, poor, they were often placed in one of the abysmally designed mid-twentieth-century housing blocks scattered through the borough, with recent disasters such as the Grenfell Tower fire displaying just how hazardous and mismanaged social housing still is.

Almost ironically, such housing projects, which encapsulate the struggle of the working class in inner London, more often than not face, or are adjacent to, tidy rows of three- or four-bedroom Victorian or Edwardian terraced properties, symbolically modelling to the working-class Thatcher's mantra of, 'If you stopped being so lazy and so poor, look at what you could achieve!' You can spot the well-to-do nuclear families in these homes; you know the type – mummy and daddy guzzling eight bottles of wine a week from the cellar, and their children perpetually laughing as if to say, 'I enjoy an abundance of extracurricular activities.' Their dog probably has a bigger lounge than you – those types. The first wave of these families setting up shop in Hackney occurred around the mid-1990s, after they realised neighbouring Islington just wasn't as cheap. At this time Hackney wasn't as upmarket as many parts of it are now, which somewhat confusingly seemed to attract the

Bugaboo-pushing parents from Somethingshire who flocked, and continue to flock, to the borough.

And thus Hackney began appealing to the appetite of the bougie: the Whole Foods on Stoke Newington Church Street has been on that corner in different forms for at least my whole lifetime, peddling organic delicacies and aspirations of healthy living, and the creative innovation and entrepreneurship that's made the borough famous in recent years has, in reality, been thriving for decades. Independent shops like The Ark in Stoke Newington have always appealed to Hackney's wealthier few by selling overpriced smelly candles and other middle-class nonsense for years. Pre T-shirt print fame (yes, I genuinely saw T-shirts being sold with The Ark name emblazoned on it – like, who actually buys that shit?), Dalston in the 1970s was home to a genuine community of hardworking artists, as opposed to the frauds living there now who claim to be struggling whilst paying £800 per calendar month for a double room above a chip shop. Despite the existence of a more affluent group within the borough, when I was growing up there, and even when my mum was a child, there was little of the socio-economic division that is seen today.

For someone without the same emotional connection to Hackney, perhaps this contrast is best displayed visually.

A concept: how the fast food establishment and the off west end theatre are actually cousins.

The McDonald's has sat on the corner for decades. It rests on the main thoroughfare of Dalston and is a hub of activity for Hackney's schoolchildren, the unemployed, parents, commuters, late-night partygoers, early-morning civil servants, the old, the young and everyone in between. It is buzzing throughout the day and night, and is the subconscious landmark and linkup point for pretty much everyone that goes to Dalston. It serves an entire community wholly through providing cheap food and somewhere warm to sit. Or on the newly added terrace, if it's good weather.

A stone's throw away, tucked away on the corner of a cobbled street, sits the Arcola Theatre. It produces pioneering work in-house, and since its inception has moved into a larger building, away from the street where the theatre gets its name, due to its popularity. It has a lively bar with music nights, a great theatre space and two studio spaces, and provides a central spot for Hackney's creatives to network, drink and enjoy the culture on offer.

Both of these institutions are merely buildings filled with people. Yet there's little crossover between the people who utilise these buildings. To generalise, those who visit the Arcola regularly would much rather buy smashed avocado on crusty sourdough for £6 than buy a cheeseburger and fries from McDonald's. Similarly, those who go to McDonald's regularly are more likely to watch a film in Stratford or hang out in Hackney Central than go to watch a play without an interval at the Arcola. These two buildings, simply bricks and mortar (and terraces), are symbolic pillars of the class division in Hackney. They encompass the differences between the people that live in the borough, and despite their close proximity, there are very rare occasions in which these two groups cross paths. Yet, somehow, I belong to both.

As I cycle from my relatively nice flat in north London into my company's office – the one adjacent to my old estate – I automatically feel a sense of resentment, knowing that every so often I'll pass old friends and neighbours who still live in the bubble of that estate a decade on, and haven't 'made it out the hood'. Not long ago I was making my way down the road into work and almost found myself surprised by the police tape that prevented me from going any further. I remembered where I was and stopped awhile, considering the fact that, whatever the incident might be, my reality is that I could very well know the person affected. Two days later, speaking to my grandparents, it turned out I did: a young, black man in his twenties had been hit by a car and stabbed repeatedly in the chest – a young black man I grew up with in church. He lived in another area in Hackney, where he'd previously had trouble with gangs in the borough, and had crossed the divide into the 'wrong' postcode to see his friend on my old estate, only to be in the wrong place at the wrong time. Luckily, he managed to survive this horrific incident, after being in an ICU at the local hospital for days afterward. The common perception is that all of this violence involving gangs and Hackney's youth more generally stopped when parents started naming their children Odyssey and Clover instead of Oluwadamilola and Chanel. It hasn't.

The fact that we grew up in replicable settings, yet I have an adequate career in the arts and moved away while my peers are still trapped there because it's the only way of life that they were exposed to, fills me with ambivalence and uncertainty about where exactly to place myself socially and economically. My line of work, well-spoken accent, rolled-up jeans and appreciation for 'white' things often leads people to believe that I'm from a stable or wealthy background. However, the only reason I cycle to work is because TfL is fucking expensive, and day to day I can't afford to top up my Oyster. It may sound like the woes of a struggling artist, but at times it can genuinely be hard to make ends meet. If anything, all this proves is that gentrification has layered effects on everyone: the less wealthy who had little access to cultural capital remain stagnant in their poverty; the wealthy who move into the areas where the less wealthy live (because it's cheap) agree to pay higher rents, forcing up property prices and pushing the less wealthy out of their own area; and the people in the middle (me) will continue being not poor but far from wealthy, creating a new purgatory in Britain's much beloved class system and perpetuating feelings of – and literal – displacement.

I know more than anyone that gentrification will continue

to spiral out of control if we continue to appease those who exacerbate it. The Dutch pot of Hackney was long boiling prior to their arrival, with all of the flavours and spices in our neighbourhoods blending seamlessly. But as soon as the gentrifiers got a whiff of the stew, they ran straight into the kitchen to rob it from us, water it down because it was too spicy, and replace the authenticity of Hackney's vibrancy with generic, 'look at the exposed brickwork, we're so edgy!' cafés that cater to the palates of the avocado-devouring, latte-sipping elite.

But this is where I am in flux.

If I'm offered a smashed avocado with a poached egg on sourdough it's very unlikely that I'll say no. If I'm at a meeting in a ridiculously pricey coffee shop, and the barista with the bad haircut and 'LOOK AT ME, I'M A WHITE FEMINIST™' armpit hair asks what I'd like to drink, it's now more likely that I'd say an organic pressed elderflower juice than a Coke. Fam, I drink coffee now. I still don't know if I even like the taste, or what the difference between a cappuccino and a macchiato is, but I drink it now, just like everyone else.

I'm stood on the periphery of change: walking past – never through – these glossy apartment complexes leaves me feeling as empty as the apartments themselves, as housing developers attempt to market a one-bedroom flat at £565,000. Yet such developments are a benefit to me, as the people that have the money to buy that flat usually also have the money to invest elsewhere, in fields such as the arts, in which I work.

Recently, I've been asking myself more and more who and what it is that I am becoming, or have attempted to become. I've subconsciously succumbed to the culture of the gentrifier, living their life completely, only without the money. As much as I protest about how the process of gentrification has led to the decimation of local family-run businesses, and how the new businesses that open in their place only appear to welcome a certain type of person, I will still go into the new establishment anyway.

An anecdote: that one time I went into an organic food shop where the turkish furniture shop used to be just to see if they would acknowledge my presence.

They didn't. I waited a good six to eight minutes before I even got asked if I'd been served. All I wanted was an orange juice.

Fin.

As unwelcomed as I may be in hipster havens, I know that plenty of Old Hackney still remains, and will greet me with open arms. I know all of the barbers in the barbershop on the bottom of Ridley Road as well as I know all of the aunties in the church I used to go to. As different as they may be, I know undoubtedly that both groups of people embody the love and spirit that once filled the borough, and being in their presence alone is enough to bring me back to times when figuring out how I'm supposed to complete a tax return and not knowing when my next invoice is coming through were just not on my mind. The subtle segregation between Old and New Hackney used to frustrate me, because the vapid New Hackneyites couldn't (and still don't) seem to comprehend that people who don't look or sound like them – i.e. a six-foot-and-a-bit black man – may be interested in theatre, too. But alas, I'm long past caring now, because I thrive not in the Arcola Theatre bar, but in the McDonald's, and all of the other alcoves and people in which I can find aspects of what home used to be.

Of course, gentrification has meant that Hackney has cleaned up a bit; for much of this decade crime in the borough has been low, employment has increased, the creative scene is booming, and when Hackney is mentioned to an individual, young white people on bikes spring to mind, instead of drug dealers and the homeless. Yet somehow both coexist in this large and confusing borough, and all of its residents call it home.

For me, generational diaspora woes will continue to cloud my view of home and what that is. But for now, Hackney comes pretty close. Just to be clear though, I'll take Irish stew at my nan's house in Stoke Newington over a fucking latte any day.

A MARKED WOMAN

Chloë Maughan

Content warning: sexual assault, fatphobia, sexism

November 2015

Weight: 236 pounds

The first page of Google says I am a crazy woman. Stacked between my LinkedIn profile, filler pieces in the local press about my former high school, and the website I edited as a first-year at university, the article sits there like a badge of shame.

In this day and age, your search history matters. Those first ten hits on a search engine will determine the impression I make on future employers before I even walk through their doors. It is embedded into my identity, and how am I read by the world.

And yet without having ever done anything of notoriety, my name has been punched into the keyboards of strangers in different cities, in different countries. Typed alongside the most vile profanities and insults imaginable.

I had known, entering my term at university as Women's Officer, that this could happen. I had seen countless articles where student activists were torn apart in student newspapers and blogs, on Twitter and in anonymous Yik Yak posts. Earlier in the year, the students' union at the University of York had reported that candidates for their student elections were being subjected to abuse via Twitter and Yik Yak. Among this spate of abuse, a misogynistic marks-out-of-ten ranking scale had been applied to the candidates for Women's Officer.

Being a woman in the public eye came with the risk of harassment – even if the eye was only that of the student movement – and that risk seemed to escalate when it came to Women's Officers, and any other student representative with a portfolio based on equality or liberation.

In 2014 Annie Tidbury, the Women's Officer at University College London, wrote an article for the *Telegraph* entitled 'Sexism, harassment and rape. Why British universities need us Women's Officers'. In her article she discussed the important welfare function that is often performed by Women's Officers – many of whom, like myself, acted as unpaid representatives and advocates. Tidbury noted the high levels of disclosures and cases that Women's Officers often work to support, which saw her dealing with high numbers of reports of sexual harassment, domestic abuse and rape. Her article was, however, met by scepticism, hostility and, of course, an added dose of objectification.

'How can anyone justify such a ridiculous job as "Women's Officer"?'

'She's not much of a role model in any event. Girls with rings through their noses aren't going to get a bloke.'

It was clear that I had taken on a role that for some is considered unnecessary, redundant and uncomfortable. Or as our critics delicately called it, 'Feminazi bullshit from the PC brigade'.

I would have a difficult line to tread. To be quiet, uncontroversial and non-confrontational, or risk vilification.

I walked the line.

Within my role, I found myself often being asked to comment on issues affecting women students. These should have felt like opportunities; instead they felt like openings for harassment. So I kept quiet. I refrained from comment on any issue that seemed divisive or controversial. I asked for anonymity when I felt I had something I really wanted to say, and I avoided the BBC interview I was asked to participate in on the debate around safer spaces and 'freedom of speech'.

I was quiet, personable, palatable.

Despite my eagerness to hide, it didn't work. I found myself included in an article on Breitbart, called 'Campus Crazies: Women's Officers Who Have Gone Off the Deep End'.

Under the headline, the poster child of campus crazies everywhere: an image of me. Breitbart is, to its fans, an alt-right news site not afraid to stray away from the truth, and not hampered by political correctness. To its critics (or as I like to call them, people with feelings), it is a far-right site that champions misogyny, transphobia, xenophobia and racism. It has featured headlines such as 'Birth Control Makes

Women Unattractive and Crazy', 'There's No Hiring Bias Against Women in Tech, They Just Suck at Interviews' and 'The Solution to Online "Harassment" Is Simple: Women Should Log Off'. The latter even goes so far as to state: 'Given that men built the internet, along with the rest of modern civilisation, I think it's only fair that they get to keep it.' And now, as a 'Campus Crazy', I was just another feature in their portfolio:

'Speaking of comedy gold, Chloë Maughan of Bristol University posted this photo of herself on Facebook the other day.'

In the image mentioned I'm holding a placard for an upcoming Reclaim the Night march that reads 'Cake Culture Not Rape Culture'. It remains unclear whether the caption related purely to my figure, which apparently reveals I'm very much the advocate for 'cake culture', or whether the 'comedy' was in me suggesting we might live within a 'rape culture' – a culture where rape jokes, victim blaming and harassment (a list that reads much like the average contents of the Breitbart comments section) are prevalent.

I shouldn't have been surprised. I'd feared that at some point the inevitable would happen. There's a new Godwin's law on the internet, a new kind of certainty: once you are vocal about sexism, even if only in your immediate circle – a hundred or so Twitter followers, or a modest Facebook following – online harassment will follow.

And feminists, in particular, are honey to misogynists. If the Everyday Sexism Project was set up to free women by giving them the space to talk about encountering sexism in their day-to-day lives, over the years the hashtag has instead become the feeding ground for men who don't find enough women to yell profanities at on the street. Indeed, lauded for giving a much-needed space for women to talk openly about the prevalence of sexism, within only a matter of months the hashtag had become flooded by misogynistic men and 'Women Against Feminism', simply to respond to women's complaints with insults and gaslighting comments suggesting they were being overly sensitive.

Indeed, when a friend set up a personal blog exploring her frequent encounters with everyday sexism and the effects it had on her day-to-day life, she was flooded with comments tarring her as a 'narcissist', 'petty' and a 'liar'. One went so far as to suggest that she was disclosing the harassment she had been subjected to not to raise awareness, but as a way of indirectly reminding people that men found her attractive. The responses on her blog were so regularly full of hostility that after just seven posts she was pushed into silence.

And these are not isolated incidents. Indeed, 'The dark side of *Guardian* comments', published as part of the *Guardian* series 'The Web We Want', extensively mapped the abuse taking place within their online comment sections. Their research, which has analysed comments made since 2006, found that a higher volume of abusive and offensive remarks are lobbed at female writers, and are more prevalent within the comment sections of articles written on topics such as feminism and rape.* Like I said: honey to misogynists.

In my case, the trigger point was that picture – something I'd shared with a small Facebook page set up to keep members of the Women's Network up to date on what I was doing. An undoubtedly feminist message: a signalling call to the bees.

That picture of me, once a snapshot of a moment of pride, became an ugly reminder of how threatening a place the internet is for women.

In the same week that I was working hours around the clock to organise Bristol's Reclaim the Night march, the Breitbart comments section began to swell with comments devaluing the cause, and suggesting I probably just needed a 'good raping' to stop me banging on about the 'myth of sexism'.

Reclaim the Night is an important event for me. It's a movement built on tackling the innate fear with which many women walk the streets.

A fear compounded by street harassment.

For most of us that fear is there even before anything has ever happened to us to make sense of it. It's innate, like the discomfort that comes with passing a white van parked on the roadside at night. It's likely that nothing has ever

---

* Becky Gardiner, Mahana Mansfield, Ian Anderson, Josh Holder, Daan Louter and Monica Ulmanu, 'The dark side of *Guardian* comments', *The Guardian*, 12 April 2016, available at https://www.theguardian.com/technology/2016/apr/12/the-dark-side-of-guardian-comments

happened to make you feel distrustful around them, and yet you find yourself crossing roads to avoid them.

But my fear was rationalised some time ago. It's now an anxiety response. A protection mechanism. A flashback.

June 2012
Weight: 148 pounds
The London street was a dense arrangement of tired-looking shopfronts, covered by metal corrugated sheets. The pavement was littered with cardboard boxes, wooden pallets and detritus that had been left to build for days. A cluster of flies and pigeons fought over the remains of the day's produce: a couple of nectarines, and the meat of some unidentifiable animal. Not a soul around to disturb them; not a soul around to interrupt our interaction. And somewhere, nestled down a staircase behind it all, the sublet I'd be calling home for the length of my internship.

It had started with an innocuous line. Ten men loitering around one of the trailers left on an otherwise empty Ridley Road. It always was come 7 p.m. The market closed for the day and the street became the territory of the rats and litter everyone was too careless to sweep up. The picture of a land left forgotten.

'Hey, baby, how are you doing?'

'Fine, thanks,' I muttered, my hands suddenly clenching.

'Can I walk you home?'

Just be polite. He'll leave you alone. 'No, thank you.'

I lowered my gaze to ground level, and stepped homeward. At this point I felt a hand catch my wrist.

'Come on, baby, where do you live?'

'It's only a minute away, it's really not necessary for you to walk me. Thanks for the offer though.'

I began to pull my wrist forward. The hand tightened around it.

Firmly, he whispered into my ear, 'I would really like to walk you home.'

He stepped in front of me, obstructing my path, and pulled me into his torso.

His hands moved to my back, to my bum, under my skirt, and between my thighs.

Beside us, his friends watched.

November 2015

Weight: 230 pounds

'Don't read the comments.'

The warning had come so firmly from my housemate that I knew there was something there, I only needed to scroll beneath the article on Breitbart to find it.

'She's proof that enough cake culture prevents rape culture.'

'The female in the picture has no worries. She is well protected by her looks.'

'That "cake…" sign isn't big enough to hide her affection for cake. OOPS… I guess I am not Politically Correct. Sue me.'

'And then there is Chloë… My Lord! A butt the size of

a Gray Hound [sic] bus! She really needs to swear off the cake culture idea… Maybe the celery culture will work out better! Just trying to help.'

'Women that would never be raped by any man are the ones most obsessed with the idea of being raped.'

April 2012
Weight: 140 pounds

He violated me two times.

First, when I told him I didn't want any 'below the belt activity', and still he slid his hand beneath my waistband, and between my thighs.

The second time when I told him he was hurting me, and he told me it was normal.

He violated me twice that night: first with the rape. And second with the condom he discreetly removed during the act.

The following morning, the pharmacist took me into the little room. I didn't say the 'r' word when she asked if we had used contraception. I told her instead that the condom had failed. I saw her eyes roll as she noted the words 'unprotected sex' on the form.

November 2015
Weight: 236 pounds

I hid the scratches on my arms from my counsellor. There was a freedom in talking to Kelly about what was going on inside my head, and there were things I could articulate there in that quiet room that I couldn't voice to other people, but there was still a sense of shame that I carried with me for being affected by it all.

'Have you had support?' Kelly asked.

'Barely, like I've talked to friends, but it hasn't really helped.'

'What did they say when you told them?'

'A mix. A few of them congratulated me. Apparently being shamed online by a complete stranger on a Republican news site is the highest award you could have bestowed on you as a feminist. So I should be happy or something.'

'And how do you feel about that?'

'Like that would be fine, if I didn't feel like complete crap right now. Like that's all fine and well, but I haven't even felt like I can leave the house, because I don't want to be looked at right now.' As I spoke it, that raw feeling, my voice began to crack.

'And what about the other responses?'

'It doesn't feel like anyone gets it. Like it just felt like people wanted to change the subject. There was no nuance in the comments for them. It was just kind of like, "So what, someone called you fat? Their opinions don't matter."' Tear droplets began to form in my eyes.

'But it does matter to you, doesn't it?'

'Yeah, I just feel like nothing that I do will matter, nothing I'm proud of, nothing I care about, as long as my body looks like this. And it's watching my experiences be invalidated, because surely the fat girl couldn't have ever experienced harassment. And like they're divisible anyway? Like my body just exists in some kind of vacuum, and harassment hasn't shaped it in any way? It's crap!'

'And how has it shaped it?'

'Like when the symptoms get bad. When I'm depressed, when I'm anxious, my eating habits get worse. And I feel like I can't win, you know? Like I was starting to feel safe again. I don't love how I look at the moment, I'm bigger than I was and than I want to be, but I also feel less at risk.'

'Less at risk from harassment?'

'Yeah, it feels like I don't experience it as much, and I need that at the moment. But then does that just mean that this is the tradeoff? Do I just go from being an object of sexual harassment to an object of ridicule?'

There were things in that room that I could voice for the first time. And yet, I couldn't tell my counsellor that I'd been looking up train times again. That I'd hidden the paracetamol in the freezer, just to keep it out of my own reach.

It didn't sound like enough to push someone over the edge.

July 2015
Weight: 180 pounds

A man stood at the exit of the U-Bahn station in Nollendorfplatz, Berlin. As I descended the stairs, he began to cross into my path.

'Hey, baby.'

My hands seized.

I ducked past him and quickly crossed the road.

He followed me.

Twenty metres further another man catcalled me.

Another twenty metres, a third man, another 'hey, baby'.

Another: 'Can I come your way?'

I turned around, hoping to find a clearing to pass them, but in each direction I turned there was someone approaching me. Their voices overlapping and crescendoing into a haze of noise. Too loud. At each voiced I flinched. My windpipe tightened. An invisible hand began to clasp itself around my throat. And suddenly I was transported back there: Ridley Road. 'Hey, baby.' His hands. My thigh.

November 2015
Weight: 236 pounds

I'd spent four months in a cycle of flashbacks. When my eyes closed, or my thoughts were allowed to wander for a moment – a daydream in a seminar, or a solitary walk home – my mind would transport me back. My thoughts would be replaced with a showreel of his bedroom, Ridley Road, the U-Bahn station, every flash of fear on a night-time walk home, and every repulsed moment when a stranger yelled at me in the street. Behind my eyelids a video of his eyes glancing up at me whilst he dug his hands further into my vulnerability replayed. My hands would clench with that same protective instinct they did that day on Ridley Road. My heart would thump in my chest to the same beat of fear I'd felt that day at Nollendorfplatz.

And when I returned to the present, my surroundings would feel just that bit too sharp. Smells too strong, noises too loud, air too thick to breathe. My breathing would become shallow and quick, my fists clenched permanently and involuntarily. Distant laughter would make me flinch. And it didn't take much to send me spinning back round the reel again. Occasionally I'd see a flash of a red hoodie (the kind he'd worn on that night), or a man would approach me in the street and my body would double over with waves of nausea. I'd be back there. His bedroom. Ridley Road. Berlin.

Catcalls had gone from an inconvenience to a health risk. On the walk home from my lectures one day, a man had looked up from the boot of his car to eye the length of my body, and deliver a 'hey, baby' to me. My body retaliated with a wave of nausea and hyperventilation. I didn't waste time on a response, but instead sought safety. As I walked into the distance, I heard him call the word 'bitch' at me. I turned the corner and threw up into the street.

These incidents became indivisible from my body. I felt caged by it. Like it wasn't mine to control, but instead an object for prying eyes and clawing hands.

As the post-traumatic stress disorder worsened, weight gain became a mechanism of control and a path to freedom.

I wanted to feel safe. So imbued with society's messages about what it meant to be beautiful, I set out to be the opposite. As flawed and incomplete as that logic is, because fat women are not immune from harassment – far from it – fatness felt like safety. It was my armour.

I'd stopped counting calories – an obsessive habit I know stems as far back as the cereal diet I embarked upon when I was ten years old, based on Kellogg's promise that I could drop a dress size. For the first time in my life I was eating without feeling guilty about it. And as my body swelled, I began to feel more confident.

Then came the article.

Suddenly this figure I'd become accustomed to recognising kindly in the mirror had become an ugly, festering mass in front of me. I shut her up in my bedroom, kept her disgusting form from the gaze of society, and I began to punish her. I starved her, cut at her, burned her with the slides of my hair straighteners. I resented her ugly appearance, her refusal to shrink and blend into crowds.

After a while, the anger shifted. I'd look into the mirror, and the mass would catch my eye, and we would share this nod, the sad eyes of hopelessness. I started to see her as something human. Something vulnerable, sore and fragile.

The comments rolled in. They continued to label the mass 'ugly', 'unfuckable', 'disgusting'. And as the words continued to form on lips that were not my own, I grew sympathetic towards her. I grew defensive.

I wanted to speak up. I wanted to talk about what they were putting us through, how we'd hurt. But I couldn't find my voice. I knew there was a risk my hurt would only amplify their ridicule. And besides, the evidence had shown me time and time again that this is just what it meant to be a woman on the internet.

November 2012
Weight: 147 pounds

'Fucking bitch.'

This was one of hundreds of misogynistic comments that accompanied a Facebook post. The 'bitch' in question had told a guy she wasn't planning on spending the night with him. The pair had met in a club and agreed to share a cab ride home.

When they reached her place, he went to exit the taxi and she said, 'Oh, you're not coming in.'

The gentleman took to Facebook to vent his rage, branding her a 'bitch' and a 'slut'.

The likes hit the thousand mark.

'But you would be pissed off...' Peter interjected, as Alice and I discussed how unacceptable the whole thing was. At university, our kitchen was regularly a debating ground for feminist topics.

To Peter it was fair game that this woman was shamed for 'leading the guy on'. To Alice and me, it was emblematic of the sexism women experience every day, in which they regularly find themselves labelled with four-letter words for refusing someone's advances.

Peter didn't understand why I avoided nights out.

He couldn't identify with the anger clubs evoked in me. Couldn't understand why a man grabbing at my ass wasn't a compliment, and instead filled me with rage.

Peter had never been, and never would be, the bitch who didn't put out. But more than once, I'd seen the words 'miserable bitch' form on the mouths of strangers whose arms I disentangled from my body. And here it was, directed at this poor girl from the mouths and thumbs-ups of over a thousand strangers. There, as a warning to the rest of us.

June 2013
Weight: 160 pounds

Within twenty-four hours Angie's pictures were everywhere. The front page of Google, in Twitter search results, on Facebook feeds, downloaded onto the phones of strangers, and on an untold number of hard drives.

The pictures which she'd sent to a now ex-boyfriend had been shared on a Facebook page with only a hundred or so likes, but had quickly been shared across the schools in my hometown. The page sought to take down the 'Facebook Famous' – a handful of teenage girls who had attracted large Facebook followings. Their status as social media celebrities was enough to provoke a group of pissed-off teenage boys to humiliate them.

None of the girls had been controversial in the posts they'd made on their Facebook pages. They were just average sixteen-year-olds, their profiles full of selfies and complaints about school assignments.

And yet the hate Angie was subjected to was unforgiving. For doing little more than existing as a popular teenager, nude photos of her had been shared across the region. On Twitter her peers blamed her, body-shamed her and slut-shamed her.

Angie deactivated her accounts. In the wake of her silence, speculation turned to whether she was the unnamed girl the papers had said had been hospitalised as a result of the online abuse.

'So is Angie in hospital or not???: "Teenage girl lands in hospital after viral facebook postings."'

Later photographs of a naked Barbie doll holding the same pose Angie had struck in one of her photographs made the rounds on Twitter. 'I've found Angie,' read the words beside the picture. Twenty-four likes.

Even as questions arose about her safety, the abuse continued:

'She'd do anything for a few more followers. Little tramp. Have you seen her nudes on Google? *vomits*'

'Angie loves a naked picture, doesn't she, all over my newsfeed the little slag.'

'Angie is the reason I'm currently raiding my kitchen for bleach to pour into my eyes.'

The perpetrators – the ex-boyfriend who'd violated her privacy, the person who posted the original photoset, and every person who downloaded or shared the images – escaped any backlash.

'I know putting those nudes up was sly as fuck but that's what you get for sending pics of yourself around.'

'Angie shouldn't have sent so many nudes, bet she knew they'd probably get leaked all over facebook. She's just a whore tbh.'

The young women of my hometown learned an important lesson that summer: when it came to the internet, we were vulnerable. We were just something for teenage boys to 'like'. Not equal citizens, but objects for humiliation and objectification.

October 2014
Weight: 157 pounds

News reports read that Anita Sarkeesian had been pushed to cancel a speech at Utah State University.

Over the year Anita's name had become well known in feminist circles. She had gained notoriety within the gaming industry for her outspoken criticism of how women were depicted. Her video series, *Tropes vs. Women in Video Games*, shone a light on the misogyny that was rife within gaming. She looked at the misogynistically charged roles that were reserved for women in videogames: the damsel in distress, used as the reward, or the background decoration. She discussed the sexualisation and objectification of female characters within videogames, from armour modelled on lingerie to camera angles that allowed the viewer to leer at the buttocks or breasts of female characters.

For women like me, who've never had a particular interest in gaming, Sarkeesian's name became known for a different reason.

In 2014, she was the focus of an intense harassment campaign that included other women in the gaming industry and became known as 'Gamergate'. For many of us this was a scary reminder of how terrifying a place the internet (and the world) could be as not just a woman, but a feminist woman.

Sarkeesian was subjected to death threats and rape threats, and had to flee her home over safety concerns. Her speech at Utah was cancelled following several death threats, including an email that warned a mass shooting would take place if she went ahead. The email was signed with the name of a man who had killed a group of women he branded 'a bunch of feminists' twenty-five years earlier in Montreal.

Now
Weight: 210 pounds

I was lucky my abuse stopped at the comments section of Breitbart. Lucky that my Twitter account was not flooded with tweets reminding me by the second that I deserved to be raped to correct my feminist views. Lucky my inbox was not flooded with rape or death threats; that my attackers hadn't threatened me, but merely suggested I'd deserve it, or that I was 'well protected by my looks' so needn't worry anyway.

But it is happening every day, to someone somewhere.

Anita's case may read as an extreme example, but it is not an isolated one. The founder of the Everyday Sexism Project, Laura Bates, has spoken publicly about the rape and death threats she has received since beginning the project in 2012. In 2016 Melanie Jeffs, the manager of the Nottingham Women's Centre, was sent death threats following her involvement in the Nottinghamshire Police's decision to categorise misogyny as a hate crime.

In 2016 a study by Demos found that over a period of three weeks, over 80,000 individuals were sent aggressively misogynistic tweets, tarring them as 'sluts' or 'whores'.* Each time I tweet and escape that risk (sometimes more akin to inevitability) I count myself lucky.

But even with all that luck my experiences, and those of the women before me – every 'bitch' who ever rejected a man's advances, every Angie, Anita, Laura or Melanie – has shaped my citizenship on the internet.

Each time I write, it's a feat. It is a dual monologue. A battle between what I want to say, and the comment section that unfolds in my head.

---

* 'New Demos study reveals scale of social media misogyny', Demos, 26 May 2016, available at https://www.demos.co.uk/press-release/staggering-scale-of-social-media-misogyny-mapped-in-new-demos-study/

Every time I assign my name to an article on the internet, regardless of whether the content could be construed as controversial, I worry if I'm heading for my Angie or Anita moment. Each time one of my tweets gets a response from outside of my inner circle, I lock my account as a fear reflex.

This is an issue that has evolved with the advent of social media. Sure, harassment and shaming are not new issues, but they take on a unique character on the internet. Perhaps most distinct is that harassment on the internet is still tolerated. We've reached a turning point where when women are harassed on public transport or in bars, most of us will firmly state that it is not OK. But when it comes to online space, women are simply being told, 'If you're offended, then log off.'

It is disingenuous to suggest that this is any solution. The internet is no longer avoidable – it is a part of how we live and communicate and learn. It is not a place we visit outside of our 'real' lives, but an extension of them. And as such it is wrong to suggest that anything that happens to you on the internet is any less real or worth challenging than something that happens in physical space. They are a part of the same.

Almost a year on from Utah, in a *Guardian* interview with Jessica Valenti, Anita Sarkeesian discussed how the online harassment she'd suffered had shaped her 'new normal': 'If someone stops me on the street to ask for directions, I feel as if I'm going to have a panic attack.' After a recent talk she gave at New York University, a young man came up to talk to her, with his hands in the pockets of his hoodie. 'The whole time I'm thinking, "Does he have a knife in there?"'

The crap that affects us on the internet is still the crap we carry with us. For Sarkeesian it's fear. For me it's shame.

Each time a stranger glares at me on the street, the Breitbart comment section scrolls through my head. Each time an article circulates in which I speak candidly about sexual violence, I wonder how many readers look at pictures of me and go to type those same comments.

In July 2017, on the day of my deadline for *Rife*, I found myself typing the following email to my editor:

Dear Nikesh,

I'm sorry to contact you so late in the day. I know today was the final deadline, but I can't finish the piece. I think I need to pull out of the book.

I know that some of it is just classic 'imposter syndrome', that it all feels too fresh and raw and I'm not yet ready to pass it on. But I also just keep coming back to the idea of the repercussions. It feels like by writing this piece, I'm putting myself out there just to experience exactly the same harm I'm discussing in the piece. And bluntly, I'm terrified. I can see people reading the piece and thinking it's oversensitivity. I can see the body-shaming starting again, and I don't know if my mental health will be up to scratch to deal with it.

And then at the same time I'm wrestling with this gut feeling that if I do that, then the only person who loses is me. That my decision is governed by fear and shame, and silence merely plays into the hands of misogynists who'd prefer I stay silent anyway.

It's a lot to wrestle with. But right now, it feels like the fear is winning. I'm sorry if it feels like I've wasted your time.

Kind regards,
Chloë

I didn't press send.

I still feel nervous putting my name to print. Still approach Twitter with caution. Still worry about the repercussions of writing about equality. But I am steadily getting more confident.

I've made peace with my body. It swells and dissipates with my mental health, like any other symptom. Hating it wasn't making me thinner, it only fuelled a dangerous tendency for self-loathing.

And nowadays it's the second page of Google that says I'm a crazy woman. That's the thing about the internet: your history is ever changing. Silence will keep it static, but keep speaking and you have the chance to wipe the slate clean.

LITTLE MISS SUNSHINE
Katie Oldham

'Olive, can I tell you something about ice cream?' her father says, swivelling to face her with a squeak from the threadbare vinyl of the diner booth. 'Ice cream is made from cream, which comes from cow's milk. And... cream has a lot of fat in it—'

'Richard...' her mother warns, a low rumble of caution in her tone.

'What! She's gonna find out anyway, right?'

Seven-year-old Olive takes her elbow from the sticky table, concern creeping into her soft expression. 'Find out what?'

A murmur of protest rises from the booth. Uncle Frank drops his face into his hands.

'I don't... Why is everyone so upset?' Olive exclaims, as her mother begins to console her, assuring her that whatever she wants to eat, she can.

'OK Olive, well let me ask you this...'

A silence falls as her father folds his hands against the table and Olive readjusts the oversize spectacles perching awkwardly atop her button nose.

'Those women in Miss America. Are they skinny... or are they fat?'

*

It was 2006 when the film *Little Miss Sunshine* hit movie theatres. A film I was too young to see at the time, so I remained as oblivious to it as I was to most things then that weren't the Jonas Brothers or the release of the next Harry Potter book. I was just beginning to enter the awkward phase of tweenhood, where you're convinced you've earned the right to be treated like a grown-up, yet to the world, you are still very much a child. And it was then that I heard it, at first from my parents, then my older sister, and later from pretty much any adult that I knew:

'Oh my God,' they'd say of the movie. 'It's Katie!'

When I found out the plot featured a young girl determined to become a beauty queen, I thought: of course! After all, ever since that ill-fated time my mum volunteered me to model bridesmaid dresses in the local newspaper, I'd been tirelessly pleading with my parents to allow me to follow my true calling to somehow become a superstar.

It actually wasn't until my mid-teens that I finally got to watch the movie I'd been likened to for years – an act that, though I couldn't have known it then, would completely alter the way I viewed my life up until that point, and would change the way I lived it from that day onward. I popped in the disc, pressed play, and the first thing I saw was the face of the young protagonist Olive, watching the Miss America beauty pageant on TV. Immediately I saw myself, a young girl, watching her, watching me. A small bubble of sad familiarity rose as I remembered how fervently I'd dreamed when I was her age, and how I somehow never seemed to make it actually happen. But I pushed down those anxieties and continued to watch.

In the first half of the movie, there's a line that's repeated twice, both times referring to Olive as if she wasn't there. The first time it is uttered by the mother, Sheryl, during a conversation about her brother's failed suicide attempt, and the second time is in a diner, when Olive orders the ice cream.

'She's gonna find out anyway, right?'

I remember how the phrase had jammed in my throat as I watched, and how all the little pieces of my own story seemed to fall into place, glueing themselves together with the adhesive of hindsight. After all the years of believing I was Little Miss Sunshine, it was only then that I realised what the grown-ups had actually meant. For it was never her dreamlike ambition that had reminded people so charmingly of me. It was, in fact, her complete obliviousness to the fact that she didn't have, and never would have, what it took to actually succeed in what she dreamed of most.

And just like her, it was only a matter of time until I found that out, too.

Growing up, I was what adults referred to as a 'boisterous' child. If I wasn't falling out of trees or trying to catch crayfish in the river at the end of our road, I was writing letters to the queen, or forming playground girl bands with my schoolfriends and demanding we play the end of year disco.

I was a dreamer with a lust for adventure, compelled by the need to make things, make things up, or make things happen.

As the daughter of early-divorcing parents with a 'problem child' older sister, a lot of this childhood daydreaming was done alone, concocting vast elaborate plans about who I was going to be and the things I was going to achieve. Perhaps it was far easier to exist in a fantasy world, or maybe it was just this 'overactive imagination' that I was so often reminded I suffered from – all I knew was that in my world, I could be anything. In the real world, however, there was one great authority that I had to win over if I wanted to do anything: my parents. And it was clear from day one it would be a losing battle. They weren't ever discouraging as such, they simply emphatically encouraged a lifestyle opposite to everything I sought and stood for, without much room for compromise or negotiation.

But it never stopped me from trying. You name it, I wanted to do it, and I had a presentation for every last dream and desire, scrawled out with scented gel pens on sheets of computer paper to present before my parents for their consideration. I had well-thought-out arguments about why I should be allowed to pursue marine biology, acting, cheerleading, painting, telekinesis, photography, modelling, dressmaking, architecture, pottery, treasure hunting, even building electromagnets to simulate X-Men-esque superpowers. My whole childhood was framed by these presentations I'd give about the next big thing I'd decided I wanted to do with my life.

I constantly escaped into books and movies and stories of heroes saving the day, dreaming of a world in which I could go to Hogwarts and become a witch, or hone my powers at Professor Xavier's academy. I was so in awe of fierce, tech-savvy heroines in shows like *Kim Possible* and *Totally Spies!* that for a while I was dead set on becoming some kind of inventor. One memorable plan at around age ten was that I was going to build myself a jetpack over the summer holidays. After many weeks spent researching jet propulsion engines on Encarta, I pulled together some pretty solid blueprints for a jetpack made from a space heater I'd found in the Argos catalogue, backed up by important data I'd gleaned from test runs throwing Barbies out my bedroom window. I excitedly sat my parents down in their respective houses and pitched them my plans. My father managed to make it to my explanation of my bin bag parachute before entirely collapsing into fits of laughter. And then, just like they always did, he swiftly cut off the idea before I could entertain it any further, telling me if I spent as much time on my schoolwork as I did dreaming, then I might actually do something with my life. Of course, in retrospect their reaction was completely justified, but to a dreaming child desperate to explore where her passions might lead, their constant dismissal was soul-destroying.

Little did I know in my young naivety that there was nothing on Earth I could've done to convince my parents to let me try a single thing. Because while the idea of making something of myself was the most magical prospect in the world to me, to everyone else, it was nothing more than a joke. A light comic relief from the everyday stress of trying to hold together the razor-sharp fragments of a broken family.

'She's gonna find out anyway, right?' was the phrase that finally shattered the illusion when I watched *Little Miss Sunshine*. Because just like me, in her innocent and wholesome optimism, there'd never been a doubt in Olive's mind that she might not be cut out for what she dreamed to be, because the blind faith a young girl has in herself is one of the most honest, humble and fragile things. And her father suggesting that if she wanted to be a winner she'd have to change who she was was a scene so striking and familiar, it felt as if he were speaking directly to me too. Because in that moment, Olive and I were united, bound by that first moment in a young girl's life when she finds out she's deemed as anything less than enough.

From that day onward, it was hard not to grow increasingly bitter toward my parents, scorned by what I perceived as their deliberate sabotaging of my potential.

I developed a fascination with genealogy out of pure existentialism – how could I possibly be the biological combination of my mother and my father when I was so starkly different from them both? I withdrew into the dusty eaves of the houses our family was scattered between, sifting through boxes in lofts, desperate to find any clues as to who I was or why I was like this. My family tree brought me no solace – my mother and father were both raised in large religious families, both with divorced schoolteacher parents, both having worked as clerks in a local bank branch where they met, married, had two kids, and then divorced. My searches weren't entirely fruitless, however. In my mother's loft I found a small tucked-away newspaper cutting revealing her at my age, beaming up from the browned paper in black and grey dots, as she received first prize for a poetry competition. A similar bounty was found in a forgotten drawer at my father's house – a framed, sticker-covered photo of four young boys in a band, which, on closer inspection, revealed my father as the gawky, moustachioed drummer, having the time of his life. I ran to them with what I'd found, desperate to find some correlation between those people in the photos and the parents who raised me, but I saw none.

'We were just silly kids,' my father said, tossing the photo back into the drawer. 'We didn't even know how to play.'

I knew whatever had happened to those kids my folks used to be, I couldn't let happen to me. So I stopped my presentations, and started going about my dream-seeking in secret, trying to find any way I could make it on my own. I wrote letter after letter to the casting director of the Harry Potter movies, the name and PO box address of whom I'd found in some strange corner of Google, begging her to let me audition to be an extra or have a small role. One time, I even enclosed a list I'd made from flicking through the entirety of the fifth book and marking all the minor characters with Post-it notes, compiling a table including which page number they appeared on, in what context, and why I'd be perfect to play them. For that, I actually received my one and only response, a rejection letter on *Harry Potter and the Order of the Phoenix*-headed notepaper, which I still cherish to this day as the closest I ever got to going to Hogwarts.

I also harboured a passionate desire to make music, fuelled by the memory of my father patting me on the shoulder as a child and telling me that while he was no expert, he knew a good voice when he heard one, and have one I did not. I saved up my Christmas money one year and bought the cheapest instrument I could find, a ukulele, learning to play it and uploading covers onto the seedlings of what would grow to become YouTube.

At sixteen, without telling a soul, I snuck out of my house at 5 a.m. and got the train alone to London to audition for the *X Factor*. I stood in line for twelve hours outside the O2 Arena in the bitter February cold, only for the producers to be far more interested in my parents' disapproval than my voice. I made it through three rounds without telling anyone, desperate to find some kind of validation that I wasn't completely deluded in my belief that I was actually good. I now dread to think what would've happened to me if I had found it there.

All the while my parents were steadily mounting their pressure for me to fall in line with their plan. The moment I was legally old enough I had to get a part-time job, I had to pass my driving test, I had to start applying for university. Their persistence had somehow got me straight As in my exams, so I was sent to an English literature open day at Oxford, the only question I could think to ask on the day being: 'Is there a good drama club here?'

I was working two jobs, starring in the school play and studying full-time when the time came to take my A levels, and I was spiralling out of control. The enormity of pressure from both parents, plus the benchmark left by my older sister, was scorching away what was left of my self-belief, and I simply buckled. There could only be one victor, and it was not me.

With mediocre grades and a mind saturated with a poisonous sense of resentment towards my parents, I packed up what was left of me and went to the only university that would have me. I completely vanished, the black sheep who finally fled her flock.

I knew from the moment I arrived that I was never going to flourish in the arms of academia. It wasn't long before a depression rose thick and fast from the depths of my own disappointment. I was friendless and alone, unable to turn to my family for support, and loath to reach out to the academic staff for whom I had such a distaste. With the final dying embers of the fire in my heart, I turned to the internet, opening up a browser window and typing into a new blog: 'Hello world. Can anybody hear me?'

For weeks that became months, while I suffered through the gruelling academic system, I wrote words that were read by no one. I exorcised the demons I'd brought with me, voiced my fears and admitted to those little childhood dreams I'd been taught were foolish, but that I still secretly harboured anyway. The words were sent nowhere, but I felt them begin to heal me nonetheless.

And slowly, they came. One by one they emerged, these complete strangers from across the world, who'd somehow found their way to my words and reached out with two words I didn't know how desperately I needed to hear: 'Me too.' Gradually, what began as my loneliness somehow started to become a shelter beneath which other wounded souls had begun to gather.

These words became essays, which became chapters of a narrative that began to stitch itself together to form the fabric of a new kind of person I was becoming. Between us, we shared our stories and our fears, all these other little girls who'd dreamed before anyone ever told them they couldn't. As my writing advanced, so did my understanding of the anger that fuelled it. I began to disassemble a lot of the hurt that I carried and learned to release the blame I held against my parents. Because in a sense, they were right. It's hard to appreciate the bigger picture when you're still so young and inevitably myopic about the world. I did 'find out anyway' that the world is a harsh place for dreamers.

I did what I did to remain at university, but this new plan was giving me my life back. Over the years, the online community that established around my writing became that buffer of support and encouragement I'd so desperately yearned for as a child, and I realised it was because they were all Little Miss Sunshines too, spurring me on to be the one who eats the ice cream and doesn't care if Daddy says it'll make you fat.

And that's how three years later, I arrived at the most life-changing decision of my young life.

Whilst I'd slowly regained my confidence and resurrected the dying part of me that cried out for more, I was still stuck in the mentally and financially crippling institution that only served to tell me, once more, that I wasn't good enough. This time, however, when something had to give, there was no way in hell I was going to let it be me.

The decision-making process was agonising. For months of sleepless nights I turned it over in my mind, weighing up my options. Could I really drop out of university? I'd come close to it multiple times over the years in particularly hard moments, but the fear of letting everybody down had kept me on the straight and narrow. But this felt incredibly real, like the final choice between surrendering myself to what other people expected of me, or claiming ownership of my own life.

After two decades of compromise and three years of healing, I knew what I had to do.

At twenty-one years old, I did what I think will remain forever the most ridiculous thing I've ever done, and with my hard-earned savings from working full-time at the local movie theatre, dropped out of university, sold my car, moved out of my flat, quit my job and moved to New York City.

Understandably, my parents were absolutely horrified, and I must admit, there was a small guilty pleasure in finally doing something I said I would, when they still never took me seriously enough to believe I'd actually do it. But my healing had brought me clarity and acceptance, and I laid it all out to them in the form of a letter, writing, 'Because if you love me, if you truly love me like I love you, then you'll let me go forth and be the person I so ardently believe I was always meant to be.'

And remarkably, they did. So, carrying nothing with me but a small suitcase and ambition the size of a nation, I dropped everything and moved to Red Hook, Brooklyn, to live and work as a deckhand restoring an old Victorian ferry on the East River.

And New York changed everything.

The sheer madness of that adventure shaped me in ways that I could never have previously imagined. Here, the Manhattan skyline became the backdrop of my coming-of-age tale, this wild, thrilling journey of self-discovery that brought me to the very fringes of my own identity. I no longer needed to seek permission to be myself, to do the things I wanted, or chase the future I sought. Of course, it wasn't without its low points, and the boat particularly was one of the hardest mental challenges I've ever endured. But even in the darkest moments, I couldn't help but revel in what I had made for myself.

I remember so distinctly on the Fourth of July, gazing over at my best friend who'd flown out to visit me, as we stood on the roof terrace of the apartment block of the new friends I had made, watching the dazzling fireworks glitter above the skyscrapers of Manhattan, and I simply thought: Wow. I really did this. I was one Olive Hoover, exploding onto the stage at the Little Miss Sunshine pageant, fearlessly, shamelessly performing the sexy dance her grandpa taught her, much to her parents' dismay, and loving every moment of it.

There's a scene toward the end of the movie where Olive finally makes it to the pageant and gets to meet a real-life beauty queen like the ones she's seen on TV. She approaches the elegant Miss California, looking up at everything she wants to be, and gingerly asks, 'Do you eat ice cream?'

Miss California smiles serenely and replies, 'Yes! My favourite is Chocolate Cherry Garcia.'

It's now been three years since New York, the place I'd fled to as girl, and returned from a woman. My relationship with my parents remains a work in progress, but it's healthier and more open than ever. For in my soul-searching I came to perhaps the biggest revelation of all: while it was not easy to feel deprived of the world, it certainly can't have been an easy thing to be asked for, either. Their horror at my choice was not because I'd betrayed them in some desertion of our family's honour, but because they were most likely desperately afraid for me. The sanctity of routine and proper procedure had always kept them safe, and I had turned my back on it all. So perhaps now it was no longer my duty to prove them wrong, but to prove to them my decision had been the right one.

Last week my family visited me in the seaside town where I live. When I first came here two years ago, I immediately began to write again, but not in the desperate, yearning way I'd so needed to before. This time, it was power. Where my dreams had turned into words, they now became lyrics, and it wasn't long before I found that stage I'd always secretly believed I was destined for.

'I actually have some news,' I announced over dinner, taking my father's hand and searching deep in his eyes for some kind of recognition. 'I've been invited to a meeting to discuss a record deal.'

While the table erupted in congratulations, my father simply nodded and looked at his hands for a moment, before saying, 'Well, make sure you read the contracts thoroughly.' But my disappointment was only fleeting. I didn't need his permission, his congratulations or his approval any longer. Although a little later, I did glance over to find him googling the name of the record label beneath the dinner table, so I guess that's something.

Today I live as Olive Hoover and am proud, and I suppose I feel a small sense of duty to my fellow Little Miss Sunshines. To any other person out there who feels the longing of their neglected inner child, to all those souls who are still waiting for that permission to become who they truly are – if you take one thing from this, I urge you to know that it's never too late to make the change. Even if you're not quite ready, just remember that one day you will be.

And don't ever, ever let anyone tell you not to eat the goddamn ice cream. Because believe me, there's nothing in the world that tastes as good.

EXCLUSION
Shona Cobb

Content warning: ableism

There are 13.3 million people with disabilities in the UK. We're your family and your friends and the biggest minority that anyone can become a part of.

And yet we are hardly listened to.

Our stories have already been written by the world around us. A world that isn't built for us.

I remember the first time I went shopping in my powerchair. I was so ready to grab back my independence and to say goodbye to being pushed in a wheelchair by my mum. Minutes after leaving my home, I came across a car blocking a dropped kerb onto the pavement, forcing me to travel on the road for over fifty metres. In town, I battled shops that you could only enter by step. My favourite shops became no-go places; their inaccessibility made me feel unwelcome. Staff were often full of apologies when I questioned the issue, but when I took it one step further and emailed companies, I was lucky to even get a response.

Nowadays I expect to be excluded from places like shops and restaurants. I have to check the accessibility of wherever I go, information that can be hard to track down. I have to plan everything, but no one gives you a starter manual when you become disabled; there's no guide to navigating this world that hasn't been built for us.

My mum was aware that she had a rare genetic condition called Marfan syndrome when she was pregnant with me and was pretty sure I had it as well. Most conditions come with a set of characteristics, and Marfan has plenty of them: being tall and slim with long arms and legs are some of the most visible, and this is what led my mum to believe that the condition had been passed on. She's told me several times before about how ultrasound scans showed my long arms and legs, and from that moment on she was sure that I too had the condition that sadly took both her dad and brother way before their time. Those experiences had equipped her with the knowledge she needed to raise me; she was confident that we would tackle everything Marfan threw at us together. I know she feels guilty for the condition being passed on to me. I can reassure her that I place blame with no one, but she's my mum, she'll always carry some guilt.

I was one of the lucky ones at this point. I was diagnosed at birth; thousands may not get a diagnosis until their teens or adulthood. Some sadly pass away from complications without the knowledge that they even have it.

As a child, I mainly just suffered from achy hypermobile joints that would slip about – bearable but not fun. All I had to do was take a step forward and feel my knee joint slip in and out of place. It definitely felt like something that your body is not meant to do. Once I managed to dislocate and break a toe from catching it on a cardboard box.

At secondary school the difference between me and my peers started to become apparent as my body crumbled. I loved school. I loved learning new phrases in French, taking part in chemistry experiments, learning. I loved the stability that school offered. I helped teachers when I could, collecting workbooks and putting out equipment. I won school awards for my efforts in some of my favourite subjects, English and history. I had great relationships with all my teachers, so it shocked me when my PE teacher reduced me to tears.

It was a hot summer. I joined my classmates outside for a PE lesson. We were running laps around the field, something I could usually manage, but this time was different. A deep ache gradually began to wrap around my knee as I ran, and soon I was far behind my friends, struggling to keep up at the back of the crowd.

'I can't carry on, my knee is killing me, I think I've hurt it,' I shouted to my teacher.

'Stop messing around,' she replied.

I carried on, and as the pain got worse, I realised I was also deeply embarrassed. She'd made me feel like a lazy liar. This is common. If I mention anything to do with my health, you'd be surprised who in my various circles tells me I am exaggerating. Friends, doctors, teachers – all people who should want the best for me. This has happened most commonly when my disability and chronic pain have not been visible. Lack of understanding contributes to this greatly; it can be difficult to understand things that we cannot see, but instead of asking questions, many people seem to jump to the assumption that I must be exaggerating, that my pain can't be 'that bad'. As a young teen experiencing pain, it was an issue that the people around me hadn't seemed to have interacted with before. Even doctors made assumptions that young people couldn't experience chronic pain, so it's no surprise that friends and teachers jumped to the same conclusions.

The thing is, sometimes you can adjust to life with one condition, and then suddenly it can all change. When I was thirteen I was diagnosed with scoliosis, a curvature of the spine. I'd noticed that my ribs didn't look even, one side was sunk in, and out of fear I stayed silent about it for months. Finally, I showed my mum.

'Mum, I think there's something wrong with my ribs,' I said as we chatted in her bedroom. I lifted my top to reveal my deformed ribs, terrified of what her response might be.

'How long has it been like that?' she asked.

'Not long,' I responded. In reality I had no idea.

By the time I was fifteen, I was suffering with back pain on a daily basis, a symptom of my bending spine. I struggled to climb the stairs at school. I was lucky to get through a week without a day or two off. Sometimes whole weeks off. Some days, even getting out of bed was an impossibility. It meant missing vital GCSE lessons, which put me two steps behind my classmates at every turn. I was permanently trying to catch up.

My hands were constantly cramping, another symptom of my condition. As we approached exam season, I started to fear them. Exams involve writing, for long periods of time. It was becoming obvious that I needed extra support during the real thing. Things like regular breaks to take the strain off my back, and using a computer, as I found typing easier than writing.

I don't say all these things as a catalogue of misery. I say these things to demonstrate to you that the world wasn't built for the likes of me.

I arrived for my English exam early. I asked my teacher where the computer was.

'I'm afraid your request for a computer and regular breaks has been denied,' she told me.

I started crying at the prospect of having to write for an hour and a half whilst trying to breathe through intense pain.

The teacher, instead of trying to understand my problem, fetched my head of year, who said, 'Sadly, you need a doctor's note to prove you need adjustments made.' My first experience of having to prove I was disabled enough for support.

This made me furious. When my mum and I had made requests of our school, and of her in particular, she had told me there would be no problem. Crucially, at no point was a doctor's letter mentioned.

'You never told me that; no one told me I needed a letter,' I blurted angrily.

'I'm sorry, it's just the way it works,' she told me, as I found myself unable to control the feeling of panic, tears continuing to stream down my face.

My English teacher took me into a side room to help me to calm down.

'Take this,' she said as she handed me a box of tissues.

'No one told me about the letter. I don't think I can do this exam, I'm going to be in so much pain,' I told her.

'Right,' she told me. 'This is what we're going to do. We're going to give you extra time so you'll be able to stop writing every now and then to help your pain.'

Sadly, extra time was not what I needed. I needed breaks. I needed a computer. Within fifteen minutes I found myself struggling to write. My hand was cramping up and panic shuddered through me as I realised that this exam wasn't going to reflect the work I had done.

I was disappointed with my results. I was in a room packed full of students and teachers as I nervously peeled open the envelope. It felt like a lot was riding on what it said. I was surrounded by friends who were overjoyed by how well they'd done. My immediate response as my eyes scanned down the page was a smile. I was, I suppose, proud of how well I'd done despite all my time off.

There are systems in place that are supposed to support people like me in schools. Every school has a SENCO, a special educational needs coordinator. I didn't seem to fit the boxes that would entitle me automatically to this support. I feel like I was overlooked due to my good grades and well-known history for being an excellent student. Even as I look back now, it's difficult to know exactly what caused me to slip through the net. I was never offered the support of a SENCO. The school didn't seem to have any experience of a student going from being fit and well with great grades to suddenly barely turning up for half the lessons, struggling to keep up and being desperate for support.

The plan that summer was to have a spinal operation, which would allow me to recover in time to start sixth form. It was my first-ever operation, and it was major. I was terrified. However, I balanced the terror out with the daily pain I felt, and I just wanted it to stop.

After the surgery, I had to relearn how to walk, sit up, wash and dress myself all over again, and until then I had nurses and my mum doing everything for me. For the first few days I needed help from three people even if I just wanted to turn over in bed.

Recovery was slow and I found myself in a similar pattern. I thought that this time the support would be there after the issues with my GCSEs. I missed more and more of my first

A-level year, without having a single piece of physical work sent home for my three subjects: psychology, sociology and English language. My point of contact was my head of year, instead of a SENCO, and I barely heard from her. There were emails here and there containing textbook numbers, and a couple of short meetings, but I got the distinct impression that she didn't want to help me, or the school didn't have the resources to. Some of my emails requesting work didn't even get a response. Looking back, it shocks me that at no point did any member of staff think to transfer my support over to the special educational needs team, who were equipped and prepared to deal with my needs.

One of the last times we spoke was during a meeting with my parents.

'When do you feel you could come back to school, Shona?' she asked.

'I'm not sure, we're waiting on scan results and my pain doesn't seem to be improving. Have you been getting my emails about the work I'm missing?' I asked.

'I have, yes, unfortunately I've been really busy.'

It was my education she was too busy to help with. I feared that I was slipping through the cracks, and my fears turned into reality. I never returned to school. I barely started my A levels, let alone completed them.

I spent evenings crying in bed, longing to be in school with my peers. I became more distant and isolated from every part of school, including my friends. If you're not there to join in, you miss the chats and the everyday jokes, the little things that happen in friendship groups. Things that never translate as well online. Messages from friends dwindled; I was no longer part of their lives each day. I was at home, coping with pain, whilst they rightfully enjoyed their youth. I was angry and frustrated, but if I wasn't equipped to deal with pain and surgeries at that age, then I certainly couldn't expect them to be. Unless you grow up with a disabled friend or family member, it's difficult to know how to handle that situation, how best to help or interact. Disability is still a subject that is avoided, and so none of my friends were prepared for a member of their social group to suddenly be dealing with such a big obstacle in life.

To this day my heart aches about how different things could have been.

I like to imagine I'd be at university, going to parties and turning up to lectures with a hangover. I wonder if I'd be working, enjoying spending my wages at the weekend. Every now and then an old friend messages me on Facebook and I find myself feeling jealous of them, how different their life is to mine. I think about the future a lot and I wonder if I'll ever achieve my goals. It can be frightening when you're faced with so much uncertainty in life.

For my eighteenth birthday I had a hip replacement. Some people get clothes vouchers, or maybe a new console, if they're lucky, a car. My hips had levels of degeneration that you'd usually see in someone four times my age. I still find it odd seeing 'degenerative changes' on my medical letters. Without replacing both I'd be at risk of fracturing my hips, so I started planning for my third major surgery. Meanwhile, my friends were enjoying their youth and celebrating university places.

I noticed a change in me during the time of that operation.

I didn't cry. I was not scared. I did not wake up in a panic. I felt numb. I felt nothing. I realise now, I felt broken. My childhood had been taken from me. I had been failed by my school, my friends and my body, and I felt nothing.

When you have suffered with exhausting and constant pain for so long though, it is inevitable that it will eventually become normal. I wake up in chronic pain and every night I fall asleep in chronic pain.

One of the best pain relief methods for me can be distraction, but it's a fine balance between distraction and pushing my body too far. I have a blog, something I've been writing for over six years, and it's something I'm proud of. My goals have changed due to my health, and now that my aims are to raise awareness of my condition and improve the world we live in for disabled people, my blog has been a vehicle for this. Thousands more people now know what Marfan syndrome is, thanks to me. I've been in newspapers, on websites, on the radio and even worked with major charities like the British Heart Foundation. I've encouraged countless businesses and companies to improve their accessibility, succeeding more often than I expected. I have plenty to keep my mind occupied. And yet, I still feel isolated.

It's common for chronic pain sufferers to experience depression and anxiety. Many of us have been forced into a completely different lifestyle, and that's without even factoring in having to deal with pain that would send most running to A&E. My blog has thousands of readers, and yet I still feel alone. I get invited to speak at events, to write pieces for charities, and yet I still feel like I'm not achieving anything. Society sets the bar so high, especially for young people, and despite my obvious difficulties I feel the pressure to reach above and beyond expectations. Being young and disabled in a world that isn't designed for you and expects so much from you can send you tumbling into feelings of despair. The reality of my situation can be difficult to stomach, but it also motivates me. I have such a drive to make changes, to use my time wisely.

Your social life might be made up of coffee dates with friends and drinks in the pub on a Friday night. Mine is a mixture of doctors' appointments and charity Skype calls. It's different, but that doesn't necessarily mean one is wrong and one is right.

It's the barriers and boundaries that society places in my way that really cause me the most issues. People are quick to blame a disabled person's impairment for the fact that they are unable to do something. We blame that person's wheelchair for not being able to enter shops with steps and have even invented stair-climbing wheelchairs because society sees the disability as the problem. This is the medical model of disability, which focuses on what is 'wrong' with the disabled person.

But the social model of disability puts forward the idea that disability is caused by the way society is organised rather than by a person's difficulties or impairments. It focuses on ways to remove the barriers that restrict what disabled people can do. It seeks to empower disabled people, to give them greater equality and freedom to participate in society.

I've had countless people tell me that I shouldn't let my disability get in my way of achieving anything, but the inconvenient truth is that if barriers are in place, then they are ones placed there by society, not by me. I can't go back into education because there isn't enough support, financially and physically, in place for disabled students. I often can't even access the bus because priority is so often given to buggies in the wheelchair space.

Even when I'm able to access the bus I often feel like an inconvenience. I see drivers roll their eyes as I request the ramp. I'm also stared at for the entire journey, as wheelchair users are forced to sit backwards on the bus. There are moments that make the battle worth it though. The email back from a local shop bursting with enthusiasm in reply to my accessibility requests. The meeting with the bus company, where they hold their hands up and change their system. The parents with a newborn baby who gladly fold their pram and hold their precious bundle of joy. I used to think to myself, what chance do I have at changing the world when I'm just a teenager? It turns out there is a lot you can change with a bit of persistence.

Bureaucracy is another big barrier I am required to scale. My life as a disabled person involves completing form after form after form to prove that I am disabled enough to receive support from the government. I even have to prove to music venues that I am disabled enough to book the accessible seating. I must prove that my spine is damaged enough, my joints dislocated enough, and most of all I must prove that I am not a liar. Everywhere from the government to festivals want my personal medical history.

The benefits system seems to have developed into a system where you start off being seen as a liar, with all the forms and assessments there for you to prove your innocence. In the past three years I've filled in several forms for ESA (Employment and Support Allowance) and PIP (Personal Independence Payment) and most have had at least forty pages for me to fill in. Then, for each benefit most people have to go through an assessment. The same questions in the form are asked again, with such repeated frequency that I start to doubt my own answers after a while. If you keep asking, then perhaps what I'm saying isn't true. I'm constantly answering questions, earning the money that pays my bills and buys me food.

In such assessments I have to explain why sometimes I'm able to do more on one day than another, and how that doesn't make me a liar. I have to explain my best possible days, even though they come once in a blue moon, just in case a neighbour decides to report me for seeing me walk on crutches to put something in the outside bin, rather than using my powerchair. That is a genuine fear that I have. I know people with variable conditions, who can walk some days and on other days they need a wheelchair. Society seems to lack understanding when it comes to such conditions.

Not all barriers are physical – some are attitudinal. If you open a newspaper, it's not uncommon to find a story about benefit fraud, about people pretending to be disabled to access certain benefits. If something gets reported on regularly, then you'd probably assume that it's happening a lot, when in reality the rate of disability benefit fraud has been below 1 per cent for years. The actions of a few are having a huge impact on the rest of us, though. The media have made out that benefit fraud is a massive issue and the government only makes this worse by reducing payments and changing the system of benefits, with the declared intent that it will allow only the people who really need support to access it. The reality is that this changeover has left an estimated 50,000 disabled people without their vital Motability car. The rate of fraud is way too low for the government to justify these changes and way too low for us to even be having this conversation so often. There aren't millions of 'fake disabled people' out there, so why must the many be punished for the actions of a few?

There is of course a general stigma that sits around benefits. People often tell me that everyone on benefits is lazy and doesn't want to work, when the reality is so different. I'm even part of this problem as I stigmatise myself. My own internalised ableism, ingrained by the world around me, makes me ashamed that I rely on benefits. Even though PIP is there for disabled people regardless of whether they work or not – it simply helps cover the extra costs that we have – still I feel shame. I know I'm not the only one who feels this way, like I'm not disabled enough to receive support. I often wonder if things will ever improve for disabled people, whether we'll ever leave behind people's judgements and assumptions.

It's easy to blame my disability for my stolen teenage years, for not completing my A levels and for not reaching my original goals. Delving deeper into the way that society deals with disability tells a different story, though, highlighting issue after issue, people falling through the net again and again. I have every chance of living a full and independent life if I'm given the tools I need to do so. The care support, the financial support, the physical adaptations. It's not something I or other disabled people can do alone. Our voices need to be heard. All I ever ask of people is that they listen. Let us be heard.

MY BODY, MY CHOICE
Mariam Khan
Content warning: Islamophobia, sexism

Sometime in 2016, I was travelling to Sweden. As I went through airport security, I had to remind myself that it didn't matter how many times fellow passengers glanced over at me and my family. It didn't matter that they shifted uncomfortably when I started talking in Pashto or their nervousness around my carry-on luggage because I was doing nothing wrong. I told myself looking visibly Muslim wouldn't make a difference to my experience.

As a Muslim woman, I find my body has become a symbol of rebellion. A way to judge whether I am a good British citizen; a way to test my patriotism. Many perceive my hijab not to be a choice, and feel entitled to police my body, including politicians, the media and white feminists. White feminism fails to consider the way in which women of colour experience discrimination and sexism. I've been told not to wear my scarf everywhere from a bus stop to a job interview.

This constant demand for explanation is dehumanising. It dilutes the authority of Muslim women's choices and ultimately attempts to make us powerless. If you believe someone has agency, you don't second-guess their choices. But this image of powerlessness allows Muslim women to be framed as helpless and it allows for interference.

As I waited in the security line behind my sister, the security officer said to her, 'Take off your scarf.'

My sister looked back at me, baffled.

'What did he say?' I asked her. Then, to the guard: 'I'm sorry, what did you say?'

Ignoring me, he turned to my sister and repeated, 'Take off your scarf.'

He said this so casually, as though it meant nothing.

Our scarves were loosely draped around our necks. Neither my nor my sister's neck was covered. If the security officer was asking us to remove our scarves because it looked as though we might be hiding something, then I was well and truly confused, because there was nowhere we *could* hide anything.

The man persisted. 'Take off your headscarf. You as well,' he said to me. Finally, my existence was being acknowledged. Now nobody else was paying attention to us, they were just shuffling through security with their clear bags and taking their shoes off.

'I will,' I said. 'But please can you explain why you're asking me to remove my scarf?'

The security officer replied to say he didn't know why. He shrugged before walking off.

I turned to look at my sister.

'Don't take off your scarf,' I said.

I didn't take mine off either. We walked through the body scanners and we collected our things, both of us bewildered and uncomfortable about what had just happened. I felt intense anger at the unfairness of the situation. As an authority figure, that man had the upper hand. We'd been treated like we had done something criminal.

Two years before, in 2014, I was travelling through Norway to get back home to the UK. As I went through security, my scarf was once again loose around my neck. The security man could see my neck. But as I went through, he asked me to put my scarf in the box that goes through the scanners. Honestly, I'm still trying to figure out what these people think I could hide in a thin piece of fabric. Without thinking, and afraid to be somewhere that wasn't my home country, I did what the man asked. I remember feeling naked. I went through the rest of security, collected my things and moved on. Only in the car on the ride home did I reflect on how odd and guilty I was made to feel even though I'd done nothing wrong. I felt ashamed for not questioning the man's command.

So now, two years later, I was on home turf, in the UK, and a different security officer had demanded my sister and I remove our headscarves, but wasn't able to provide a reason. I was not about to let history repeat itself. I was not going to let my sister feel guilty or ashamed for simply being 'visibly Muslim'; neither she nor I had done anything wrong or suspicious. With regard to head coverings and face coverings, the gov.uk website states: 'It is a requirement that Border Force Officers always establish the nationality and identity of all passengers.' My sister and I weren't covering our faces, and by removing the loose scarves draped around our necks our identities weren't going to be discovered; our passports would reveal our identities but we were not asked for our passports. If we'd been white, secular women, with scarves draped around our necks, I'm sure we'd have been treated with respect, and if asked to remove clothing there would certainly be an explanation. Even a criminal who is being cuffed is legally required to be told why they are being arrested. I wonder how many nuns are suspected and demanded to remove their wimples when they pass through airport security, or does their religion make them appear peaceful and not suspect? Though the rule may be the same for all head coverers, I can't help but wonder whether it is applied in a discriminatory manner.

I angrily stuffed everything else in my bag, and then walked towards the lady on the end of the security conveyor. I told her what her colleague had done and that he hadn't explained why I needed to remove my scarf. She apologised and explained that they needed to see my neck area and didn't really have much else to add. I was dumbfounded. I couldn't make sense of the situation. I was a visibly Muslim woman in an airport, nobody was on my side, and I was afraid asking for a manager would mean being detained in some way, so I got my things and carried on through.

In the lane opposite us, my mother and two other sisters went through security. My sisters, wearing their hijabs like me, were not questioned. Neither was my mum, who had her hijab wrapped around covering her hair, neck and chest area. If they weren't a threat, why was I? Why was this rule about seeing necks selectively applied? Especially when my mother, the only person whose neck you couldn't see, wasn't asked to remove her hijab. These *rules* would make anyone anxious and paranoid as they travelled through the airport.

I am ashamed to say I didn't press the lady or the man further, and I really wish I had. If the person in power was telling me to remove my clothing without being able to justify it in a very public environment, what would happen if I made a fuss? Could I be detained unfairly? Strip-searched in the name of national security? I wanted to believe I had the same rights as any British citizen, but with the way I had been treated, I knew I didn't. These situations aren't isolated and I've come to realise it's impossible to constantly kick against oppressive systems as an individual.

Attempts are being made every single day to control Muslim women's bodies. In 2010, UKIP called for all face-covering Muslim veils to be banned. In September 2013, Home Office Minister Jeremy Browne called for a 'national debate' about Islamic veils in public places. Not a fringe party member. A government minister.

In 2014, UKIP leader Nigel Farage said full veils were a symbol of an 'increasingly divided Britain', that they 'oppress' women and are a potential security threat. In 2016, a YouGov poll showed that 57 per cent of the British public supported a burqa ban in the UK. In 2017, the *Guardian* reported that the European Court of Justice 'issued a joint judgement in the cases of two women, from France and Belgium, who were dismissed for refusing to remove headscarves.' The ECJ decided that these garments could be banned, but only as part of a general policy barring all religious and political symbols in workplaces. I wonder how many Christians will be asked to remove their cross necklaces, or Sikhs asked to remove their turbans or karas. This ruling didn't bring justice for Samira Achbita, who was fired from her job because she decided to wear a hijab and refused to remove it when asked to by her employer. I am certain this law will systematically and unfairly target Muslim women in the workplace, who are once again powerless to decide how they choose to dress.

During the 2017 election, UKIP's then-leader Paul Nuttall set out the UKIP manifesto, which included a commitment to ban the face veil. He attempted to justify his ludicrous commitment by aligning Muslim women with terrorism, saying, 'In an age of heightened terror, you need to see people's faces.'

This need to control Muslim women's bodies isn't new in our politics and doesn't appear to be going out of style in a hurry. My worry, as a British Muslim woman, is not only that my rights are being threatened, it's also that the decisions I make are being discredited. The Western narrative describing Muslim women – that we are being oppressed by our own religion – denies that we have agency.

But we have agency. I can tell you that the hijab or the veil is not forced upon me. There is no compulsion in religion. In Islam, we all have free will, and if not wearing the hijab is someone's choice, then good for them. It's between them and God. For some women, however, wearing the hijab has become mandatory because their cultures have interpreted the hijab as something you can impose on women, and I don't agree with this at all. This kind of cultural compulsion is not Islamic.

Even online, I'm unable to completely escape these narratives, as my profile picture makes me a visibly Muslim woman. I have been called everything from a terrorist to a cockroach online by Twitter users who don't like what I have to say, because it deviates from the narrative they have curated around Muslim women. Though being online and sharing my opinions about Muslim women feels empowering for me, for haters, bigots and racists, their anonymity emboldens them.

The narrative around Muslim women has long since been co-opted. We are all perceived through the lens of a single story: weak, voiceless and oppressed.

In 2004, France's national assembly began debating a bill to ban religious symbols including the Muslim headscarf. Then, in 2011, under a decree made by the French prime minister, François Fillon, Muslim women were banned from wearing the niqab (a veil worn by some Muslim women which covers most of their face except their eyes) in public spaces. French politicians argued that banning the veil for Muslim women would be liberating and would follow France's principle of *vivre ensemble*, or living together, because of course:

- Women can't liberate themselves.
- Everyone has to dress alike to achieve national unity and solidarity – because Maoism worked out so well.

This ban has not liberated women. It has created further hostility between the French state and French Muslim community, and has encouraged hate crime. A report by the Open Society Foundations found, after speaking to thirty-two Muslim women who wear the niqab, that thirty of those women strongly believed that being spat on and called names was a normal part of their everyday life.[*]

The report found: 'A minority of cases involved physical abuse, such as passers-by spitting on the woman or attempting to tear off her veil. At least five women also reported that members of the public had photographed them without permission as if they were animals in a zoo.'[†] This law has emboldened and empowered racists and

---

[*] *Behind the Veil*, Open Society Foundations, available at https://www.opensocietyfoundations.org/sites/default/files/behind-veil-20150401.pdf

[†] Ibid.

misogynists to abuse those in society with whom they don't agree. The study found that these women actively avoided certain areas and tried to avoid travelling alone. A law that was put in place to free Muslim women has crippled their social lives and put them under house arrest. This law in France promotes segregation and fuels stigma to make Muslim women afraid, othered and alienated in a country they call home.

And the reality of these French Muslim women could soon be the reality of many Muslim women in the UK. In 2016, UKIP leadership hopeful Lisa Duffy said the Islamic full-face veils should be banned in some places. She described the veil as 'a symbol of aggressive separatism that can only foster extremism', adding, 'There's no reason why we in Britain should allow it to be worn anywhere and everywhere.' Because apparently when a Muslim woman decides to dress herself, she needs permission from the whole of Britain before she's allowed to leave the house.

At the time of the ban in France, the burqa was only worn by about 2,000 Muslim women in France. The population of France is 65 million. Did this small number of women really pose such a massive threat to French culture and society that the French government needed to create a law targeting them specifically? I want to know how the banning of the burqa has impacted on Muslim women integrating into French society. Surely if it was important enough to ban, then someone somewhere must be keeping watch of how the ban has impacted on integration. I agree we all need to live together and follow the laws of the land, but I refuse to support governments that prioritise one group's freedom prioritised over another's. Just because something is the law, that doesn't mean it's right. Laws can be wrong. If you can't think of examples of when laws were wrong then you are either white or really didn't pay attention in history lessons.

I personally would not wear a niqab to cover my face. That doesn't mean I won't fight for the right of a woman who willingly decides she wants to. She should be allowed to dress her own body. Isn't the idea of free will and choice the glue for Western civilisation? Or do the rules change when you identify as a Muslim woman?

In 2016, French mayors banned burqinis in thirty French coastal resorts. In August of that year, the country's highest administrative court ruled that the ban was illegal. However, nearly all the mayors refused to lift the restrictions. As the French quibbled about what to do, the worldwide media published an image of armed French police standing over a Muslim woman on a beach in Nice, demanding she remove her burqini. We saw pictures of the woman undressing herself, and it was reported that people on the beach shouted, 'Go home!' Where were the anti-burqini politicians and their supporters when Nigella Lawson wore the burqini in Australia? Why didn't the media question Nigella's agency and ask if she was being oppressed? Nobody talked about how she wasn't integrating into society. And even if she had worn a burqini on a French beach, I doubt anything would have happened. This is a double standard. Supporters of the burqini ban argued that it was a matter of national security. These people seem to think that controlling Muslim women's bodies will be a victory against terrorism. How many terrorist attacks have been carried out by Muslim women in the UK? Almost none. How many committed by women in swimwear? None. Between the burqa ban and the burqini debacle, the French have become used to abusing the rights of Muslim women and dictating how they should dress. In turn, this has had a knock-on effect throughout Europe.

In May 2015, the Dutch cabinet approved a partial ban on Islamic veils in some public spaces. In January 2016, former UK Prime Minister David Cameron ruled out a full public ban but said he would back institutions with 'sensible rules' over Muslims wearing full-face veils. In December 2016, German chancellor Angela Merkel endorsed a partial ban on the burqa and the niqab, claiming 'the full facial veil is inappropriate and should be banned wherever legally possible', and Austria prohibited the full-face veil in January 2017. How long before this full-face veil ban turns into a burqini and hijab ban throughout Europe? Specifically, in the UK? The polls already show the majority of the British public would support the banning of the burka/full-face veil.

Sitting on Andrew Marr's couch in the BBC studio, UKIP Leader Paul Nuttall claimed Muslim women need to fully integrate into British society and that they 'can't do that hiding behind a veil'. Conflating the idea of wearing a hijab, niqab or burqa with oppression is a classic example of racism and misogyny disguised as concern. It is yet another way for politicians to win votes and pretend they care about Muslim women – even if the people whose votes they're gaining don't care about those women, this tactic allows them to at least pretend they do. It gives them plausible deniability about their own racism. As the discussion moved forward, Nuttall sat, evincing faux concern for the lives of Muslim women, while claiming that women who wear the veil aren't integrated, labelling those who wear the burqa as ignorant and unable to speak the English language, and fuelling the fears and prejudices of his potential voters. The joke here being that when the British colonised, did they all give up speaking English, convert to local religions, and integrate fully, respecting the laws of the land? No, they imposed their own language and customs – including the odd traditional British massacre.

In 2016, the Casey Review was commissioned by the government to look at how social integration could be improved across the UK. It has been reported that funding for ESL (English as a Second Language) provision has dropped by 50 per cent between 2008 and 2015. The Casey Review urged the government to look into this area and improve it to further social integration and to provide a resource to those who didn't speak English. If learning English is such a key part of integration, then why does the government keep slashing funds for it?

★

There is a growing demonisation of Muslims in much of the mainstream media, and in the minds of many, Islam and terrorism have become inseparable. Islamophobia is rising rapidly, with hijabi Muslim women being easy targets, as they are marked as 'visibly Muslim'. After the London Bridge terrorist attack, figures released by the Mayor of London, Sadiq Khan, showed a fivefold increase in Islamophobic attacks. Hate crimes rose to fifty-four incidents a day. In June 2017, the *Guardian* reported that Tell MAMA 'recorded 141 hate crime incidents after the Manchester attack on 22 May, a rise of 500 per cent compared with a daily average of twenty-five'.

Nearly every Islamophobic hate crime I hear about is against a woman. As a Muslim woman in the UK, every time a terror attack takes place I'm worried about leaving the house, and I'm worried about my family and friends who are visibly Muslim, because I know they could be targeted.

Where society and people have disappointed me several times, my religion has not. For many, me saying I want to wear a hijab because I just do isn't acceptable. I hate having to dig deep each time and reveal what's between me and Allah; it feels such an invasion of my privacy and faith. Though wearing a hijab at times has been difficult, simply put, I wear my hijab for Allah, and because I believe it is an important part of my faith. It is silly to think that wearing a hijab is the beginning and end of being modest or a good Muslim; the principles around hijab are about more than aesthetics.

I want to believe that non-Muslims of my generation

are more accepting and respecting of my decisions to wear my hijab, but that isn't the case. Although I acknowledge for some this could be pure curiosity, most of the time it feels like a demand, where entitled individuals expect me to justify my decision and my identity. I am often frustrated that many non-Muslims expect Muslims to educate them, as though it's our job. People need to understand that Muslim women are not seeking their permission to wear a hijab or any other type of veil. If your version of liberation is revealing skin and hair, then great. For some Muslim women, it is the opposite. Your choices aren't wrong, but neither are ours. This is my body, and how I choose to dress or not dress myself should be my choice.

HALF-TRUTH HISTORIES: HOW ERASING EMPIRE MAINTAINS THE STATUS QUO

Ilyas Nagdee

Content warning: racism, classism

This is a story of immense frustration about educational inequality and what got me passionate about tackling it. Central to this essay is some terminology and a key statistic that will help you understand what forced me into action. It's something widely known within the higher education sector as the BME attainment gap, or ethnicity attainment gap. This means that students of colour who start university with the same, or even higher, qualifications as their white counterparts are 18 per cent less likely (nationally) to get a first or 2:1 than their white counterparts.* The national average currently stands at 18 per cent, but there are differences within individual institutions and courses. This gap is another manifestation

---

* 'Degree attainment gaps', Equality Challenge Unit, available at https://www.ecu.ac.uk/guidance-resources/student-recruitment-retention-attainment/student-attainment/degree-attainment-gaps/

of the institutional racism faced by students of colour in predominantly white institutions. White in their teachers, white in what they're taught and white in their success. White in their teachers – two years ago a report came out that shocked the higher education sector: of the almost 20,000 professors in the UK, eighty-five were black, and of those only seventeen were black women. White in what they're taught, with a rigid Eurocentric curriculum. White in their success, with graduates of colour two and a half times less likely to be in employment after graduation than their white peers.

There are lots of cited reasons for this attainment gap: an unrepresentative curriculum, imbalances of power in the classroom and the terrible way in which young people of colour are made to understand their history.

Wanna know what my first experience of learning about history relating to India, where my family was from, was?

Unfortunately, this isn't a story of how a second-generation Indian immigrant sat on his mum's lap as she painted for him a rich story of farms surrounding our village, buffalos roaming the streets, or tearing into the deliciousness of a sugar cane that grew in the fields. Nor is it a picture of a group of enthralled children sitting down on Eid as their granddad tells them of writers and warriors of the past.

No, my first experience of Indian history was 'Queen Victoria'.

In an overcrowded classroom on a relatively cold and wet day (it's Manchester: of course it was raining), this was the first thing a fourteen-year-old Indian kid heard about his ancestral home.

Bloody colonialism.

That was way back in Year Eight, where in all of five minutes I was told about how the British had travelled across the world, travelled thousands of miles, to save India. That they improved our trade a thousand-fold, brought civilisation to us, and – most importantly – gave us the railways (cue applause). The class reacted as all students are taught to react – with complete acceptance of history as it's presented to us. But having my country's entire history reduced to a footnote about how backwards we were before being saved impacted me in ways I didn't even realise at the time. I wanted nothing more than to distance myself from that history, from that culture – shouting at home about how I couldn't take stinky Indian food into lunch, rolling my eyes at the Bollywood movie my family insisted on watching, horrified at my mum for wearing her kameez when dropping me off at school. And God forbid I was asked to wear one myself! Because Indian culture was inferior – why was I the only one at home who could see it?

History had taught me that. It had to be true.

I think about that history lesson a lot. I think about the long-lasting impact it had on how I saw myself and my family. I do not want young dual-heritage kids to have to reject part of themselves. Nor do I want British white kids to look at me and see a conquered Indian.

In classrooms across this country, children are not being taught history. Instead they are being taught a whitewashed version of history, which even now paints the British Empire as the saviour of the world's savages. So is it any wonder that last year a YouGov poll found almost half of the British public were proud of the empire, with only 21 per cent feeling negatively about it? The remainder did not have enough information to make a call – and that in itself is a whole different issue.*

The reality is that the story of the empire is a story of an infrastructure which propelled Britain into riches and wealth on the backs of black and brown people. And yet this is a reality that is rarely explored in schools. You'll never hear about things like the Bengal famine and the horrifying role Churchill played in it. One of my favourite descriptions about the lack of study of the British Empire is 'collective amnesia'. This term was well explored by Shashi Tharoor, the Indian MP and author, who spoke in the Oxford Union about whether Britain should pay reparations to India, and who continues to speak out about how British society and its education system are plagued with an unwillingness to learn about the evils of empire. By not teaching young people the true consequences of empire, we allow them to grow up

---

* Jon Stone, 'British people are proud of colonialism and the British Empire, poll finds', *The Independent*, 19 January 2016, available at https://www.independent. co.uk/news/uk/politics/british-people-are-proud-of-colonialism-and-the-british-empire-poll-finds-a6821206.html

in ignorance, an ever more dangerous position in an ever-globalising and multicultural world. There needs to be a deep re-evaluation of what we consider worthwhile teaching in schools, colleges and universities.

Imagine learning the names and stories of all the wives of Henry VIII but never even hearing the name Mansa Musa, the richest king (and man) who ever lived. And imagine being taught Pythagoras' theorem but not being informed it was Indian mathematicians whose work was translated into Arabic to form the numbers we use today – the numbers that constitute the basis of everyday transactions, from the stock market to the supermarket.

Imagine being taught your ancestral home was gifted railways from the British but not of the absolute atrocities of colonial rule: from the kidnapping of the young by the empire to continue systematic slavery to the destruction of natural resources with no regard to, nor reward for, the local population. Imagine having hidden from you something on the scale of the Bengal famine in which 4 million starved to death in order to keep British non-essential reserves stocked. (Not to mention the real reasons the railways were there in the first place – as an instrument of colonialism to facilitate the continuous exploitation of an oppressed people.)

Imagine all of that – and still being unable to enjoy your tasty, oily keema in a tub at school, because if a drop of that deliciousness falls it'll stain your white shirt!

The importance of education is a central discussion

amongst communities of colour and those hailing from immigrant backgrounds. If my grandparents, who came here with little, had one wish, it was what my parents repeated to us as a ritual growing up: 'You have to study, you have to do something with your life, [and of course] you have to become a doctor.'

The medical profession has become for migrant communities the pinnacle of social mobility – education is the great liberator, but to become a doctor is to reach the very top, with those who become doctors able to bridge class divisions and have the hope of finally being comfortable, attaining that better life for which they had crossed countries and oceans. Hence, for many of us, our parents were resolute about one point – we were all to become doctors.

From the age of ten I was in tuition a few nights a week and every weekend for years trying to make my parents proud. The pressure put on me at that time seemed unfair, like the world's burdens sat on my shoulders, and to be honest a parent's aspirations can sometimes weigh as much as the world. I always remember thinking, 'Why is Dad spending so much money?' (sometimes it was twenty quid for an hour) when we had so little. Dad worked weekends in the family newsagent and every morning he'd call home from the shop to check I had prepped all my work for the tutor. All I wanted to do was sleep in and go on the PlayStation, but he had other plans for me. At the time I found his pestering annoying, but soon enough I was grateful when I saw the fruits of their labour in the A4 sheet of my degree. Now I find myself wanting to push my nieces and nephew just as hard – wanting for them the opportunities my parents provided me.

Even so, university was not a path I imagined for myself. Yet, as luck would have it, on a rainy day (again: it's Manchester), I found myself following a friend into an information session about an access programme at the University of Manchester, lured by the promise of food. Never did I expect that I would end up applying for it and that it would be the start of my journey to university. I remember the first time I went onto the campus – I thought it was so far away. I got on the bus my friends said to get, had no idea where to get off, and ended up being half an hour late, roaming round the vast campus. Later I would learn that this huge collection of buildings was less than a five-minute drive from my house, but at the time, I felt lost.

That feeling of being lost summarises a lot of my time at the access programme. I was required to go onto the campus twice a month to take part in workshops. One in particular stands out to me. I had to work in a group with other seventeen- and eighteen-year-olds and prepare a presentation. It was only when I was on stage that it dawned on me that I had never done any form of public speaking before, and I panicked. Just standing up there made me go bright red, and I sweated more than when going through airport security on a bad beard day.

Just being in those rooms and those buildings was preparing me for university, because all of this was new. So many of the students on the scheme were second-generation immigrants, as were the university students mentoring us. That link alone relaxed me enough to ask questions about how the finances worked and subjects besides medicine.

Just as the India I was taught about was different to the India I am descended from, the university on my doorstep was very different to the Manchester I grew up in. Even though I lived with two of the UK's largest museums and art galleries on my doorstep (both owned by the university), I'd never visited. Quite often, in big cities like Manchester, huge universities are close to areas with low levels of progression into university, and the communities around benefit least from these gigantic institutions. I wonder how many students from Moss Side, Longsight and Ardwick make it to the University of Manchester. We have world-leading institutes a few minutes away from council estates lacking investment. Universities have started to do more work with local communities – but they have a long way to go.

That's why, on that strangely warm results morning, upon the hundredth refresh of the UCAS website, when I found out I had got into the University of Manchester, I knew one of the first things I wanted to do was work with young people from backgrounds like mine: young, working-class kids who thought they had no chance in hell of going to university.

Two months in, I got the opportunity to become a mentor and had to pick the school I wanted to mentor in. There was no doubt about it: I was going back to my high school. The feeling of going back, for the first time since I'd picked up my GCSE results, was surreal. It was strange being sent to the staff room to wait until the session started and striking up conversation with old teachers (I still called them Sir and Miss). Most of the kids were people of colour – most of my high school was – and I saw myself in their questions, in their enthusiasm and in their curiosity. I wanted to make the idea of going to university more real for them, to transform it from a distant goal into a reality they could expect. Last year I bumped into one of the girls in that group as she started her first year in pharmacy.

Education continues to be central to communities of colour, but over the last few years we've started to have difficult and different conversations. This mainly revolves around how well the new generation are taught their own history. Many immigrants are now faced with the reality that their children know very little about their countries of origin. Having finally fulfilled my father's goal of getting myself into university, I thought back to that history class and about what I had memorised to pass those exams.

I was forking out £9,000 a year and saddling myself with decades of debt to be taught some half-truths from people who didn't see people who looked like me as equals. Wanting to engage with some material that felt remotely connected to me, I enrolled in Middle Eastern studies. I wanted to learn about Islamic history, try learning the Arabic language and start to understand the history of the Middle East. Part of this is because of how difficult it is to be a Muslim in modern-day Britain – for some of your earliest memories to be of Saddam Hussein's statue falling and a plane going into a tower. I thought by learning more, I'd understand a bit more. Studying Middle Eastern studies, you'd think I'd constantly have my nose down in the writings of eighth-century Arab theologians or nineteenth-century Egyptian feminists, but instead I was reading what some old dude from France thought about his one visit to Cairo. Slightly disappointing, to say the least.

With the seventieth anniversary of Partition in 2017, I'm more aware than ever of how I didn't know about this important piece of history until I was eighteen. And even now, my education on it is limited, despite the fact so many elders in my family lived through it. The gaps in our history are more profound than ever. These conversations have spilled into campuses as well, with students in small classrooms learning from each other and creating book clubs to learn more about themselves. How many young people of colour are aware of the triumphs and tribulations of those that came before them? The history of our people is either minimised to slavery and empire or completely ignored. Any heroes we are taught about are American – we learn about Martin Luther King Jr whilst ignoring Olive Morris and

Jayaben Desai. We learn about the Montgomery bus boycott but not the Bristol bus boycott.

Learning facts to pass exams was easy. Learning about my own ancestry, and going through the process of unlearning my perceptions of India, proved to be much more difficult. For one, I was doing it alone. I started to learn about Surat – the region in India my family stems from, which was the first port the British took control of. I found photos and documents highlighting the introduction of girls' schools there before 1900. The various ways in which my people had resisted oppression fascinated me; they were not savages saved by the empire, as we'd been taught. This was coupled with stories coming out of India of the continuous challenges around stigmatisation and marginalisation of those with different sexualities, those who are Dalit and those who are currently facing horrendous pressure under the current government.

The more I researched the history of the global south, the more I felt settled, as if some deep void which had existed was slowly being filled. As if suddenly so many power imbalances I saw made sense. You see, being taught about the places of our parents' and grandparents' birth in a negative way affected the way I saw myself, the way I saw my parents and in effect the way I treated them. I resented them trying to get me to be more Indian, because I wanted nothing more than to be absorbed by whiteness – that was, after all, the ideal I had been taught to aspire to.

That's when I first heard a phrase that turned out to be the name of a national campaign, the Why Is My Curriculum White? campaign. This was born out of the frustrations of students of colour and academics at University College London, SOAS and other London universities wherein they identified a gap in learning and the imbalances of power in their institutions.

They were interrogating the way their history was being taught, and through whose gaze – because what is being taught, how it is being taught, where it is being taught, what purpose it is being taught for and who is doing the teaching are crucial questions, rarely spoken, that shine a light on the nature of education and its function in society. These critiques and conversations have been circulating within institutions for years, but have most often been dismissed or re-routed into dead-end discussions on diversity.

But those top-down proposals failed to properly address the impact that the education system was having on students of colour.

Continuously telling students of colour that their respective ancestral countries had contributed very little to the world through a warped and often whitewashed version of history has consequences, both seen and unseen. Seen in the sense of disaffected students becoming disengaged in the classroom, but the unseen consequences are far worse – impacting on a student's confidence, turning the student into the disempowered 'other'.

Slowly but surely, things are changing. Campaigns like Why Is My Curriculum White? aim to shift the conversation through lectures, seminars, reading clubs and protests. In Bristol, students are protesting to remove the name of slave-owner Henry Overton Wills from one of its most popular sites – the Wills Memorial Building. This is the very centrepiece of the institution, hosting exams and graduations in its great hall. It is the university's most iconic building. The profit Wills made from the tobacco industry and invested into the university was how it came to get its Royal Charter, earning him permanent glory in the university's most iconic building. Students at Bristol are calling into question whether the same hall that hosts progressive speakers can hold the name of a slave-owner.

The campaign was met with similar remarks to the Rhodes Must Fall movement throughout Oxford, where international stories broke about the huge numbers of students protesting the celebration of the colonial figure Cecil Rhodes. The campaign originated in South Africa, where students at the University of Cape Town were frustrated by the ongoing inequalities as a result of apartheid coupled with the celebration of this figure in an institute of learning. The campaign grew from one against a statue to one that looked holistically at the institutional racism prevalent at Cape Town, using various forms of direct action like occupations, sit-ins and other tactics to get the removal of the statues. In the UK, at Oriel College, the statue of Rhodes stands above those of kings, queens and saints.

Resistance to this campaign involved comments like, 'Why can't we just learn the history about these people?' again coming back to the acceptance of history as pure fact. It begs the question – do statues teach histories, or are they there to glorify certain histories? Before young people of colour, and in both these instances primarily young black people, protested the glorification of these individuals – whose gifts to these historic institutions were only possible through the exploitation of peoples and lands halfway around the world – who knew that Wills owned slaves and Rhodes aimed for British rule from 'the Cape to Cairo'? The glorification of their legacies through buildings and statues enshrines in the minds of the unsuspecting visitors and passers-by that they were great men. Universities are, by their own admittance, plagued with institutional racism, and that cannot be tackled until an honest conversation happens about all of its manifestations, including their own histories.

Melissa 'Melz' Owusu, the former Education Officer at Leeds University Union (LUU), provides a great example of the kind of cultural and institutional change that can be made on a local level, from lectures and panels to a poster campaign explicitly unveiling problematic history of the topics being taught there: how gynaecology was born through the experimentation of pain on black women because J Marion Sims believed they had a higher threshold of pain, or how the father of ethics, Kant, was a white supremacist. Melz forced discussions and coupled this with mobilising students of colour to create change on her campus, resulting in the creation of a module on black British history – the first of its kind in the UK. Melz has also been a Sabbatical Officer during the two years in which students and student officers across the country have been demanding change in their education system and challenging the attainment gap.

The attainment gap has existed for a long time, but thanks to the work of several organisations – including student groups like the NUS Black Students' Campaign, which seeks to represent over 1 million students of colour from across the UK – it has now been made a national priority. An incredibly important transformation in the approach was the slow move away from the 'deficit model', wherein students of colour, especially black students, were seen as a problem that needed to be resolved (it was the students who lacked the ability to succeed, not the institutions that exclusively catered to whiteness). This was eventually overturned by the Birmingham BME Ambassadors Scheme, set up by Jane Tope and Malia Bouattia. Tope and Bouattia took students of colour who were traditionally perceived to be 'the problem' and gave them a seat at the table – namely on academic and decision-making boards. This, in turn, enabled them to change and shape the student experience, the methods of teaching and the culture of the university, thereby drastically reducing the attainment gap which existed there.

This process of viewing students of colour not as a problem and an attainment deficit but as students who could transform their institutions is ongoing. The Birmingham Black Ambassadors Scheme has been internationally recognised as a model for good practice and formed the basis for what we're doing in Manchester. We're recruiting students, training them and pushing them to engage with their peers on how to create a greater sense of belonging within universities. The hope is that this, alongside pushing for a more representative and decolonised curriculum, will help stop students of colour feeling as disillusioned with universities as they currently do.

This is being done in conjunction with dozens of other universities now looking at tackling this gap on an institution-wide basis, with some exploring socio-economic backgrounds and others looking at intersections within students of colour. This is crucial given how poorly used the terminology around access and attainment can be. I remember attending a sector conference on access and attainment and once again being one of the only people of colour in the room. I was chatting to a friendly white woman who worked in a widening participation department (the sector which aims to get those from backgrounds unlikely to go to university the information and resources necessary to make a decision about whether to go or not) in a university. We began talking about perceptions of students of colour by white professors, and I noticed she had used the term 'low socio-economic background' in the place of 'students of colour' at one point. I didn't mention it, thinking it was a slip-up, until she repeated it again and again. She actually thought all students of colour were working class and had put us all neatly into a box. This says a lot about the way students and communities of colour are perceived by elite institutions.

It's when all of these things are taken holistically – the attainment gap, the white curriculum, the rise in hate crime and the perceptions of students of colour – that you begin to realise why some, like me, felt like they didn't belong.

Young people of colour are changing the institutions they exist in. They are transforming the very spaces which in so many ways have failed them. They are resisting and liberating at the same time. It's been so tough trying to play a small part in that change. You say goodbye to your social life, your family will be annoyed at you for not spending more time at home, your mental health is in tatters, and your bank balance – bruv, don't even get me started on that.

But we continue. We persevere and we continue to try and transform our places of learning into liberated spaces so that those who come after us aren't introduced to their histories in the way we were. So that those that come after us don't fall prey to institutional racism and merely contribute to the attainment gap.

I do it so an Indian kid in a classroom isn't introduced to their ancestral home through a colonial lens.

I do it so a Muslim kid can be unashamedly political.

I do it in the hope my parents are proud.

WORKING WITH ANXIETY
Chloe Kitching
Content warning: mental health

I have generalised anxiety disorder (GAD) – spiced with depressive episodes and panic attacks – which has always been a loitering figure in my life. I try to consider it as a strength and embellishment to my personality as much as it is a gargantuan menace. It impacts most aspects of my life, but having lived with it for as long as I can recall, I have become pretty efficient at managing it. The only place I still have not mastered my mental health is in the workplace. I have had three full-time jobs since graduating and a couple of part-time roles, all of which have provided me with varying experiences illuminating the way in which mental health is dealt with in the workplace.

I've experienced a mixed bag of responses to mental health issues. In my first proper job, I had a 'code word' with my boss, which I could use to duck out of situations at the last minute if necessary. For the most part, I can handle demanding and pressured situations, but occasionally, the anxiety gets the better of me and at the drop of a hat, my head fills with dense grey cloud, my sweat glands become over-productive and all clarity of thought goes to shit. One morning I remember walking into a room full of colleagues for the weekly catch-up and suddenly feeling an overwhelming sense of dread. I gave the code word and was able to retreat to the bathroom, just in time for a panic attack. She would only really bring up my mental health in our scheduled catch-ups, which was a relief. The expectation of this meant I could be prepared for that discussion, or if I didn't want to discuss it we would just breeze over the topic. A friend of mine used to have panic attacks on the way to work, from the sheer suspense of starting the day, but once she was around her colleagues she would feel OK again, and her colleagues never batted an eyelid at her slightly dishevelled appearance or lateness. They just knew that's the way she worked.

I've also been party to some pretty poor responses to mental health issues. This includes micromanagement to the point of puppetry, being deliberately excluded from social occasions due to being too quiet, or being referred to as 'the crier', which, by the way, I don't think lexically applies unless you are referring to someone wielding a bell, shouting 'hear ye! hear ye!' in a town square. I think crying is a fruitful way of expressing pent-up emotion; it's truthful, it's time effective and has less of a knock-on effect than carrying suppressed emotion around like a storm in the stomach. In general, it seems that people who experience mental ill-health are regarded as not normal and therefore less trusted to carry out their roles. These are just a couple of examples. But I'm going to relay to you my recent and significant experience of how mental health issues are handled in the workplace.

Last year, I started my 'dream' job, which I'd applied for on a starry-eyed whim and miraculously was offered. I moved to London, cut my hair into a bob and started wearing statement clothing, as I'd learned all successful young people do in those HP tablet adverts. This was a big fist pump 'fuck you, anxiety' moment for me. I was, naively in retrospect, convinced this meant I had overcome mental adversity and from now on would be a full-blown legitimate adult human, able to laugh in the face of the shit-flinging monkey we call life. Alas, this was not the case. Having moved away from my support network, I was quite mentally unwell for the majority of my time in London, which provoked physical illness. The deterioration was rapid. One week in January, after suffering from anxiety, depression, the flu, a urinary tract infection, not to mention other afflictions that further contributed to my misery, I sat in bed and decided it was probably time to give up the ghost. But for the sake of the story, let's rewind...

I had decided, as a new, self-assured, healthy adult woman, to seize this fresh start with a positive gung-ho attitude, throwing myself at the situation like a catapulted starfish. This was a chance to re-invent myself – I'd never have to fear my own company again. It was lovely; I could have conversations over ten minutes long without breaking out into a cold sweat and later revisiting the conversation to critically analyse every word I'd uttered. I walked down the road and could give other people legitimate eye contact, iris to iris. It was as though getting this job offered me the gratification I'd needed. It proved that I was a worthy professional, that I was not a fraudulent infant in a woman's body, but in fact the person that I'd always hoped I might be.

This, I think, lasted for around three weeks before the familiar face of old father anxiety rocked up and decided he was ready for a showdown. How foolish I had been to think it would be that easy. I started to notice the usual behaviours creeping in, but to the best of my ability, I ignored them. Such behaviours include obsessing over conversations and circumstances which have happened in the past, framing these experiences through a lens of shame and guilt and regret, taking the long route home to avoid spending time alone at home or rushing home to be alone and drinking to excess once there, convincing myself I'm pregnant and spending hours on Mumsnet, self-diagnosing myself with various disorders and spending hours researching them, watching entire TV seasons in a matter of days, convincing myself everyone knows I'm a mad woman, deleting Facebook and Twitter to avoid anyone else finding out, stopping washing, stopping looking after myself and crying every day without fail.

I try and do this all secretively, of course, and for the most part I still appear to my friends and colleagues as a healthy person

(I think). Most of the 'madness' exists in my own internal workings: mind-reading, catastrophising, emotional reasoning, etc.

When I am suffering from mental ill-health, there is no break from it. Sleeping provides no restorative effect, but only temporarily mutes my mind's frantic administration of anxious and disturbing thoughts. Waking up feels like returning to work to discover a full inbox of red-flagged unread messages. There are simultaneously not enough hours in the day to deal with all the mental commotion, and too many hours in the day to endure. Things like human connection and conversation are a source of dread. Enjoyment and pleasure seem non-existent, with the exception of activities that drown out one's thoughts and feelings, e.g. drinking. Empathy or care for any other human being is absent. It is a narcissistic and self-loathing world. It is a great shame, and shame is felt in abundance.

I knew I needed to get some help, but between working, travelling and self-medicating, I was incapable of even organising and attending an appointment of my own volition.

After six months at work, I decide to disclose to my managers. Yes. This is good! This is a good thing. Finally, I can take these hurtful scary thoughts and yank them out of the depth of my skull. Extract them like spaghetti from a strainer, lay them out on the table, and someone will say, 'How brave you have been, it's all going to get better now.' They will take it all away for me and I'LL BE FREE. FREE FROM THE PRISON THAT IS MY PREFRONTAL CORTEX.

So I disclosed. I feel strongly that I had left it too late, and rather than disclosing in a space where I felt confident to explain how my anxiety impacted my working life as coherently as I could, I instead ended up disclosing what can only be described as an inconsolable nervous breakdown, in front of my two managers, in my ten-week review. In hindsight, using my review to do this was a regrettable decision. It detracted attention from the job I had been doing and the chance of receiving an honest assessment of where I had been doing well and where I needed to improve. Instead, it focused the meeting entirely on my illness and current mental state.

I think this is where things got tricky for me. Following disclosure, my managers' behaviour towards me began to change (understandably, out of a desire to be helpful) but I was unsure of how my anxious behaviours would manifest in the workplace, and so was unable to give them appropriate guidance to deal with this change in behaviour. I didn't know exactly what support I needed or how I was going to be proactive to make the situation better. Any counselling I had received previously was a referral via university, or via a friend's contact at school. In truth, what I wanted from disclosing was for someone to acknowledge my situation, take the reins and make everything better, telling me exactly what I needed to do to feel well again and do the job to the level I should be. I wanted an immediate, simple and concrete solution, and I wanted to be assured I would be better soon and to believe it. This was naive of me and perhaps even a little selfish. I would quickly learn that my mental health is primarily my responsibility, and to keep it in good shape takes hard work, therapy and self-help. Unfortunately, I had all this to discover, and in that moment, I was desperate for some magical intervention.

When I have an intense spell of GAD and depression, reality can become blurry and confused. My sense of self is no longer concrete, but a shape-shifting wisp of immediate response and paranoia. This became an issue after disclosing. My managers were brilliant in responding and kept an eye out for unusual behaviour. On occasion, they might gesture me a thumbs-up 'everything OK?' as an informal check-in. Due to my inability to identify my own thinking, I'd worry that I actually was having a 'bad day' without knowing it, triggering a wave of self-doubt. This then started a loop of hyper self-awareness and a sidelining paranoia that I was exposing my madness more than I should be: I thought I entered the room in a normal manner, but it seems I in fact entered the room as a mentally ill person. Where does the distinction lie? This is a complete overreaction to a kind gesture, but this unfortunately is the nature of the beast. On the flip side, disclosing will put pressure on managers to intuitively recognise when you are struggling. This, though done with good intentions, is not always helpful. Say goodbye to using colloquial office expressions such as 'today is not my day' unless you want panicked expressions, seven cups of tea, a sympathetic squeeze on the thigh and a 'you're doing really well'.

I remember sitting at my desk whilst the rest of the office excitedly packed up their things for the staff Christmas meal. I had told my managers I was not going to join. A sit-down two-course meal in central London with the office sounded like torture in my current frame of mind. However, my absence from the meal had remained confidential from the rest my colleagues, who, much to their confusion, had clocked my lack of movement...

'Are you not coming?!'

'Oh, no. No, sorry.'

'Why not?'

'Er, I've just got loads on. Sorry.'

'We've all got loads on – come on! It's Christmas lunch!'

'I don't have much money, sorry.'

'We'll cover you, it's fine!'

'No it's not that. It's...'

'Yeah, come on!'

'No, I, I, I...'

Cue sweat, red face, toilet, panic attack

I became convinced I was useless and everyone knew it. I'd read into emails like a teenager decoding a text from a love interest. I would pay extra careful attention to the direction of people's gazes and facial expressions in meetings – any slight wrinkle of the nose or quick glance would be used as evidence to confirm that I was shit and everyone agreed. I never contributed or spoke up in meetings and started wearing headphones at my desk to deter conversation. I was shattered constantly, doing things like going to the bathroom to spray cold water on my neck and face to try to stay alert or closing my eyes on the toilet for two minutes as an attempt at a power nap.

I knew I needed time off to rest and to do some internal rewiring, but I didn't know how long I would need. Although there was no pressure from my line managers to give a specific timeline of recovery and return, I was acutely aware of 'letting the department down', concerned about who would be burdened with my workload, and how that would impact their view of me. Unlike physical illness, the recovery time for mental illness is much more difficult to predict. The fear that you will return much the same, if not worse, is also a factor in refusing to take time off.

I was able to get some CBT quickly; however, I felt as though the damage had been done. I felt so ashamed of my poor mental health and of the occasions I'd sat in my manager's office hyperventilating or having to ask for something to be explained to me for the third time because my brain wouldn't compute. I had given up. I felt I'd already exposed myself, and there was no going back from that. I felt I had misrepresented myself as a competent human being by not disclosing in the recruitment process.

Ultimately, this drove me to leave my job completely. I couldn't trust that I would recover whilst on leave or get better whilst continuing to work. I'd already wasted enough of everyone's time, so the right and gracious thing to do was to leave and just apologise profusely for everything.

This boils down to the stigma of mental health and the fear of it. I understand that unlike some physical illnesses it doesn't come in a box or with a straightforward description. Symptoms can vary, and it takes all sorts of shapes. What I'm beginning to learn is that you can have a day where your mental health feels poorly, but it doesn't mean this has to follow you into the next day, or the next week, or the next few months. I also realise now that it's good to be honest about your mental health, but you don't have to share everything. Sometimes it's a positive thing to safeguard yourself by only telling the finer details to people who you trust until you feel you have more of a hold on it yourself.

Often the protocol for companies after disclosing is to pass you down a long line of managers/nurses/consultants who will probe you to describe how you feel only to pass you on to another person. I do not believe this is helpful. It is exhausting. What is helpful, in my experience, is finding your local council's talking therapy unit, and self-referring yourself for some CBT. Tell your GP, but you don't have to take any medications if you don't want to. Read some books, listen to a podcast, join an online forum. It's difficult to be proactive when you are ill, but signing up for CBT/therapy involves a quick internet search, an easy form to fill in and then a wait for the phone call (which might take some time). This means there is no need for you to leave the house, talk to anyone, or even change your pants (all those things you dread).

I think what could have been helpful to me at the time were solid options I could select from. It was made clear that I could have flexible working time or start times depending on what I thought would help; however, I couldn't quite decide for myself what would be best, as I wanted to put the demands of the job first and make sure I wasn't letting down the team. I think each institution should have their own plan of action, which contains a statement outlining the organisation's attitude to mental health and a framework of defined options of flexi-time working and support that work for both the department and employee. The employee can thus be confident in the knowledge that they are not having an adversely negative impact on the department. It cannot be solely up to the individual to determine the parameters. Pre-established options would mean the employee could select or suggest a plan of action, which could in turn be adapted accordingly dependent on the needs of all parties. Also, any meetings to review mental-health-related performance should be penned in the diary and kept to. Find a time that works and that can be protected to the best of everyone's abilities. Moving or cancelling these meetings can serve to create more uncertainty and doubt in the mind of that individual.

When it comes to disclosing at work, each individual is completely different and has their own unique needs dependent on how their health impacts them. I think it's also vital to note that not everyone will have mastered this. It's probably fair to say that many young people (and people of all ages) are doing this all for the first time and coming up against new obstacles both in their heads and physically in the workplace. This is going to cause some unknowns, and it might not always be possible for an individual to tell you exactly what's best. It's not black and white, but we can make the support structures and modes of helping a little stronger.

Since leaving my job, I have completed some CBT, started eating better, drinking less, walking more, and spent more time talking to friends and taking an interest in new things. I have stopped mind-reading and started to have more confidence in my own thoughts and feelings without criticising myself for every little mistake. I occasionally view my anxiety as a small child – it might want to stay up late or eat bad things, but I know what the ramifications of that are and that it's not worth it. I also started a new job, where I flagged my history of anxiety in the interview as an explanation for my gap in employment. I'm glad I did. It is a part of who I am and the way I work, and this felt important to mention. The honesty was appreciated, and since starting this new job, I now feel I am much better equipped to support myself.

Despite all this, I'm acutely aware that I am one young person, of many, who must experience and manage their mental health in the workplace. My experience is both unique and remarkably un-unique; everyone experiences mental ill-health differently, and there are a lot of us with mental health issues! I believe it would be safe to say that my experience is pretty standard for young people today. These experiences have taught me a lot, both about how I manage my own mental health and about how organisations can best place themselves to support their employees. It seems that conversations around mental health are starting to become more frequent, open and more at the forefront of the consciousness of employers. This can only be a good thing.

Ultimately, I believe it is the responsibility of the individual to best support themselves with regard to their own mental health, but I hope what I've articulated is that understanding from colleagues, and structures within organisations, can go a long way in actively supporting that person to get the most out of themselves and the work they are doing. I don't consider myself to be at the 'end' of the road with my mental health, and it is something I will continue to work on every day. But there are small changes in attitude and protocol which will help to make working environments better, to give anyone with a mental illness a chance of being the 'best' version of themselves, and to finally normalise anxiety and depression as facets of the human condition.

CONVEYOR BELT SOCIALISING: AN EXPOSÉ ON MODERN DATING

Ellie Ford-Elliott

Content warning: sexism

'I want to write about sexuality, I think,' I said to my friend, hungover in my living room after a night out.

'I don't feel like I even know anything about my sexuality. Except for like, having sex,' she replied.

I laughed. Then I paused. She was just pouring coffee and making a blasé comment. My mind, however, was suddenly a whirlpool of activity.

It dawned on me that up until right then, my conscious thoughts about my sexuality had been overwhelmingly preoccupied with who I was attracted to rather than the ways that I'd expressed that attraction. I have always asserted that I'm bisexual, slapped a label on myself and sent myself down the conveyor belt.

In 2015, a YouGov study showed that as many as half of all eighteen- to twenty-four-year-olds considered themselves 'not 100 per cent heterosexual'.* In my experience, the idea of sexuality as a spectrum, characterised by its potential for flexibility, is generally accepted by most people born after 1960. This attitude shift towards non-heterosexuality has affected everyone – especially young people – in the dating world hugely.

The ways in which we have relationships with one another and express our sexuality in practice – whatever gender we may be – are also shifting. With new ways of communicating through social media, we have developed new kinds of romantic connections, where the rules of engagement have changed – Tinder, anyone?

There have been a lot of moments in my life that have felt like the low point of a rom-com where everything goes wrong. None more so, however, than on one bright autumn day when I was living in halls at university. I was taking out the rubbish bags and I saw, through a window, my then-boyfriend kissing someone else. There I was, dragging along this gigantic, bursting rubbish bag… an apt metaphor, no?

Three months, a road trip and some heartfelt spoken word performances later, however, I was back on my feet, and my friend encouraged me to download Tinder one afternoon on campus.

I was hesitant. 'Isn't that for people who only want sex?'

---

* Will Dahlgreen and Anna-Elizabeth Shakespeare, '1 in 2 Young people say they are not 100% heterosexual', YouGov, 16 August 2015, available at https://yougov.co.uk/topics/lifestyle/articles-reports/2015/08/16/half-young-not-heterosexual

'I don't know, really,' my friend replied. 'I've never met anyone from it, it's just fun. It's an ego boost.'

It sounded great. An ego boost was what I needed. My first three swipe rights were instant matches, and it had been months since anyone had properly looked at me (break-up face isn't my best look), let alone looked at me with the IRL equivalent of swiping right.

The first few months of using Tinder were fun, despite the fact that there is not another place on Earth where bisexuality is so ill-understood. I'd have conversations with people who were interested in me, occasionally duck when I recognised someone from the app on campus, and laugh with my friend about all the atrocious pickup lines that had been used on us; I generally came to accept that it fitted in quite well with my university lifestyle. I never really thought about meeting anyone from it. This was the fun kind of 'keeping your options open'. I felt like there were no pretences – you know these people are also talking to lots of other people. And talking to lots of people at the same time – maintaining several options – is a lot easier when they're all in one place.

I wasn't thinking about sex then, though. Lots of people think sex can stay casual. Our generation has endless songs and movies based around whether or not that's true. For me, being naked and sexual involves a great deal of intimacy. I've never been able to separate the two, not least in the kind of relationship that seems to want me to. The pre-sex conversational dance is casual enough. Flirting is great. Flirting is a show, a performance, a persona. Intimacy, on the other hand, is different. It's defined essentially as 'familiarity', which I think is apt. I'm familiar with my body; I'd like to be familiar with someone else before the two can meet. That doesn't sound particularly strange, but sexual fluidity and flexible identities have challenged the concept of intimacy. My experience of social media, especially apps like Tinder, proved to me that many people feel quite comfortable with a certain amount of emotional separation from sex. And I don't blame them. After all, we're incredibly intimate in relationships, and when relationships end, it hurts. Why not spare ourselves that pain? Why not have our cake and eat it too?

The moment Tinder stopped being fun and became more serious was when I began speaking to some of the people on other forms of social media, rather than keeping it confined to the app. Texting is old school now, so texting someone from Tinder felt more real, even though it's still just pixels on a screen. Having somebody's number feels real – there's a reason we try to get phone numbers from people we find attractive. Conversations progressed differently when these people weren't just a picture confined to an app. What used to be 'let's play the twenty-questions game ;)' became 'I'd love to meet you'.

However, I was still a total chicken. I didn't arrange to meet anyone from Tinder during my first year at university, though there were a couple of times that I almost did. I made excuses and busied myself more and more with university work and less with the app, on which I'd once spent every day flicking through people like they were playing cards. Somewhere along the line, I deleted it. I didn't know it yet, but I wasn't cut out for casual relationships. What I did know already was that this kind of dating was nothing like anything I'd experienced before.

I'd had two long-term relationships by the time I was twenty – four years, then two years. Both were boys I knew from school, where, most of the time, boy–girl relationships form easily through mutual friendships and shared social pressures. These were naive relationships, based on a kind of mutual safety that we offered one another in an otherwise turbulent time characterised by tough decisions and self-discovery. However, I was not about to throw myself headfirst into the adult dating pool before I felt prepared for it – something my past relationships hadn't remotely helped with.

So I deleted Tinder. Then summer happened, new friendships happened and I found myself downloading it again. And funnily enough, back in my hometown, drunk on summer air and wine, I ended up meeting someone from Tinder.

David didn't look like his pictures. It was him in his pictures, don't get me wrong, but he had definitely found an incredibly flattering light and the very best angle. I wondered if he thought the same about me. We all do that these days, don't we? Find the best light, the best angle, the best filter? Make ourselves look like the brightest, prettiest versions of ourselves?

We got milkshakes. However, it was so awkward between me and David that I finished my milkshake in five minutes flat. Back on my home turf, a little confident and not wanting to spend any more money, I asked him if he wanted to come back to my house. Bad move. I meant it innocently; I had no idea if my family were home or not, I guess I was just being friendly and making a terrible excuse to leave. I don't think that's how he took the suggestion, because he lit up. I tried to make more excuses on the walk back to my house, but he ended up sitting on my sofa next to my brother, who thought it was the funniest thing that had happened all year. Once David realised that I definitely wasn't about to banish my family from their house and have him lay me by the fire, naked and impassioned, he 'received a phone call' and had to leave. We ignored one another forevermore; he appeared as a potential Facebook friend months later – thanks so much, Mark Zuckerberg – but I was glad to see he now had a girlfriend. For his sake, I hope their first date went better.

My second Tinder date was with Jack, and it was perfect, storybook stuff. It was the fourth of July. He and I had a coffee, went adventuring in the countryside, kissed under a gorgeous sunset and talked until midnight on a hill in the middle of nowhere. Then he walked me back and gave me his coat to take home and a promise of a second date. The only negative? In a flurry of emotion, when he asked me to tell him a secret, I said I rather liked him, and he laughed. I would spend days analysing that laugh, wondering if it was part of a much larger game that he was playing with me. I felt that way a lot, though of course, I never did know the rules.

The second date with Jack was a group affair: a party my friends threw in my honour, a few days after my dismal birthday. But he said he was coming today, to camp out with my friends and me by the river. It was a mission and a half to get him to come and meet us, but I managed it (persistence is something I'm good at, but not particularly proud of). He was charming, articulate and seemed into me. In retrospect, I can see that I had romanticised him massively, but I didn't think it was unreciprocated at the time. At 3 a.m., I left my own party to accompany him to his place, both of us starry-eyed and drunk. I awoke at 6 a.m. to an angry phone call from my friend, and I realised that, yes, I was being *that* person. I had ditched my friends for sex, after making them bring tents out into the middle of nowhere to camp whilst I gallivanted off for a dick appointment. I hadn't even told them where I was. I quickly got dressed and he let me out of the house so I could walk back to meet my remaining friends by the river. He kissed me goodbye with a smile and said he'd text me later.

I never heard from him again.

He didn't even delete me from social media. I was like a ghost. Later I found out that was a real thing: ghosting. A friend showed me the definition on Google: when they ignore your entire existence after pretending to be into you, whether for sexual gain or not. It had happened to her too, she said. I found a slight comfort in that. I'd sent him one or two messages afterwards, but it became clear that, as my friend put it, I'd been 'humped and dumped'. I was floored. Hookups are one thing, but to pretend to genuinely like someone, lure them in and then never speak to them again… I was incensed. I must admit, he never actually promised anything. We'd both let the other assume what was happening. Romance isn't romance if it's all planned and talked about, right? Turns out, I had assumed wrong. Romance wasn't at all what he had in mind.

How I wish I'd realised then that I wasn't a 'casual' kind of person. Not romantically and not sexually. No, that came later. Instead I fell into a dreaded 'situationship' – a newly coined term which describes two people involving themselves in every aspect of a relationship without the exclusivity or the communication, and often ends without closure. It's similar but also incredibly different to the phrase 'friends with benefits', which describes a sex-based friendship that, at least in theory, is built on mutual respect and solid communication but without any romantic feelings. A situationship, on the other hand, is characterised by its lack of communication and mysteriousness.

Perhaps I should have deleted Tinder after my ghosting experience; instead I used it to try and make myself feel better, because that's always worked out so well. I messaged back and forth with a boy for about eight months, deleting Tinder once he and I began talking on other forms of social media. We even had a few phone calls, which left me spinning with the dizzying happiness I'd been waiting for since I started dating. Even though it wasn't technically exclusive (these things are always technical when you don't talk about them), I wasn't interested in talking to anyone else. We spoke every single day, and everything about the way that we talked was like being in a long-distance relationship. He began to remember things about me and say sweet things, and I began to trust him, regardless of the fact that nothing was set in stone and I'd never met him in person.

Eventually, I got tired of him saying that he would come and see me and called his bluff by offering to go and see him. He turned it back on me and told me to chill out. He hadn't 'signed up for anything'. Oh, to be young and naive. I thought with enough time he would probably want to meet me. He didn't. When he popped up in my inbox days after ignoring one of my pointed messages, with a chirpy subject-change to get us back on track without actually defining anything, I knew I was in a situationship. My friends had mentioned the term before, and now it finally made sense. I was on the hook. A distraction from his daily life. An interesting toy that hadn't become boring yet. He was 'breadcrumbing' me, a friend of mine explained, a term that meant giving me just enough attention to keep me interested without being genuinely invested in our relationship. I laughed, but slowly I realised she was right. He'd compliment how I looked in my latest profile picture and tell me how funny I was, but he'd never say I meant anything to him specifically. He'd tell me how gorgeous he thought I was, then accuse me of 'catching feelings' when I wanted to meet up for a casual drink.

Eventually I deleted him from social media. Even writing that feels weird, knowing that you can 'delete' someone from your life like they're nothing, with no sense of closure and an empty feeling in your stomach. It felt like a horrible break-up... except we were never together. Later, I found out that he'd had a girlfriend the whole time, who had been travelling in America when he first began talking to me. I think I actually laughed when I heard, because at least it was some semblance of resolution. For months he'd been telling me I was too intense, I needed to chill, I needed to calm down. I read something in *Cosmo* a few months afterwards that made me hoot in agreement: 'You can't make someone crazy and then accuse them of acting crazy.'

I had wanted to go on a date with a woman, but unfortunately that never materialised. It's a lot easier to find straight men, it turns out, than bisexual-friendly WLW (women who love women) in the Tindersphere. Not all my dating experiences were tragic though – I had a few that weren't so bad, but still ended up going nowhere. It made me wonder where it was that I actually wanted to go. That was when I realised I probably wasn't the right kind of person for Tinder, because the 'where' for me was 'a relationship'. I was fine with being single and independent, but I wasn't casual. Not even remotely.

In the year or two that I used Tinder, I did at least expand my dating vocabulary greatly. I even had a date with a guy who wanted to 'Netflix and chill' – a term which has famously become synonymous with watching a movie and having sex. Except when it happened to me, he came over with popcorn, said very little and didn't make a single move on me save for an awkward hug when he left. He worked at Pets at Home, though, and let me hold one of the rabbits, so he'll be forever remembered as the best Tinder date ever.

Then there was my brush with 'negging', which is as grim as it sounds. It is a practice in which a dude (yes, it's usually a dude, I've never seen women do it except to prove a point about how stupid it is) deliberately insults a woman's appearance before softening the blow, so to speak, with a surprise compliment. It first surfaced decades ago amongst the subculture group of 'pickup artists', and is described on Urban Dictionary as men who 'use a variety of underhand tactics to try and get laid because, having serious problems with misogyny, a roaring inadequacy complex, [and] a deeply warped image of what constitutes being a worthy person, [they] have never developed a healthy way of interacting with the other sex and seem to believe that the only way to get laid is to trick them'. Horribly, this happens often to my friends of colour in conjunction with casual racism: 'You're pretty for a black girl,' for example. That's a whole kettle of issues in and of itself, highlighting the problem with how exotification and Western beauty standards affect dating, right down to a specific tactic that is already gross enough. For me, it was a guy at a bar (yes, I'd moved on from Tinder!) who told me, 'You look quite sweet without your glasses on.' No, dude, do not come near me.

My experiences with women have been very different. Most of my sexual encounters with women have been with long-standing friends, for one thing, and so there was a mutual respect established that precedes gendered behaviours. Still, I couldn't imagine these encounters being so uncomplicated with male friends. I've always felt an intuitive understanding with women, but due to my lack of experience, I have never been confident approaching a woman romantically. There was one girl I met whilst at university, not through any dating app either, who I crushed on for months from afar, and for months we shared small smiles and moments where I was like, 'Does she...?' However, by the time I had the opportunity to get closer to her – hell, by the time I found out she was bisexual too – I had found a new relationship.

Thankfully, it was an honest, loving, adult relationship with a man who managed to break down all the barriers I had put up when it came to dating men (with a lot of patience and compassion). It began to feel like the years of feeling lost and bitter had been worth it. However, I continued to watch in fascinated horror as my friends and their friends navigated the dating minefield. It wasn't just me. This was happening everywhere. The vigour and speed at which the situationship can turn from a nice, casual way to get laid into a vengeful and angry mess is astonishing, and happens only because, in these arrangements, emotions are demonised and communication is deemed uncool. It doesn't only happen to women, of course – wanting a basic level of respect and care is universal, but because of pesky gender roles, we women are generally socialised to prioritise emotional connections and men are taught that sexual prowess is power; so in my experience at least, it tends to happen far more to man-attracted ladies. A close friend of mine had a situationship with a guy she worked with, who also 'hadn't signed up for anything' but was asking her to stay over and cycling over to her place in the early hours to throw stones at her window. Then, instead of 'catching feelings', my friend found out she'd caught chlamydia. She'd been the exclusive one in this situationship, but nonetheless he blamed her for it, claiming that the other girls he'd been sleeping with were people he trusted 'implicitly' – thus making it obvious that my friend was the one he didn't trust. My friends and I worked a new term into our vocabulary for guys like this: the fuckboy.

'Fuckboy' is a term that I've seen on social media more than any other. It's considered to have come from prison slang (in which context it means something very different) but now has many long and detailed definitions on Urban Dictionary. There are various types of fuckboy out there in the wild, and their respective characteristics fluctuate. However, every fuckboy shares a fundamental lack of respect for women and an inflated idea of what they are 'owed' by said women. Fuckboys use the phrase 'nice guys finish last'. Fuckboys love to complain about the friendzone, as though having a female friend is the worst thing on Earth. Fuckboys text you at 2 a.m. asking for nudes and then ignore you for months. Fuckboys pretend they're busy for weeks at a time, but suddenly have time for you after you post a great selfie. They are feared and loathed by women everywhere, regardless of sexuality, since they can be anywhere and hide their true colours excellently. Even men fear fuckboys, since they might snake into your bed and steal your girl. Or your man. Or they'll verbally abuse them on the street.

Pre-Tinder, I was aware of those magazines touting articles like 'How to Get a Guy to Like You', where they examine feminine behaviour that straight men historically find attractive. Post-Tinder, I'm now seeing articles with titles more along the lines of 'How to Spot a Fuckboy', and I don't think that's just a coincidence. Whilst hookup culture has been around for decades now, it has never been as rife as in recent years, and we have never before coined so many terms for the different dating woes we're experiencing. It strikes me that all these terms describe behaviours which avoid real relationships and honesty. Why is that?

All my life I've watched romantic movies. All my life everyone I know has watched romantic movies. Recently, though, I watched a film that changed my view of this kind of film irrevocably. In *Don Jon*, written and directed by Joseph

Gordon-Levitt, Scarlett Johansson plays a woman obsessed with romantic films. Her expectations of a romantic partner, shaped by these movies, are contrasted with the main character's (played by Levitt) expectations of a sexual partner due to his addiction to porn. It struck me as an incredibly accurate societal observation. A lot of women I know will demonise porn (often with good reason) but then gush about Christian Grey in the same breath. Of course, in *Don Jon*, this is exaggerated and streamlined for cinematic effect, but it does make sense that the 'chick flicks' we've grown up on – *Sleepless in Seattle, Titanic, Pretty Woman, The Notebook, Love Actually,* etc. – have had a massive impact on the kinds of romantic partners we look for and how realistic our expectations are. However, that isn't exclusive to our generation. With so much of our lives being lived online over the past decade, the effects of that shift are inevitably going to affect relationships. Porn is undoubtedly one of these effects, considering how readily available it is on the internet.

Freedom of choice is fundamentally important to me, so I have never been fiercely anti-porn. However, do I think porn has negatively affected the way that men treat women (and how women see themselves) within the parentheses of modern hookup culture? Yes. It predisposes them to objectification and an exaggerated view of how available women's bodies are, which contributes to that separation between sex and intimacy which I mentioned previously. Do I think all men who watch porn see women's bodies as objects? No. Communication, near-infinite environmental factors and common sense all still exist. I'm not a scientist, but it would be naive to discuss hookup culture without acknowledging the influence that porn has on it – particularly when it comes to relationships with men, and particularly when it exists in the same sphere wherein many relationships are coming to fruition – the internet.

Having unrealistic expectations of anyone you're dating, as with anything else, cannot be solely blamed on societal factors. At many points in my dating life, I have wondered if I am 'enough' for the person I'm seeing, or if they are 'The One' for me. Now that I've grown up a bit, I prefer to focus on whether or not I have fun with them, how honest they are with me, and how similar our desires for the future are. Grand notions like 'The One' are all well and good in romantic movies, but there are no solid terms for what makes somebody 'The One', only a vague idea that you'll 'know it when you feel it'.

The flip side, of course, is total disillusionment with the idea of 'The One' and 'soulmates', preferring instead to engage exclusively in emotionally detached sex and hookup culture. Hollywood has utilised this trope too, churning out movies like *Friends with Benefits* and *No Strings Attached*, which still somehow end up with the two leads in a romantic embrace and a fully defined relationship by the movie's end. It's also resulted in films like the previously mentioned *Don Jon* and *How to Be Single* though, wherein the characters learn realistic and difficult life lessons which prove that not only are rom-com expectations bullshit, but that bog-standard, flawed human beings are fantastic when you find something that works.

Of course, it's hardly surprising that we're surrounded by commitment-phobes. My generation has grown up in the era of meteoric divorce rates, where almost half of all marriages break up, and many of us, including myself, have seen our parents go through the hellish stages of a marriage breakdown. We've watched them dealing or not dealing with questions of their own perceived failure, wasted time and sometimes betrayal. We have been conditioned to be cautious. After all, it proves that relationships require work, and who wants that when being young is supposed to be fun? Who wants to lay the foundations for something real when it could all be destroyed in a matter of seconds or, even worse, gradually deteriorate before your eyes?

Keeping our options open is also clearly going to be more prevalent when it's so easy to do so. Contraception is more accessible, and people are prioritising childbirth much later than they did just a few decades ago. Our exposure to lots of different kinds of people has never been this high. Online dating has become so incredibly popular and widespread that there are even TV shows like MTV's *Catfish* which focus on making sure the person you're dating online is who they say they are. Tinder allows you to swipe through hundreds, even thousands, of people without having to worry about anything other than what they look like. The options are endless, so why would we waste them by sticking to one person?

Hence the proliferation of new terms for the myriad experiences this kind of 'conveyor belt' dating can lead to. 'Benching' is when you put someone on a metaphorical bench until things go south with your 'main' person. 'Cushioning' is when you do this with lots of people – making them the 'cushions' in this scenario – and both are done without those people's knowledge, so that they think they're the only ones. This is pretty dishonest and mean, but not exactly surprising when you consider everything I have already discussed.

In fact, none of the dating woes I've experienced strike me as being particularly surprising anymore, which would be worrying if I wasn't now looking back in retrospect at how these experiences helped me to grow and become more resilient. In some ways I do think that they've made me a bit cynical, but then, perhaps that's just adulthood.

Whilst I feel jaded because of my experiences, though, there are stories all over the internet of people enjoying similar situations, so I will say this:

The freedom of choice that you are awarded in online dating is very worthwhile, and it is a great way to meet new people. As with many things on the internet, though, online dating can come at an emotional price for many people like me and spawn some unsavoury behaviour (read: ghosting, negging, benching). All things considered, I remain hopeful. I remain hopeful that the people we have long-term relationships with will be more suited to us due to our ability to test the waters more than previous generations. I remain hopeful that as we collectively grow accustomed to our new online lives, we will treat each other better and with more respect, and that we will consider the person behind the screen more than we do right now.

Most of all, I remain hopeful that when it comes to the internet, love will eventually prevail. Until then, well... nothing beats real life.

PLAYING THE PART
Aniqah Rawat

All I want is my parents' blessing to audition for the National Youth Theatre.

I'm sitting on my bed, looking out of the window as cars race by in their rush to get home. Home. That is where I am, and have been all my life, and there's nothing new when it comes to watching the rain trickle down my window.

Cold, wet and miserable – three words commonly used to describe Preston, especially in winter, when snow turns to grey sludge and umbrellas are often seen inside out. But the cold doesn't stop at my window. It seeps in through the cracks of this century-old house, and into the voice of my dad as he snaps, 'We'll talk about this tonight.' So I am sitting on my bed, wrapped in my duvet, trying not to shiver, as I wait for the ominous knock.

Knock, knock, knock.

'Come in,' I say, and my dad opens the door, the hallway light illuminating him and my mother from behind whilst my little lamp throws shadows across their faces.

'OK, so we're… we're not happy with this,' he tells me. 'Why do you want to do this thing?'

'Because I enjoy theatre. It's… it's…' I'm scared and angry. There's a whirlwind of emotions coursing through my body, and amidst the confusion, I struggle to convey, without crying, just what theatre and performing mean to me.

'It's what? It's something you can do for a bit of fun, but it's not like it's going to get you anywhere in life,' he replies, finishing my sentence for me. 'We let you do drama at GCSE…'

'Exactly!' I can feel the tears of frustration starting to build up as I try and plead my case. 'It gives us skills and helps us talk to others and work with people…'

'But it's not going to get you anywhere!' he snaps back. I can sense his anger lurking, and so can my mum, as I fail to understand where he's coming from.

'OK, stop,' says my mum calmly to my dad, before turning to me. 'Say we let you do this, what then? What happens if they ask you to kiss someone? Would you do it?'

I pause, but not to think. I now understand exactly where they're coming from and I just shrug and laugh. 'Yeah, it's a kiss. It doesn't mean anything.' And my dad turns to the hallway and takes a breath whilst my mum replies, 'But it does. Where does your modesty go, and respect? The things you have been taught…'

'This has nothing to do with Islam,' I reply, finally breaking into tears, admitting where their issues lie, 'It's an incredible opportunity…'

'It goes against Islam and how we've brought you up. We won't sit here and let you go ahead and do this,' my dad interrupts.

'I'll just find another way to pay the audition fee online. You can't stop me,' I say, defiant. I can see the sadness in both their eyes, that I am disappointing them. What neither of them realises is what their lack of support for my ambitions is doing to me. And whilst, after a few days of silence and tension, they did pay for my audition, it in no way meant that they had opened up to the idea of me pursuing theatre.

That night ended up being the turning point for me, a moment of revelation, and the start of a conscious decision to acknowledge the differences between the two cultures I am trying to navigate. It was the point at which I had decided I could no longer let my life be forcefully led by the beliefs of my parents, but by my own decisions and understandings of the world I live in, and the faith I have been raised in.

There are Five Pillars of Islam: Shahada, Salat, Sawm, Zakat and Hajj. Shahada, in its most basic sense, means 'faith', but it is so much more than that. It is an oath, a commitment to wholeheartedly devote yourself to the wonders of Islam, and unless you believe it yourself, that 'there is no God but Allah, and Muhammad (PBUH) is his messenger', you cannot call yourself a Muslim. But what about faith beyond the religious sense?

My parents have raised me with religious beliefs, but in the community I found amongst my peers, within my generation, faith goes beyond a higher power. There is a bond formed through our shared experiences and the trust we have in each other. There is something that keeps us, as a generation, behind each other, whether it be our love of avocados, or our despair at rising house prices. We have faith in each other. But more importantly, through our sense of community, we teach each other to have faith in ourselves. And whilst religious faith and a belief in yourself are not two mutually exclusive things, within my upbringing, emphasis was definitely placed on the former. But I like to focus on the latter, which is what propelled me to the National Youth Theatre in the first place.

Faith and trust are important when it comes to the relationship between a daughter and her parents. And since my bedroom door slammed shut that night, my parents have watched, part in awe, part in disappointment, as I continued to vault myself into rankings and a national final, race my way to the Northern Indoor Championships and perform on stage to reviews better than I could have imagined, all whilst maintaining a grade A average.

My mum and dad have grown up in a community where your neighbour is your brother and the whole street your family. They are part of a culture where dawaats (feasts) are held frequently, and not just for a special occasion, and a culture where men and women are segregated.

Mum was born in India but has lived most of her life here in the UK. Engaged at sixteen and married at eighteen, her dreams of joining the mounted unit in the police force were quashed by my grandparents because that was too dangerous. Too different. It was something that a good Muslim girl would never do, especially when she was just about to be married and have a husband, house and, in the future, children to look after.

Growing up, we'd often have huge family barbeques, and being young, it was OK to go and mess around in the garden, blowing bubbles everywhere, playing piggy in the middle and almost always hitting the food with the ball. There was one particular gathering where the sun was strikingly hot, so we decided to get out the water balloons. With about twenty kids running around, hiding out in all available bathrooms, as the mums prepped food in the kitchen and the dads were laughing in the small garden by the three barbeques, there was a plot to ambush the adults. After we'd had fun throwing and missing each other and being told 'enough is enough', we crept to the windows of the second floor before dropping the ice-cold bombs on our fathers and uncles. Crying with laughter, we went downstairs to resume playing in the garden, but I was pulled aside by my incensed mum.

'You need to start behaving like a girl,' she hissed. 'Let the boys go and play and come and help in the kitchen.'

'But I'll just get in the way.'

'It doesn't matter. You can watch and learn.'

And so I watched, as my brothers enjoyed the sun on their backs, kicking the ball and stealing bits of food while I sat in the shade of the kitchen doing nothing.

When you try to combine the culture and traditions my parents know with the culture I see in my everyday life, it can become a little messy. It's hard to navigate – what do you do when your parents expect one thing from you and your friends another? Navigating the corridors of my high school was easy, but finding my place was not.

From the get-go I established myself as the teacher's pet, just as my parents had hoped and expected from me, with a pristine plait the length of my back and a work ethic that kept me at the top of the class. I was the annoying girl who could do everything from playing centre position in netball to writing in fluent Spanish to solving complex mathematics equations. I was smart and lacked a social life. I don't know what the switch was while I was at school – perhaps as simple as a change of friendship group in Year Nine – but I went from hardworking teacher's pet waxing lyrical about Shakespeare and quadratic equations one month to discussing who fingered whom behind the bike shed the next.

From that point, I had a social life. Everyone knew who I was and I would always have the homework answers, but as time went on through high school, I learned that some people appreciated me more than others. However, all that actually meant was that at lunch breaks, my new friends and I would go and watch the boys play football, giggling away as we purposely got in their way, pretending it was an accident, so we could get as close as we could to any lad we found attractive. There was one particular boy, with blond, windswept hair which fell in his sparkling blue eyes, that I just had to try and be near to at all times.

It wasn't like boys were a foreign concept to me. I'd spent time in primary school and Madrassa pratting about and getting into trouble with them, but in high school it was suddenly different.

Hormones were flying everywhere, and when all the popular girls had boyfriends, of course I wanted one too, despite not knowing what it would entail. It's not like dating is a common thing amongst strict Muslims. I couldn't exactly tell my mum about a boy I liked and then cry on her shoulder about how he just wasn't interested in me. (Turns out small, nerdy Asian girls with long hair and big noses weren't quite his type.) It's not like I could tell my parents this when they asked why I was upset. Maybe if I could, my dad would do what I'd seen many fathers in movies do, and tell me that I'm beautiful and how 'he's just a silly boy who doesn't deserve you'. Instead, we talked about my academic progress and report cards, and not much else. Speaking of my grades, no matter how good they were, they were never good enough. I remember on A-level results day, while I was planning the rest of my life, Mum said, 'I thought you'd get more As. What are you going to do now?'

'What do you mean, "What am I going to do now?" Couldn't you have at least said "well done" first?' I said, seething.

'Well, no, you didn't get what you thought you would, so what are you doing now? What are you doing with university?'

'I don't know. I'm waiting on Bristol to get back to me…'

'And if they don't accept you, then what?' she asked, snappily.

'I take a year out, resit some exams and reapply.'

'And who's paying for that, and what are you going to do on your year out?'

'The plan was always to take a year out, Mum…'

'Right. OK. But what are you going to do?'

'Just tell Dad when he gets home, please? Thank you.'

I was sixteen when I joined the NYT in the summer of 2014, the summer between high school and college. After arguing with my parents, and with the generosity of my high school, who paid for half the fees whilst I fundraised for the other, they agreed to let me go complete the induction course. It was an opportunity for self-discovery and freedom from my parents' gaze for two whole weeks. I was very eager to get myself down to London, crossing off the days on my calendar and obsessing over things like how I would get there, what food I should take, and how I would cope with living away from home in student accommodation for these two weeks.

We arrived early on a warm Sunday morning after a five-hour drive. I got out of the car and immediately felt like I was a long way away from Preston. Everyone talked differently, everyone dressed differently, the air tasted different. It was different. I was nervous.

My parents were impatient, as it slowly dawned on them that I was going to be here, by myself, for what felt like an entire summer, getting up to God knows what, with people who were not from their tightly knit corner of Preston.

My room was nothing spectacular. Lots of blue, and simple furniture, but it was mine, and that counted for a lot. My mum helped me unpack my groceries before telling me, 'Don't get into trouble.' Dad was waiting in the car. She left me to unpack my clothes, with a quick kiss on the cheek and a 'stay safe, enjoy yourself', before rushing off to get back home.

In those two weeks, I was free. Free to not conform to the good Muslim stereotype imposed on me by my parents. Free to have my first kiss. Roam the city with boys. Take part in courtyard rap battles and dance-offs till dawn broke. Dancing. Drinking. Staying up late. I also learned theatre and performance techniques during the gruelling 9 a.m. to 6 p.m. days. And then I came home on results day to my mum asking why the one B amongst my As and A*s at GCSE wasn't also an A.

I met someone at the National Youth Theatre. Not the first boy I ever kissed. Someone else. He laughed at little things with me and one night offered me awful noodles while I sat on his lap playing Cards Against Humanity. We were best friends. I even mentioned him to my parents.

While my dad's eyebrows rose at the thought of me having a boy for a friend, ultimately he was only that, a friend.

A year later, after numerous phone calls and group messages, I met up with my flatmates from NYT, drinking wine and laughing at each other's stories as we hung out as friends at one of their homes. They were amazed at how much I had changed. I was no longer a small timid girl trying to please her parents all the time. I was bold and crazy, telling half-truths to my parents about where I was and what I was doing. The next day, I went to see him.

Throughout the year following our summer course, we had stayed in touch through Snapchat and phone calls, keeping up to date with each other's lives, not quite realising what our friendship was slowly developing into. So the day after catching up with my flatmates from NYT, he and I met at Waterloo.

He held himself with confidence, tall and handsome with swept-back hair and brown eyes flecked with green, and I couldn't help but smile when I saw him, or when he hugged me hello. 'We're just friends,' I whispered to myself, as he put his arm around my shoulder and I put mine around his waist. Or at least that's what I repeated to myself the entire day until the moment, stolen out of nowhere, when his lips were gently pressed against mine, and my hands reached for his hair, my fingers running through it, and his body drew me closer as we said goodbye under the clock at Waterloo Station.

I was head over heels in love with him, but a physically intimate relationship and emotionally intimate relationship are vastly different things. The only relationship advice I'd been given growing up was that I was a good Muslim girl and my eyes should not wander. I'm being harsh, but I come from a world of arranged marriages, attending at least one wedding a year, where relationships are built by good familial connections and a trust in one another. The most intimate thing I've seen my parents do is kiss each other on the cheek, or hold hands, and compared to the rest of my relatives, that is pretty out there, as segregation of genders is commonplace – not just in the wedding hall, but at smaller, simpler family events. Physical intimacy is put to a halt after the shaking of hands and a welcoming hug when greeting each other within my culture.

It's a long way away from the public displays of affection this boy was used to.

Of course I was a little shy when he first kissed me. I had no idea what I was really doing, even if this wasn't my first kiss; it's not like you can casually practise kissing. It was almost endearing when he asked for a 'proper kiss' before he left, and being so swept up in it all, I thought, 'What the hell? Why not?' But when we managed to meet up in person every couple of months after this, and he asked for more, I felt the compulsion to hide, because we were out in the open. To me, anything more than a kiss should be behind closed doors, but that didn't stop him trying. Even when we were sat kissing on a bench next to the river, I felt like everyone's eyes were on us. I couldn't, I wouldn't, let him slip his hand under my dress. I was already dishonouring my family and committing a sin in the laws of my religion. But to him, this pleasure wasn't a sin, and although I could understand that, it was hard to go against the things I had been taught since I was little. And even though I wanted him, at the time, I had to say no, even though it made neither of us happy.

Two days later, after about a year of seeing each other, he broke up with me. I felt lonely; there's nothing that feels more isolating than the end of a relationship you can't talk to your mum about, because it's forbidden. How could I tell my parents that I was in love with a white boy that I met through theatre, when they envisioned my future partner to be a good Muslim man, whom they would arrange for me to meet after earning their approval?

He once asked me if we could run away and get married, and I almost laughed in his face. It is commonplace within my community for most women to be married by twenty-two, and at every wedding I go to, someone will always ask me when I plan to get married or if I am looking for a husband, or feel the need to tell me that it is my turn next, as if it's a particular rite of passage I should be planning for already.

Since our break-up, through time and experience, I have learned how to better navigate my two worlds, from the hidden debauched nights with nothing but blurred memories of familiar voices in unfamiliar rooms to the long nights full of song and laughter with little or no sleep. At the end of the day, my parents still love me. They may not approve of my life choices, but they respect who I am. They no longer interrogate me about my whereabouts or coming in past midnight, but instead trust me to be the responsible girl they've raised me to be and not do anything dangerous. They still question some of my outfit choices, but I've also learned how to layer and hide my cropped tops from them before heading out. There is a mix of half-truths being told, and more freedom to breathe being given to me, as they understand how different the world they grew up in is to mine; slowly we are working out a balance that keeps us all happy. It's hard work, but I have earned this, and bringing the idea of embracing these two cultures and letting them coexist harmoniously to life isn't something that can be done overnight.

I'm still at home, watching the rain through the window, even though it's the middle of July, and soon I'll be leaving to start a new life down south. I told my parent's that after I've moved to university, I won't be moving back in again, only providing them with yet another half-truth: 'Once I've moved out, I won't be coming home very often.'

'Sure you will, in the holidays and on weekends…'

'I'll have a job, and it's not like trains are cheap. I mean if you're paying for them, then sure.'

'Well, what about summer?'

'I'll be travelling or doing an internship. And once I've finished my master's, I'll stay down south, because I'll have a job, and that's where I want to be.'

'Yeah, OK, but you'll still come home. You won't actually stay there.'

'I will.'

'No. You won't.'

And again, my mum walked out of my bedroom, while I sat wrapped in my duvet, wishing I could be completely honest and tell her I won't be coming home not just because of my future career, but because once I've left, embracing the two cultures I've tried to navigate my entire life will be so much easier. The strength of my parents' faith is something I admire, but their faith resonates within our home and means bringing certain aspects of my life into its four walls just cannot be done. We have been raised differently, and they can't erase their upbringing just like I can't ignore the world I live in. I am part of a generation that is much more open and adaptable in comparison to my parents', and while they may understand this, it doesn't lessen the truth that our interpretations of Islam differ. To me, it's not just about faith in Allah, but about who you are as a person. Faith and morals can exist separately from each other, and to me, in the modern world, Islam is about being open, respectful, honest and true, but without a necessity to adhere to cultural conventions about clothing and the company you keep, or even praying five times a day. I know many Muslim girls who have a similar understanding, some of whom party on the regular, others who pray but will still have a drink, and others who will happily cover up, wear a scarf and follow the expected ideals, but not pray. It goes back to this idea of trust, and not judging others, because ultimately, our faith, our Shahada, is meant to enhance our life, and only Allah can judge us on our actions and the life we have led. I may not actively practise my faith, but I respect and see the beauty in it, just as I do in the cultural norms of Western societies, especially as I hear the pitter-patter of rain drops on my window, knowing each one is a blessing from my Lord.

THE UNIVERSITY MYTH

Brandon J. Graham

Content warning: mental health, alcohol abuse

There is often a disconnect between the fantasy and the reality when it comes to university. The fantasy usually goes as follows: in university you will experience the best years of your life. Opportunities lie around every corner, lifelong friendships are made, you become an expert in your field and leave not only with a degree but with a fulfilling future ahead. The financial sacrifices you make at university will inevitably pay off in your future career. It's a time of both work and play. You have liberating independence, your own place, money and your first taste of adulthood all neatly wrapped into three years.

It's a fantasy that rarely comes to fruition. The reality is that university is not so straightforward. In fact, university can be some of the worst years of your life. I was first introduced to what I call the University Myth in secondary school, when choosing my GCSEs. We were all eager to cut out the subjects we disliked and the conversation turned to university. We were excited that one day we would be able to study the one subject we loved and discussed what that would be. Our teachers, when we showed promise, would say, 'You could do a degree in that!' and we imagined a time where our favourite lessons were our only lessons. This intensified during A levels. Posters for universities were everywhere, and the screen in our sixth-form common room showed the same three slides reminding us to apply to UCAS so we wouldn't miss our opportunity. We would share stories about older siblings or close friends who were off to uni and the amazing time they were probably having, our rare assemblies focused on university, and teachers told us, 'You want to attend a great university, right? Well you have to work hard now and you can reap the benefits once you get in!' When I attended open days, I was given pamphlets plastered with pictures of smiling twenty-somethings engaged in their fascinating work and a few leaflets advertising student discounts at various clubs. I pictured university as a place in which I could just focus on the one subject I was good at, alongside equally passionate people.

Some may say this was naive, but the reality was I was never directly told about the negative side of university until I entered it, or that these negatives were universal rather than situational. I believed that some people just did not enjoy uni – I would hear stories of them leaving in the first term, or the odd person in my life telling me that they found it stressful, but they always emphasised it was enjoyable too. Therefore I took it to be much like the rest of my school experience, demanding but nevertheless fulfilling. As the first person in my immediate family to attend university, I was in a unique position. I was going to be setting the example for my younger brother, and I was set on making my mum proud of me. I knew that most of my family had worked hard their whole lives, climbing up the ladder, and I felt as though university was going to move me up that ladder both academically and financially in the future.

Because I was attending the university in my own city, Bristol, I decided that I should stay at home to save money, a decision I do not regret. The truth was I was incredibly stressed about the financial burden uni was going to place on my family. I had been the one eager to attend, and yet I was also acutely aware that it was going to cost a small fortune. I decided to make a compromise: I was going to spend the money necessary to get a higher education, but I would remain in my hometown. I resigned myself to not going into dorms, again for financial reasons that my family agreed with, and I could tell it gave my mum peace of mind knowing I was focused on my studies rather than partying. However, in the back of my mind I always desired to have the freedom of moving out in the second year to a studio dorm, and while I saved money in the first year, it wasn't enough to justify the cost of moving out in my second year. I was paying a small amount of rent at home and the leap was too much. I wouldn't move out on my own until my third year, something which caused me financial grief but also gave me peace of mind, knowing it was only for the year and that I was making enough money to live week to week. The thought of moving out of my city had crossed my mind. I had applied to two other universities in England – but I always knew that attending them was another story. Before even opening my A-level results, I had resigned myself to Bristol, and I was prepared to ring up and make my case if I had been rejected. I was trying to find a balance between financial responsibility and getting a good education.

Little did I know that commuting and remaining in your family home can create other burdens that are not financial but rather mental. The strain of having to get up hours earlier than my classmates to catch a bus that never seemed to arrive, then trek to class, and then make the same trip home each afternoon was leaving me exhausted. On top of this I was carrying many heavy books, and on the rare occasion I did want to go out, I either had to crash at a friend's place and come home in the same clothes the next day or fork out money for a taxi, money I didn't have. I was inconvenienced by the cost and time of travel but always comforted myself in the knowledge that I hadn't taken out a loan, yet. This commute, of course, also had an adverse effect on my social life, but I chalked that up to being my own fault for not moving out to student accommodation; I had cut off my own wings.

That being said, the regret really hit home during freshers' week. I spoke to a few people within the first three days or so, but my nerves were getting the better of me. I felt alone in this mass of people. Even when I did psych myself up to talk to someone, it was hard to find them again in the sea of students. I had also only recently acquired Facebook and my friend list was about ten people, so I was embarrassed to give it out. My family had discouraged me from being on social media during my childhood, which I am grateful for; however, it did interfere with my ability to fit in. I remember meeting the English department freshers, and when they would ask me for my Facebook I would offer my phone number. I didn't realise how unusual this was at the time and I realise it most likely made me appear somewhat sheltered. I didn't go out once during freshers' week, and when I did start to add people on Facebook I saw endless photos of them out on the town, making friends with their new dormmates, living it up. I kicked myself for not moving out. I assumed it was my fault I was having a bad time and decided to keep myself to myself. I saw that my secondary school friends were also on Facebook, and stalking their profiles I saw them also enjoying themselves with new faces or, worst of all, on a gap year, riding elephants and climbing mountains. Everyone had something going for them and it suddenly felt as though I had nothing to be proud of, nothing I wanted to share; my profile was eerily bare. I mentioned to my mum that I was feeling very out of place and she reassured me that it was perfectly normal. I thanked her for the advice but remained anxious about the future.

I read an article during freshers' week about what to do when it doesn't go well. The author simply stated that she had kept her head down and focused on work. I had decided this was what I should do too; I felt that the uni experience had already passed me by and it was only the first hurdle.

Slowly, over the next few weeks, I picked up a few friends in my classes, and before I knew it I was saying yes to every night out on offer. I so deeply wanted to be the social butterfly I felt I was supposed to be. I drank far too much, too often, and was combining this with a workload I had never had before. To me, reading two books a week for my literature class was harder than I realised, simply because it involved so much dedicated and focused alone time. On top of commuting to and from uni every day (and with the inability to read on the bus without being sick), I was attempting to read under a lamp at night and falling asleep before I could finish. By the time the first essay rolled around I was deeply confused as to why I wasn't finding uni enjoyable, since I was studying the one subject where I was completely in my element. I had an A* in A level and yet I felt like an amateur. Moreover, I felt dumb. No one had told me it was going to be this hard out of the gate – if anything I was told that it would be so enjoyable I wouldn't feel as though I was working since I was focusing on what I loved.

By the end of the first term I had changed a lot in a short period of time. I had met many people but befriended few, I had gone out a lot but rarely had a great time and I was bitter that I had to work all the way through Christmas. Uni wasn't the oasis of calm study that I was hoping for. Having just completed my A levels, I felt as though I'd been flung right back in the deep end.

As soon as term two came around I stopped going out as often, worked harder and became far more mellow. I took university for what it was, not what I had hoped it would be. My mental health was pretty bad during this time. I had suffered from depression from a young age, but I believed I was coping with it better as I was getting older, and I secretly thought I would grow out of it. Now I found my depression was taking a toll on my work and I was starting to lose the drive I had when I arrived. All around me, I saw my peers having a better time than me, though they all seemed just as defeated and tired during the week. I started to wonder why no one had warned us this was going to be so demanding. I didn't suffer from homesickness but I saw it plague my friends, especially when returning to uni from the holidays, and the excitement of living away from home became the reality of living with strangers. Our struggles were different, but I realised that not all of my issues were stemming from me living at home – they seemed to just come with the territory of university. Our previous excitement had fizzled out; we were back at school, except this time it was a far more independent and honestly a lonelier experience than we had experienced previously. I wondered what would happen if students knew this before they arrived, especially if they were the first in their family to go to university and therefore had no prior knowledge. What would I want them to know, and what should universities know? I don't wish to turn students away from university, but to give them a more realistic look at how it is. I want to extend a hand to those who are still at university, to let them know they're not alone. These don't have to be the best years of your life.

The first and most poignant question is whether there really is a mental health problem in universities. The answer is yes. The statistics reveal that one in four students suffer from mental health problems, with the most common illness being depression, and these stats are confirmed when speaking to current students.* Furthermore, the number of university dropouts due to mental health problems has trebled from 2009 to 2015.† There is a dangerous narrative in many universities that emotional instability is normal, that it's a byproduct of working hard. It resembles a competition: whoever is the most exhausted is the most dedicated. If you haven't slept, have been working all week non-stop and you essentially live in the library knocking back coffee, you are deserving of a good grade. To be calm and well rested is

* 'One in four students suffer from mental health problems', YouGov, available at https://yougov.co.uk/topics/lifestyle/articles-reports/2016/08/09/quarter-britains-students-are-afflicted-mental-hea

† Sarah Marsh, 'Number of university dropouts due to mental health problems trebles', *The Guardian*, 23 May 2017, available at https://www.theguardian.com/society/2017/may/23/number-university-dropouts-due-to-mental-health-problems-trebles

your way of letting your fellow classmates know that you are behind in your studies, and it is common to laugh at how so-and-so must not have started the essay since they look alive. There are a few students who work diligently and therefore are able to divide their work up in ways which don't cause them mass stress, but they are rare. If you want to make friends waiting outside the lecture hall, simply ask how everyone is doing with the essay and an outpour of anxiety and sighs will emerge. It is normal to find work challenging, but at university to not be tired is to resign yourself to poor marks; the calm ones are always the ones with the most to worry about – don't they realise the deadline is tomorrow? Late nights, emotional breakdowns, homesickness, bouts of depression, anxiety about the future, constant stress – it's all seen as part of being a student. Overeating, failing health, excessive drinking, smoking, a persistent lack of sleep – again, it's all seen as part of university life. Taking care of ourselves is overshadowed by the pressure to succeed at the higher education we entered ourselves into. The vices of adulthood are used as coping mechanisms rather than signs of independent liberation.

The pressure university places on its students, aside from just the work, is greater than ever before, and it is largely financial. The decision to attend university is usually made in order to increase the chances of getting a job, but given the financial precarity of many students' families, it must be a plausible job. Understandably, parents want their children to have a happy, successful life with a steady income, and many families feel there is no point studying something you are passionate about if it won't lead to employment that will pay the bills. However, dedicating years of your life to a subject you don't particularly enjoy at university level is a lot of work for something you don't necessarily want. It can weigh on you. This disillusionment doesn't happen to every student, but many aren't sure what they are getting into until it feels too late to turn back. Students complain about their syllabus, how it doesn't challenge them intellectually, that it requires useless knowledge. They speak of an absence of real engagement; you can feel as though you are teaching yourself your subject. It can sometimes feel like homeschooling without a live-in teacher. They begin to fantasise about subjects they might have preferred, or universities they would have rather attended. It begins to affect how they approach their life at university. We are asked to make a huge decision about our futures at the age of sixteen (which A levels you take will determine which courses you can take at university), and these decisions are irreversible. By the time you enter university, you can be doing so due to the mistakes your teenage self made. Who can honestly say they truly had enough footing at sixteen to make decisions that would determine how their adult life would pan out?

Then the obvious question arrives: why don't you just leave? The answer is more complicated than one may think.

The truth is many students feel stuck, not wanting to

drop out and disappoint their families or harm their future job prospects, and believing they should grit their teeth and bear it as it's 'only three years'. Knowing that this decision will have real implications for both their future and their current home life, students feel as though they owe it to their parents to succeed, especially if they are from a low-income household and are the first in their family to go to university, when there can be a lot of pride in this and a lot of people cheering for you. This is heightened for those students who have come from abroad, usually thanks to the financial sacrifices of their parents.

This pressure from family is, however, only the first problem that students can face when it comes to the question of dropping out. Another equally important consideration is the future financial repercussions. Students tend to see their education through the lens of future employment. Our futures are no longer as clear as those of our parents or their parents. Our generation has been hit with a double blow of recession coupled with a government bent on austerity measures. Politicians' promises of scrapping tuition fees or the imminent arrival of a thriving economy are just promises, and while we may be profiting from the technological age, even this has its downside. As more and more non-traditional jobs emerge, there is a huge crowd of qualified graduates all competing for the same placements. The degree alone is no longer enough. You need to 'add value' with your experiences during uni. Did you do an internship? Did you make the most of your summer to flesh out your CV? Do you engage with enough societies? The truth is, you won't get anywhere if you simply have a degree; it is what you do outside your degree that counts. Therefore, you tend to juggle the cost of university with part-time jobs or unpaid internships. It essentially feels as though you are paying to work multiple jobs on the side, many of which demand time without pay. However, the overarching message students receive is that they will not get anywhere without a degree. That the degree is essentially necessary if you wish to have a good job, and that to miss out on the opportunity is to do great damage to your future prospects, despite a large part of your work at uni not being related to your studies. This is why students are willing to get themselves in heaps of debt – because we feel as though it is the price we must pay for a good pay cheque in the future.

We students began to feel as though we took the prospect of £3,000 a year for tuition fees for granted when it tripled to £9,000 per year, and for current undergraduates even a student grant to help with living expenses has been taken away and replaced with a larger loan. But what else was there for us to do? We were working on our A levels and university was not a suggestion, it was a must. Those who didn't go were seen to have thrown an opportunity away and apprenticeships were scoffed at by my teachers; they saw it as limiting – you were now only qualified for one single job – whereas university would open you up to an array of opportunities. 'None of us can afford university anyway, and everyone else is going,' we said, as we took out loans and overlooked the price. This degree was going to guarantee us a well-paid job that would allow us to pay off this debt quickly. We looked around Europe and the rest of the world and saw increasingly free universities (in Germany, Norway, Denmark, Sweden and Finland to name a few), but our country relishes putting its students in debt for the right to be educated to a higher degree. Students in England have the highest graduate debt in the world – yes, even higher than our American counterparts. And compared to France, we pay twenty-five times more despite being a stone's throw away from one another, and as the world moves towards not wanting to punish its students for desiring a better education, our country seems to revel in it.

Many students, especially those studying the humanities, feel as though they aren't sure where the money is going, on top of having to pay for our own large reading lists. Once a friend of mine calculated the price of each of our lectures in relation to our tuition fees, and this would cause us to joke with each other at the end of each one, 'Well, that's money I'm not getting back!' I feel as though if we didn't laugh our moods would be much lower. I was lucky – I was in the last year of university students to get a grant (I began in 2015), which is a complete lifesaver. I thought back to my friends taking gap years; it was unfortunate timing and I wondered if they would even regard uni as an option when they returned. Many did, fearing that they wouldn't fare well in the job market without a degree. Had I been born a year later I believe I would be in a very different situation. The truth is, there is no such thing as cheap university education in England.

So, if university is both expensive and exhausting, what is the pay-off besides the degree? We're told that university is where you make your lifelong friends. Forget those secondary school companions back home, here you will make close friendships with like-minded people from around the world who are open-minded, friendly and approachable. This only applies, of course, if you lack social anxiety. I have heard students worry that someone in their residence has not left their room in weeks, especially if they are an international student. Being away from home, feeling unprepared for the workload of university and being alone can be a horrific mental cocktail. Therefore, some students turn to alcohol, which is advertised abundantly around campus.

Despite heavy drinking being generally thought of as 'fun', alcohol dependency appears to be an issue during first year, and for some it extends until they graduate and beyond. There is a group mentality that if we are all doing it, then it's fine. It's a mark of adulthood for many that you can now finally and legally do these things without sneaking around. Freshers' week is notoriously filled with eager new students out on the town, exploring the bars and clubs, pre-drinking in their halls, and raiding supermarkets for cheap vodka. Alcohol can be great for alleviating social anxiety, making it easier to talk to people and creating a feeling of camaraderie. Student unions push social drinking as a form of escape – advertising the student discounts at clubs and bars, student societies have regular events during which drinking features heavily, and it seems cheap booze is around every corner. Students deserve a break from their studies, and going out for drinks can be an enjoyable way to do so; however, this doesn't mean that drinking should be used as a coping mechanism for the pressures we are put under. But where do you turn when university is saturated with alcohol and this may be your only way to make friends? You don't want to be that person on the sidelines. Why did you bother attending university if you are going to be a bore? This is your time to let loose – otherwise feel free to never leave your room and potentially face having no one to live with next year. The first term is an arms race to find people you are willing to live with for a year. Those who get left behind are more prone to drop out, as I have witnessed. Making friends isn't just enjoyable; it comes with adult responsibilities. It's true that university is a place of education and new experiences, but the more stressful and deeply responsible side is less frequently highlighted, and these conflicting feelings can cause students to abuse alcohol.

The signs of an alcohol dependency are laughed off. Constant hangovers, blackouts, late nights, and loss of memory are party jokes and embarrassing breakfast stories, not to be taken seriously. But whilst eighteen-year-olds may feel as though they are fully developed adults, the brain is still growing, and alcohol can interfere with our development. This extends beyond some unfortunate mistakes on a night out, and can result in a higher rate of depression and memory loss. Eva Cyhlarova from the Mental Health Foundation summed up the reality of heavy drinking on young adults: 'People who drink heavily are more likely to suffer from mental health problems.' Those with mental health problems are more likely to drink heavily, creating a vicious cycle. We are encouraged to go out and drink and this can grow into an unhealthy habit. Whilst I must stress that only a small percentage of students actually become alcoholic, alcohol dependence is definitely an issue. Two of my friends suffered from binge drinking, which wreaked havoc on both of their lives; luckily they were able to kick the habit just before graduation, otherwise I fear it would have leaked into their work and family life. One had to even take a year out of university to recover properly, as the depression he was experiencing in uni was causing him to relapse.

Learning to look after yourself also includes learning to take responsibility for your own time and how you use it. Universities are not always helpful on this score either. How independent you are when working at university differs depending on which subject you take. There is a huge difference between the number of contact hours in English and physics. Unistats, the official site for comparing information on university and college courses across the UK, states that contact between English students with their tutors constitutes 12 per cent of their time, while for physics this rises to 32 per cent.* The subjects demand different levels of engagement, but this does not mean that the workload is any less difficult. You are alone and know that the work must be done for a deadline, especially if your subject is essay-based. So you sit down and work. You read, make notes, gather together a plan and begin to write and write and write. And then you stop. Maybe boredom sets in, maybe you are stuck on what to write next, or perhaps you aren't sure what you should be doing. You will try again tomorrow. Which turns into the next day, next week, and suddenly the deadline looms. Procrastination strikes and is often hard to overcome when you feel overwhelmed. We have to learn from scratch how to create our own timetables and stick to them, all whilst being bombarded with the new experiences that come with living alone and potentially navigating a new city/country. In the humanities we are usually given a very small handful of office hours, and by the time you get acquainted with one member of staff, the next term arrives and you are moved on to a whole new array of strangers. These constant shifts make it difficult to keep your footing, and although we are told that we should flag our issues up with our tutors, suffice to say that many get little help there, myself included. We

---

* Declan Rooney, 'Science students like me have too many contact hours', *The Guardian*, 21 July 2014, available at https://www.theguardian.com/education/mortarboard/2014/jul/21/science-students-contact-hours

are told to build a rapport with people who may not even recognise us in the crowd of faces they see each day. My own personal tutor forgot who I was each time we met, or that I was even supposed to be arriving, and this caused me to feel as though I was intruding into the office of someone who would rather I wasn't there. This is a common feeling when you are consistently moving around and it feels like the help is designed to fit the staff's time more than your own. Many a time the door would appear to be open when I needed it least, and therefore students can find themselves losing motivation.

And then there is social media: a cure for boredom and a poison for productivity unique to this generation. When you take a break from reading to open Facebook and see that everyone else is out, laughing, drinking and enjoying themselves, you can't help but ask yourself, 'Why are they juggling work and play, yet I seem to do neither?' Which inevitably leads to feeling, 'I'm not having the university experience.' I myself have scrolled through Instagram and seen fellow students out on the town each weekend, and this carefully curated window into their lives makes me feel like they have everything together. It makes you feel inadequate, but the persona you manifest online can induce exactly the same feelings of inadequacy in others when you display the same behaviour. I've caught myself not having a great time out but still wanting a picture, as if to prove to other students that I am having the best university life. I am part of the deceptive cycle. I was fully subscribing to, and contributing to, the University Myth. I wanted others to think I had it all together when I felt as though my mental health was crumbling under the pressure I was under and the thought that these were the best years of my life made my future appear incredibly bleak to me.

If you were to ask me if I wished to do a master's before I went to uni, I would have eagerly said yes. Now I can't imagine staying in education any longer than I need to. I can now count on one hand the number of students I know who want to stay after their three years are up. Many are desperate to throw themselves into the workforce rather than continue in education, even part-time. This does not mean to say these students do not love their subject, but their specific courses or universities have soured the prospect. Graduation is no longer a day to celebrate all of the work you have achieved, but rather a day of celebration that university is finally over. Students at their best are happy, independent, intellectually stimulated and social. At their worst they are over-worked, depressed, deprived, self-conscious, regretful and disheartened. If students had a better idea of what they were signing themselves up for, we might see them seek help faster, or perhaps consider another route to future success. It's time that not only universities but students themselves put their mental health above their education. I believe that the biggest contributor to students' poor mental health in university, aside from the debt, the social anxiety, the workload or the fear of the future, is the idea that we are not getting what we paid for.

The truth is that university education is a business. Unlike your previous comprehensive school experience, it comes with a price tag, and therefore the education you receive is the education you explicitly pay for. If students in England have the highest debt in the world, this must mean that we have the best education in the world, right? Well, it appears that sometimes that money is abused, an example being the national outcry around the vice-chancellor of Bath University, who was revealed to be receiving £468,000 annually. Even after stepping down from her position, she was still set to be paid an additional £600,000 between her resignation and retirement by the university. Her salary had risen far beyond the salaries of the university staff and the whole fiasco really shed a light on the financial gain those in power within universities can make, despite their performance not being worthy of the pay increase. Students are investing a large sum of borrowed money into an establishment that many fear is taking advantage of them for financial gain. We question whether our chosen university has our best intentions at heart, or if they merely see us as customers going through a process. When a student remarks that they are 'paying for a piece of paper', this really hits the nail on the head. Many students feel as though they are investing in the degree certification, rather than their own intellectual pursuits.

There is a conversation emerging around the fees of students and whether we are being treated like banks, and it is affecting our mental wellbeing. In an article by the *Guardian* focused on the marketisation of higher education, Amyas Morse, the head of the National Audit Office, was quoted as saying, 'Young people are taking out substantial loans to pay for courses without much effective help and advice, and the institutions concerned are under very little competitive pressure to provide best value.'* This echoes the outcry of students nationwide: who are these universities being held accountable to if they fail their students? Once they receive our tuition fees it can feel as though their job is done. The same article suggests that one in three students say they receive value for money. University is a huge financial decision, but there is a dissatisfaction with the pay-off that must be addressed. We need to know exactly what we are paying for, in detail, before we are can even consider paying for it. Feeling as though you are teaching yourself whilst your university invests millions in new buildings and equipment can be jarring, especially when a very limited number of students will ever use the facilities. In early 2018, with sixty-one universities striking over changes to their pensions, students were left to their own devices during 'the most extensive strike action ever seen'. Rightly, students

---

* Richard Adams, 'University students failed by rip-off fees, says watchdog', *The Guardian*, 8 December 2017, available at https://www.theguardian.com/education/2017/dec/08/university-students-failed-by-rip-off-fees-says-watchdog

were demanding compensation for the disruption, not because they did not believe that university staff had the right to strike, but because it was at the expense of their own financial investment. The University of Bristol released a statement in February 2018 stating their staff didn't wish to strike but had been forced to and that they had 'no plans to provide financial reimbursement for any specific missed teaching sessions due to industrial action. Student tuition fees pay for a wide range of student facilities and services, in addition to tuition, which will continue to be available.' It is at times like this where you wish you could see the breakdown of your tuition fees, since we know that our money has in essence been spent even when we are dissatisfied with the end result. No matter how it treats you, what you received or even how it affected you mentally, it feels as though there are no repercussions for bad service. No matter your experience you will be in huge financial debt because of it. Sometimes it seems only the university is profiting from your attendance at the expense of the students and the staff.

The University Myth thrives on this, because it lures you in and then traps you, in doing so taking not only years of your life but also a massive financial and mental toll. In the first term one in every ten freshers drop out; it appears they come to the realisation faster than the rest of us that this is not for them, that it is an investment they are not willing to make. I believe that true change can only come if universities are upfront about what they are offering. University is a place of education, but nothing like the previous education you have had – it doesn't simply ask for your time and good grades. It asks for a large portion of your young adulthood, time you will not get back. Moreover, it asks for this without necessarily providing the dazzling social life and large group of friends you may have seen on your prospectuses. Those pictured students laughing and throwing their graduate hats to the sky may not be doing so out of accomplishment but out of relief. My excitement to graduate comes from a desire to escape, and I know I am not alone in this feeling. Many students feel as though they made the wrong choice and the only way to get through it is to go through it. I am one of these students.

I believe that the mental health resources being given to students are plasters on a larger wound. They are offering a cure for a sickness without addressing the problem, this problem being that students don't truly know what they are signing up for until it is too late. Students have every right to demand the best from their institutions: the best quality of teaching, best support services, best opportunities for personal growth and development. At its best, university can provide all these things, but at its worst, it is putting students at risk in pursuit of profit.

SWEET SIXTEEN: KISS, MARRY, VOTE
Amber Kirk-Ford

On your sixteenth birthday, you're legally allowed to leave home, get married, bring a brand-new human into the world, join the armed forces and give your life for the UK. Sixteen, then, appears to be The Year. You're young, vibrant, bursting with dreams and hopes and ideas, and you're in that limbo between the innocence of childhood and the heavy responsibility that comes with being a fully grown adult. Chances are, you've been forced to buy 'adult' tickets for tourist attractions and public transport since the age of twelve, but that's a rant for another day. The point is, you're finally growing up. You're almost there. And showing you how well you're adulting in the run-up to an election or a referendum are the endless letters and flyers from the government and various political parties, addressed to you, encouraging you to vote. This is new.

You can't vote, though. You don't get a say in who runs your country or whether or not you leave the European Union. Snap election à la 2017? Nope, can't vote in that either. The government may be sending letters addressed to you saying that they want you to vote, but it's their rule that says you can't. (Honestly, won't somebody think of the trees that gave their lives so we can be encouraged to vote two years before we're legally allowed to?) You're responsible enough to create a new human and look after them for the next few decades of your life, but you can't cross a box – anything but that. Sorry, I don't make the rules.

I do, however, make lots of Internet Things: blog posts, videos, photos, the occasional freelance piece of writing – mostly to do with books I've read or books I'm looking forward to, but also about my life: who I am, what I get up to, what I like, what I dislike, how I feel about an array of different things. I have a lot of opinions, and I am not afraid to share them online. Being an outspoken internet person, I have taken part in many a debate about lowering the voting age to sixteen, with everyone from teens with their heads screwed on, to random men on the internet who think we shouldn't be allowed to vote because we buy too many avocados and not enough diamonds.

The 2015 general election was the turning point for me in terms of being openly political.

A few months before the election, I'd bought tickets to a book signing in London, and later realised that the event was on polling day. Despite it being an evening event, getting to and from London would take up most of the day, and my mum – who has always voted and likes to watch the results come in –

agreed that she would vote and then take me to the event. On the way to London, we stopped off at the polling station and I went in with my parents, excited but unable to vote. I was sixteen and desperate to be involved in this national event, which hadn't happened since I was eleven, a significant portion of my life.

I remember sitting in the car that night on the way home, pitch-black except for the headlights in front of us and the glow of my mum's phone. She was updating us on the exit polls, and even though I was already interested in politics and had a definite idea of which way I would have voted, I felt changed, part of something. 'I can't believe I won't be able to vote until 2020,' I remember complaining. Little did any of us know that the next election would be just two years later – and, surprise! I could vote.

Whenever I've talked about lowering the age of voting, the argument always crops up that sixteen-year-olds are not mature enough to decide the future of their country. There is some truth in this. I've witnessed far too many sixteen-year-olds spit in the street, or bully a much younger kid, to be able to genuinely say that all sixteen-year-olds are completely 100 per cent mature. A lot of them don't care about anything, never mind politics. Part of me doesn't blame them; watching people in stuffy suits roast each other about their outfits is hardly appealing (looking at you, Dave; Jeremy's suit was fine). But if some sixteen-year-olds are disengaged or badly behaved, that is equally true of apparent grown-ups. I've seen enough adults catcalling women or even bullying people in the workplace to know that many adults aren't 100 per cent mature, either. We're all different. Yes, there are lots of young people who don't care, who might not vote, or who might vote irresponsibly for 'bants', but there's an equal number of adults who act like this too... and they can vote. Let's not forget the episode of *Gogglebox* where a woman based her decision to vote for Theresa May purely on the fact that she liked her shoes. So this generational divide that says sixteen-year-olds – people who are already treated like adults – can't have an official say is based on the myth that all young people are exactly the same, and are less mature than adults.

I left my mum watching results roll in at about midnight the night of the EU referendum and went to bed, beginning what would be a rubbish night's sleep. My brain clearly knew something was Up with a capital U because 24 June, results day, began for me at about 5 a.m. I shifted, my eyes adjusted, all was silent – and then my heart started pounding. I was weary, anxious; I wanted to know but didn't want to know all at the same time. Throughout the referendum campaign, I had been fairly confident that the side I would have voted for, had I been legally allowed, would win... but I remember thinking before my head hit the pillow the night before that I had no idea how it would play out.

I can't remember how I found out the news. It's possible I googled 'Brexit' and found out from the top result's headline. Maybe I found out via the group chat I have with my friends which, at 5 a.m., was already going crazy. Yes, four teenagers politically engaged at 5 a.m. – who'd have thought it?

I cried. Natural, I suppose, when you want something so immensely but there's not a lot you can do to make it happen simply because of when you were born. I felt let down, scared and perhaps more worryingly like my opinion didn't matter and wouldn't matter until a few months later. That hurt, too – the fact that I was just shy of eighteen at the time. I felt out of place. The future was uncertain. The group chat, which was 20 per cent emotion and 80 per cent determination to make a difference, updating each other on each wave of breaking news as it happened, continued for hours and hours, and even when I was walking down to the train station to see a film with a friend, I was glued to my phone. Still discussing, still shocked, still disheartened. One of my tweets from that day sums it up:

'I'd say good morning, but… "morning" will have to do.'

That said, Catherine Russell from *Holby City* liked one of my tweets, and that – pretty much – was the only highlight of 24 June 2016.

But the nightmare was not over. Statistics came in that said if sixteen- and seventeen-year-olds had been allowed to vote, 82 per cent of them would have voted Remain, closing the gap and potentially keeping us in the EU.[*] Giving young

---

[*] Aftab Ali, 'EU referendum: UK result would have been Remain had votes been allowed at 16, survey finds', *The Independent*, 24 June 2016, available at https://www.independent.co.uk/student/news/eu-referendum-uk-result-students-votes-at-16-remain-brexit-leave-a7101821.html

people a say wouldn't have made it seem like a referendum had never even happened, but our identity as Europeans and the things my friends and I are passionate about would not have been thrown up in the air, spun around and set on fire. You know… our wonderful healthcare system, easy travel between countries, actually having a say in our futures. The NHS would have received more support and not been under the immense pressure it's under now. Newspaper front pages would presumably, you would hope, have more important things to report on than the colour of our passports. Maybe future elections and referendums would be more accepting of the youth vote idea, having given it a 'trial run', so to speak. And maybe David Cameron would still be our prime minister – you know things have gone downhill when you find yourself missing Dave. In all seriousness, 75 per cent of eighteen- to twenty-four-year-olds voted Remain, suggesting that the Leave result was largely swung by the over-sixties.[*] It goes without saying that I'm not against any age group expressing their views at the ballot box, but things could be a lot different now if sixteen-year-olds had had the vote.

Not only are sixteen-year-olds unable to vote due to a perceived lack of maturity by the public, but according to the Electoral Commission, it's because of comparisons with

[*] Elena Cresci and *Guardian* readers, 'Meet the 75%: the young people who voted to remain in the EU', *The Guardian*, 24 June 2016, available at https://www.theguardian.com/politics/2016/jun/24/meet-the-75-young-people-who-voted-to-remain-in-eu

other European countries, many of which share our voting age of eighteen. Sixteen-year-olds are also excluded from voting because most of them are in the midst of revising for exams and applying to sixth forms or colleges. Apparently, learning about each of the political parties, strategic voting, and the process of going to a polling station would be too much at this stressful time. I wholeheartedly disagree. For one thing... lots of eighteen-year-olds and above are studying for exams, too. And yes, exams are stressful, but for something as important as the running of our country, we need to make the time. After all, the voting age in Scotland was lowered for the independence referendum – and the voting age has been kept like that for elections to the devolved Scottish parliament and for local elections, too. (That said, they still can't vote in general elections to the Westminster parliament... UK government, come on, please.) As I said, lots of people don't care about politics... so catch us early, make it a topic of which everyone has a fairly equal understanding. Because later in life – heck, even now – we need to be fully equipped to create change. From pre-school we learn maths and English because we'll need to handle our finances and be able to communicate later in life. We'll also need to understand what's going on in the heads of the people in charge of us, and we'll need to know how to vote. These are basic skills, but they're severely lacking. If we want society to progress, we need to learn about politics at a much younger age.

It's all very well to leave it to the parents to teach their children about this topic, but there are so many issues with that, too. What if you don't have parents? What if you do have parents but the kind who don't care, or the kind who don't think to teach you about that kind of thing? What if they don't know anything about politics themselves? What if your parents' politics are vastly different from your own? Not everyone goes to school, but for those who do, factual and unbiased lessons on our current political climate need to be given. There needs to be a clear, unbiased, easily accessible political resource available to all children, too – not just for people in school – and of different levels and mediums, suitable for all paces and abilities. Politics is taught at GCSE, A level and at university, but as an elective subject – and that's bad, because politics isn't optional. We all have to deal with the consequences of politics, and knowing nothing about it can be downright dangerous.

A perfect example of the mistrust and suspicion thrown towards young people with opinions: someone I know suggested that sixteen-year-olds only want the vote so they can choose whoever promises to lower the cost of alcohol. This one shocked me the most. Why is it only likely that a sixteen-year-old would base their vote purely on a policy of cheaper alcohol? Could a twenty-five-year-old not do the same? They could. Maybe they already have.

Some people are even arguing for the voting age to be raised, because eighteen-year-olds 'don't know everything'. Who does? Do twenty-five-year-olds know everything?

Do forty-year-olds know everything? Do eighty-year-olds know everything? Tell anyone over forty about a dank meme or some lit eyebrows and you'll see what I mean. In all seriousness, though, if we're saying that eighteen-year-olds shouldn't be allowed to vote simply because they don't know everything, then logic would suggest that no one should be allowed to vote – and then we're under a dictatorship. Uh, no thanks. We're also too easily swayed by politicians, according to a respondent to research conducted by YouGov, and so we shouldn't be trusted with the responsibility of the vote.*
I'm pretty sure the woman in the audience for *Question Time* who admitted that she switched from Remain to Leave after learning that we would get bendy bananas if we left the EU was older than eighteen, but OK.

And according to someone on debatewise.org, sixteen-year-olds who are informed and want to make a change are in the minority.† Regardless of your age, your gender, where you live, where you go to school and where you work, there will always be people perceived to be less smart than you, and there will always be people who seem smarter than you. Some of them will want to make a change. Some of them will be quite happy where they are.

---

* 'For and against: Lowering the voting age', YouGov, available at https://yougov.co.uk/topics/politics/articles-reports/2012/02/15/and-against-lowering-voting-age

† 'Should the voting age be lowered to 16?', debatewise.org, available at https://debatewise.org/debates/27594-should-the-voting-age-be-lowered-to-16/

★

On 25 March 2017, I attended Unite for Europe, a peaceful two-mile march in London from Park Lane to Parliament Square. The organisers hadn't been expecting an amazing turnout and were predicting 20,000 people or so. The chance of it being a sizable march became even slimmer when, a few days beforehand, there was an attack on Westminster as Khalid Masood decided to speed across Westminster Bridge in an attempt to enter Parliament, killing five people and injuring around fifty. #PrayForLondon trended on Twitter, eerily reminiscent of the Paris attacks from just over a year previously. But if Masood had been trying to bring London to its knees, he failed. A staggering 100,000 people were reported to have united for Europe on that march and showed that we will not be divided.* I hate crowds, but it was amazing to be part of something so big. All of us marching knew that the protest was unlikely to change anything (and, sure enough, Article 50 was triggered less than a week later) but it was the principle of the thing. People of all ages were in attendance, including happy babies decked out in blue and yellow, with gold star-shaped balloons clutched in their little hands. Lots of teenagers were there, too.

I probably spent about ten hours on my double-sided sign altogether. One side was painted with flags for most of the

---

* Chris Johnston, 'Brexit protest: thousands march in London to "unite for Europe" – as it happened', *The Guardian*, 25 March 2017, available at https://www.theguardian.com/politics/live/2017/mar/25/brexit-protest-thousands-march-in-london-to-unite-for-europe-live

EU countries, surrounding a navy-blue box in which yellow letters proclaimed 'WE ❤ EU'; the other was a simple navy-blue background with yellow stars surrounding the message 'LOST WITHOUT EU'. How punny of me.

There were lots of other good signs, too. For a while, I was walking behind a man whose sign simply read: 'HEY MAY, TRIGGER THIS', with a middle finger drawn underneath. Later, I was behind a heart-shaped sign which said, 'I'm in love with the shape of EU,' in reference to Ed Sheeran's latest single, which had been released earlier that month. At one point, two young boys were stood on a wall with signs proclaiming 'BREXIT MEANS BREXSHIT' and 'I'M STILL REVOLTING #BREXSHIT'. Someone else taking song lyrics for inspiration had the sign 'Want EU Back for Good', and another detailed the life-saving treatment the carrier had had from consultants, doctors and nurses of all different ethnicities thanks to the NHS and the EU. Some weren't carrying signs at all but were showing their support with blue and yellow clothing. One woman in particular was wearing a bright-blue wig woven with shiny yellow stars. Hordes of people gave us thumbs-ups from their red buses, and people in the backs of black cabs were taking photos as we walked past. Getting closer to Parliament Square, with Big Ben looking over us in the distance, 'Love Is All You Need' by the Beatles was blasting from somewhere, turning the crowded, modern, angry streets into a street party of sorts, celebrating us. Here, I saw one of my favourite signs, which simply said, 'LOAD OF OLD BOLLOCKS' – simple yet effective.

There was an exhilarating and heartening sense of community, with people I'd never met before from all over Europe stopping me for photos, or complimenting me on the artwork, or – for the people behind me – using the flag side of my sign as a way to pass the time, by guessing which flags belonged to which countries. This was very British in that it was very hushed. Pall Mall was crowded and noisy with our chants ricocheting from wall to wall, but I could still hear the whispered 'What about the one that looks like Donald Trump's wig?' from the elderly lady directly behind me, followed by 'He doesn't wear a wig' from the younger man beside her. 'Doesn't he?' she replied, bewildered. It was Cyprus. I'm going to assume the Donald Trump comment was based on the colour of the flag rather than my art skills.

And for the first time, I noticed our police in action, who I'll admit I'd never truly paid attention to before. These people with their own families and, hey, maybe even different political views to the protesters, protected us all the way to and inside Parliament Square just days after one of their officers had been fatally stabbed there in the line of duty. For the first time in a few months, I felt proud to be in this country thanks to the police in attendance, and people were constantly stopping them to say thank you. I passed a police van with a daffodil tucked in the hollow of the door handle.

To quote Dumbledore, 'Happiness can be found even in the darkest of times,' and it showed. Approximately 100,000 people of all different ages, nationalities, sexualities, abilities and social classes came together to fight for a common goal and, considering the events happening at the time, put themselves in an arguably risky position to make their thoughts and feelings heard. It was peaceful, respectful, perhaps everything politics should be. And amongst this crowd were teenagers who gave up their weekend to actively support a political cause, who knew what they were fighting for, who believed in it wholeheartedly just like everyone else, but who continue to be disenfranchised by the government.

The discussion surrounding the issue of young people and their political engagement, or lack of it, comes around time and time again. We need political education in schools, but it won't work if it's not engaging. Campaigns are launched, innovative and interactive websites started, YouTube channels full of youth-friendly political language begun, and I'm sure these are helpful to a vast number of young people. But it doesn't make much noise. It's a ripple in the water when it could be a splash. Do you know where we hatchlings are most of the time? Social media. Make an account and get in our faces. Pop up in our feeds so much that we can't avoid you. Come to us rather than expecting us to already know you exist, and you'll be in our pockets all day, every day, I promise. The Labour Party targeted our age group amazingly well in the 2017 general election, and look what happened – their engagement skyrocketed. In a world of adverts and gifs and videos and tweets and threads every single way you turn, this isn't the time to be standing on the sidelines. Be bold and we'll be engaged.

I believe that ageism is a huge problem in our society, but one not often given attention or taken seriously. I mean, the *Oxford English Dictionary* literally says that it's a term used to describe discrimination 'especially against the elderly'. Yes, even in the word's very definition, ageism against the young is pushed aside. Calling for more attention to one side of the problem doesn't mean to say that the other side – discrimination against the elderly – is less important, rather that a stronger connection that works both ways between the generations is needed. When it was announced that we would be leaving the EU, a woman told me about a boy she knew who was just two weeks too young to vote, yet that night he was in the middle of the action, counting ballot papers. This shows me how invested young people are in the future of the country.

Speaking on the BBC's *Westminster Hour*, Theresa May suggested the idea of mock elections, and said that being able to participate in the real deal is not necessary for young people to become 'engaged' in politics.* How patronising! Mock elections might as well be lumped into the same category as playground weddings and childhood games of

---

* Jon Stone, 'Theresa May says the right to vote is not necessary to participate in politics', *The Independent*, 15 May 2017, available at https://www.independent.co.uk/news/uk/politics/theresa-may-voting-age-16-right-to-vote-engaged-politics-general-election-2017-a7736091.html

'Mums and Dads'. Interestingly, whilst some young people do support the Conservatives, the party is massively unpopular with our age group. More popular with us happen to be the parties which think the minimum voting age should be lowered: Labour, the Lib Dems, the SNP and the Greens. Perhaps this is because these parties actively try to engage us and take us seriously. When Labour MP Jim McMahon put forward a bill on lowering the voting age to sixteen on 3 November 2017, the outcome was disappointing. Debating time in the House of Commons ran out before it could be put to a vote, and it was actually only discussed for less than an hour and a half. According to the BBC, the debate would likely be resumed a month later, however it cited that the youth vote would be so low on the agenda it probably wouldn't get any debating time.* Nice.

But I was so excited when my first ever polling card arrived through the door. It landed much earlier than expected thanks to the 2017 snap general election that Theresa May said wouldn't happen. I was actively involved, I joined a party for the first time, I rallied up my friends and on polling day made sure that they remembered to vote. I was probably fairly irritating to be around, but I was so excited, because what a privilege! People in so many places don't get to have a say regardless of whether they're sixteen or forty. But we do.

---

* Georgina Pattinson, 'Bill on voting at 16 falters', BBC, 3 November 2017, available at https://www.bbc.co.uk/news/live/uk-politics-parliaments-41804082

And no matter how often I joke about my younger friends being 'children', I do not see them as inferior to me. Being eighteen or older does not automatically make you better or more able. Some of them are smarter than me, and some of them have more experiences than I do. When I was sixteen, I had as much political insight as I do now. At eighteen, I had more experience due to Brexit and the whole Trump debacle, but that doesn't mean my vote would have been any more considered then than it would have been at sixteen. Two years seems like ages. It isn't.

We need to educate young people about politics, we need to take their views seriously, and we mustn't stop there. We must let them vote. We're constantly talking about the fact that teenagers are growing up quicker than ever, and it's usually meant in a negative light, but regardless of whether or not it's a good thing, we need to get with the times. Things are changing. The world is evolving. We have to keep up; to not keep up would be dangerous. In some ways, it could be argued that we're already going backwards, and we cannot afford to go that way any further.

No, sixteen-year-olds don't know everything. But who does?

THE DINNER PARTY

Brenda Wong

Content warning: racism

I shift uncomfortably on the chaise longue. My stomach, churning after downing the remnants from my champagne flute, threatens to growl in unfeminine protest. Of all the things I'd wanted to be doing on a Saturday night, filially tagging along to a dinner party hosted by my parents' acquaintances wasn't one of them.

The host, T, hasn't stopped moving since our arrival half an hour ago, fussing in the kitchen, putting the final touches to the starter, and bringing out the finest of his china to serve nibbles on. The plates sparkle with pride. It is not in my family's nature to surround ourselves with opulence. I think back to our home in Kuala Lumpur. Modern and slick as my mother has tried to make it, there is still a large plastic bag filled to bursting with a collection of other plastic bags on display in the open kitchen. Function over form. I have replicated the same bag collection habit in my own home in south-east London.

No, nothing in this home is out of place. The chaise longue I'm sitting on is vintage. The new chairs in the bedroom have been transported by a dealer in France. The oak bookshelf spans from floor to ceiling, and, perhaps it's the champagne talking, but I can almost see the shelves shift under the weight of all the le Carré. In awkward situations, I usually communicate with my mother in Malay, an act that has bonded us in strange times like this. Not today, though. T is a friend of my father's from sixth form, and although out of practice after decades spent away from Penang, he still speaks the language fluently. All we can do is exchange furtive looks as we fake-laugh our way through the evening.

G, T's partner, has largely been ignoring me, my mother and my sister. Settled in his chair next to his beloved bookcase, he has, instead, locked my father in a conversation about his and T's recent visit to his French hometown. 'I don't go back often, especially after T and I got our citizenship here. It was an unpleasant visit, but deaths in the family always are.'

Jarred, we listen on as G skips over the particulars of the funeral and moves straight on to his elderly mother's penchant for red meat, and then to the very particular inconvenience of having to stop over in Salzburg to buy a specific type of carafe to suit T's taste in glassware. G's stories feel a bit like going through six roundabouts in a row, never knowing which exit you'll be taking. Dizzy, it's almost a relief when he doesn't ask us to weigh in as he informs us about the subtle differences in Bordeaux wines. But when he mentions last year's referendum, I feel my back straighten. Sitting with just the balls of my feet on the carpet, I plant my heels on the ground and wait. Come on, G. Don't be who I think you're going to show me you are.

'Tch, we both voted to leave, T and I,' he says, matter-of-factly.'

'But why?' I speak hoarsely, my first words after an hour of silence. I clear my throat and ready myself for battle. The revelation throws me. A year ago, two immigrants who pride themselves on beating the odds to become fully welcomed into this country's fold, voted to rescind this right for thousands of EU nationals. It beggars belief.

'Tch,' G spits again. 'If T and I had to jump through hoops to get where we are, why shouldn't everyone else? We're happy it turned out the way it did. Honestly, if it were up to me there should be some voting reform. There are some truly stupid voters out there who don't know what they're doing.'

'Stupid voters. You mean young voters?'

Mum sees my hackles rising. Her eyes communicate a single message: 'Abort mission.'

'Ha!' G guffaws, throwing his head back, his chair creaking with the sudden movement. 'I knew nothing when I was your age. If you ask me, I wouldn't have trusted myself to vote correctly. Young people shouldn't be involved in politics at all.'

★

It's the autumn of 2011, and my right hand is slapped to the side of the bathroom stall. There is nothing left in me, but my gut heaves regardless. Am I really sick? Or is my mind telling my body that flying 6,000 miles away to a country I have never even visited, where I know nobody, where my eyes and accent and skin and habits mark me as different, is unpalatable?

We had been talking about the London riots in the car to the airport. The jury is out on whether or not the subject matter contributed to my queasiness. It probably didn't help. My mum had insisted on riding in the back seat with me, which thrilled my sister, who didn't have to fight her way to shotgun position. I rested my head on her shoulder. She grabbed hold of my hand. In the years to come I will learn she does this every time she knows we have to say goodbye.

'It's no different to what we experienced in Bangkok,' my sister piped up. To a degree, she's right. In the seven years we lived in the capital as expatriates, we had survived two political coups d'état, and a long-term people's rebellion. We had seen tanks on the streets where we lived, heard the sirens blaring, smelled the smoke billowing from high-rises in the city centre. The aftermath of these events was always quiet – an eerie contrast to the usual noises of yelling som tam vendors, motorcycle taxis and the grinding 'eeee' of the Skytrain. Once, when we emerged from our house after holing ourselves up without leaving for two weeks, we saw the main road barricaded with chairs and makeshift spikes. If the people had sung, I didn't hear it.

Every time this happened, my dad would Skype us from Kuala Lumpur and beg us to fly home immediately. Every time my mum said we would stay until the situation got serious. 'Keep your head down, and stay inside,' my father would say. 'Don't get involved.'

'Don't get involved' is a Malaysian citizen's true motto. They've been trying to foist *Malaysia Boleh* on us for as long as I can remember (translation: 'Malaysia Can'), and most recently, it's been 1Malaysia or *Satu Malaysia*, an attempt to unify a politically divided country. The 2008 and 2013 elections were mired in allegations of electoral fraud, gerrymandering and vote-buying, but the disengagement started much earlier. In the seven elections my parents had been eligible to vote in, they'd only voted once.

At home, we don't talk about politics. Not in our tiny Bangkok flat where we safely watched the red-shirts and yellow-shirts clash violently on the BBC. After all, the government wouldn't show it on national television. Not in our home back in Kuala Lumpur, even at the height of the Bersih anti-corruption movement. We weren't forbidden. It just had nothing to do with us, so there was no need to talk about these things.

Yet here I was. Eighteen, slightly nauseous and about to tear my roots from the ground and replant myself in the West. Why? Because things will never change here. Because, even if we wanted change, one lonely voice wouldn't matter. Because opportunity is guaranteed to anyone who gets into an English school of law.

'Boarding announcement: flight MH004 flying to London, gate is now open. Please proceed to the gate for check-in.'

The halogen lights of the women's toilets do no discernible good for my pallor, but it's not like I'll have anyone to impress on my solo cross-continental journey. I could do a runner. I could grab my family and beg them to take me home. But this won't happen. What will happen is a long, teary goodbye, followed by fourteen hours of the purest loneliness I've ever felt. All this for a better life.

During freshers' week I meet Ali. He's a ginger boy from Hereford. He's never travelled outside Europe.

Within the first few minutes of our meeting he bestows upon me a new nickname: 'Chow Mein'. He thinks it's hilarious. As the rest of the flat are both English and four Jägermeister shots in, they think it too.

'Wokeness' was a concept that had yet to permeate our imaginations. Yet, if I had to pick one moment, a single snapshot in time I would jump in a DeLorean to change, it would be this one. Racism, no matter how casual, is still racism. We had yet to go through sombrerogate. We hadn't experienced the furore of the racist banana. So, there I am, stunned for a millisecond. What other choice do I have but to laugh along? It's just banter, mate. It's just banter.

★

It's been a tumultuous three years. Nothing surprising. Ask most people and they'll probably tell you their university years were 100 per cent melodrama, 0 per cent chill. Sitting in the library café, laptop at fingertips and fry-up half finished, I'm bleary-eyed.

As I stretch to shake off fatigue, my phone buzzes in my jacket pocket. Shit.

I'm sorry.

He probably isn't. Five hours earlier he'd woken the whole street up by calling me a cold-hearted bitch who hadn't a chance in hell of winning a Sabbatical Officer race. My flatmate Cat, the current Welfare and Campaigns Officer for our student union, had convinced me that it was a good idea to run, despite me being an absolute student politics dilettante. Here I am, with a freshly completed election manifesto and a fuckboy who is trying to restart a relationship that was toxic at best. It is still far too early for a drink.

I was stupid. Let me make it up to you. Please.

When I met Cat I had moved back into halls for my third year, thinking that being on campus might actually make me study harder (it didn't). She, along with fellow Sabbatical Officer Zoe, were the first Sabbatical Officers I'd had contact with in three years. That probably says it all about the student union's engagement levels with international students. Yet in the months leading up to me submitting the web form that would nominate me as candidate to run for office, I'd been charmed. The idealism of it all. Hungover, we would lie on Cat's bed and stare at the ceiling, talking about putting a cap on fees, improving the university bus frequencies and introducing gender-neutral loos to the union. To the revolution. A seed of thought had been planted. Not only did I care about this stuff, I really cared about this stuff.

I'm sorry about what I said about your election thing I was out of line I'm sorry I'm sorry I'm sorry I'm...

Not interested. He wouldn't be the first person to not take my run for Welfare Officer seriously. He wouldn't be the last. The revolving door of white, straight, cis-gendered men telling me what I can and cannot do is equipped with its very own perpetual motion engine. There is only one person's faith I can truly control. My own.

I activate the 'do not disturb' mode on my phone and head to the union.

There's a manifesto deadline to meet.

Tights on, heels in bag, reading glasses packed. Of all the days to be running late. I was to join a private roundtable at

Number 10 Downing Street as a youth marketing consultant for the European Union referendum in less than an hour.

Sweating, I charged out of the exit at Charing Cross to meet my boss. I'd overheard him talk about being invited as a representative, and had convinced him the day before to get me an invite too. As he'd been out and about pursuing sales leads in the past few months, the team had been supporting him with our research and insights. In short, if pressed the man probably knew sod all about engaging eighteen- to twenty-four-year-olds. So, he needed backup.

By some Tube miracle his backup ended up arriving on time. We walked to Number 10, stopping a few buildings before so I could put on my heels. They were the only pair of shoes I owned appropriate for the occasion, and somehow, overnight, they'd grown a half-size too big.

After losing my student union election, I'd surprised myself by continuing to care. They don't tell you once you're woke it's hard to go back to sleep. Helping to empower my generation to thrive became a passion that would drive my career in ways I could have never predicted. So there I was. A girl, standing in front of Downing Street, waiting to be security screened.

Perhaps being kept waiting outside the gates was a power move. Perhaps the powers that be were late – human like the rest of us after all. Perhaps. Waiting with us were a political reporter from BuzzFeed and the chief of marketing for LADbible, Mimi Turner. I marvelled at the latter as she introduced herself. Friendly but clearly formidable, she was one of LADbible's newest recruits, and if you knew anything about the new money media giant, you would know they were a left-field choice. The clue is in the name 'LADbible'. I would later read an article where she was quoted to say, 'A quarter of "lads" are women.' I'm pretty sure you won't find me in that demographic.

We were gathered to discuss a pressing issue. The referendum was taking place in three weeks' time, and analysis had predicted a low youth turnout.

When we were finally let into the building, I mentally checked off my predicted Fantasy Roundtable bench. Facebook, check. Twitter, check. Tinder, Uber, the Student Room, Bite the Ballot – the list went on. The Avengers of the youth vote, or so Downing Street were hoping.

Trying not to succumb to anxiety, I made a feeble attempt at networking. The BuzzFeed reporter told me how he'd been in this room a few times before and how it had stopped fazing him a while back.

'It's no big deal anymore,' he muttered, one hand holding a glass of water, the other on his hip. He looked very much the dictionary definition of a hack.

'If things like this stop becoming a big deal to me, it's game over,' I replied.

The room was called to order by Daniel Korski, head of digital communications at Number 10 and chair of today's roundtable. As we took our assigned seats a sceptical thought occurred to me. Why was this roundtable happening now? What possible action could arise from a meeting taking place only three weeks away from a country-changing democratic decision? Could Facebook and Twitter engage the most cynical generation yet out of their current political disillusionment? My gut feeling said no, but we still had the roundtable to go. I hoped to be convinced otherwise.

Instead, what we got was a 'mine is bigger than yours' competition from Facebook, Google and Twitter for half an hour. Internally, I screamed as they talked about past initiatives like the 2015 election Google Doodle and the Facebook voting check-in. There weren't any attempts at suggesting new ideas, and every minute celebrating a past win was a minute of wasted opportunity.

'So, how are we doing?' a voice from the room's left entrance boomed. The room fell completely silent. A man in shorts who thought himself too important to adhere to the business casual dress code suddenly had eyes as wide as saucers. Prime Minister David Cameron had just dropped into the room unannounced. My boss gave me a look that screamed, 'You have to say something in front of this man, and goddamn it, don't forget to mention which company you come from.'

Facebook and Twitter just stared for a moment, bravado draining from their faces. They recovered quickly and started catching the prime minister up on the subject matter. The game was back on.

David Cameron looked exactly how I thought he would. Not taller, not shorter, exactly how I imagined him. He asked the room, 'What can we at Downing Street do better to encourage the youth vote?' Before my brain could catch up with my tongue I found myself saying, 'In my opinion, your voter registration website load speed is abysmal.' A stern-looking man from Downing Street's communications team stood up to protest. 'We've recently updated the website servers to cope with the load.'

'It still takes more than a minute when you try,' I replied, maintaining my seat. 'If my phone wasn't in a box downstairs, I'd show you. If you're trying to engage the youth vote, do it where it's native for them. I barely read articles that aren't Google AMP or Facebook Instant. If I'm on a bus and I'm trying to read something on the internet, I move on if it doesn't load quickly enough.'

'She has a point.' The prime minister thought I had a point. 'Make sure to look into it.'

'Yes sir.' The man glowered at me and sat back down.

The rest of the meeting passed by in a surreal blur. The prime minister stuck around for another five minutes but left to attend to other matters shortly after our conversation. The main outcomes were that Tinder and Bite the Ballot were to join forces to do a 'Swipe the Vote' engagement campaign, and that Uber were to incorporate a pop-up encouraging riders to vote. We left Downing Street, but not before we petted Chief Mouser Larry – a contented tabby and white cat – on our way out.

A few days later I was at the pub telling my friends about the roundtable. 'Is David Cameron's face as flat as it looks in photos?' they asked. I declined to answer.

'You don't think young people like me should have the right to vote?' I say it with a smile. My bubble had been burst long ago by the double-Trump-and-Brexit-whammy, but G's is still very much intact. I intend to do him a kindness by bursting it gently.

DUMPING THE GREEN BELT

Nicholas Preston

Content warning: mental health

For all of us, there will be times in our lives when we'll experience transitions that will change the trajectory of our lives dramatically. Perhaps one of the more difficult and dramatic transitions is our integration into the working week. This is partly because, for those of us who grow up in the confines of educational institutions, every second of our day is accounted for. Ultimately, someone else has responsibility for us. The transition of leaving school, starting out into the world of work or of university, and taking responsibility for ourselves looms ahead of us.

At the age of nineteen, I made two of my more profound transitions. After failing to get the necessary grades to get back into my school's sixth form, I was without a job, college placement or any other kind of routine to anchor me to the world. I was broke, like so many of my peers, navigating my way through some difficult mental health problems and confronting my own identity, initially through the lens of class, and ultimately through acknowledging my sexuality as bisexual.

I grew up in Greater London, in a suburban area of Zone 5. It was me, my mum, my dad and my brother. We were a JAM family – we were 'just about managing', a newly emerging type of household, as described by politicians. The think tank Policy Exchange describes JAMS as 'people who just manage to get by each month but whose resilience to economic shocks is not high'. Since that's the income bracket which most families in the UK live within, it's basically a term used by government to avoid acknowledging a failing economy.

Being at home was my idea of hell; my mental health was always contingent on whether I was there or not. I found the suburbs stifling and always had a desire to 'break out'. Living there seemed to thwart any ambition that stretched beyond its borders. Staying there, in Zone 5, I'd probably find a girlfriend, work in retail, get married and have a few children by the age of twenty-eight. I did not want that, but it seemed like an inevitability that would be imposed on me – lots of people around me took exactly the same path and I didn't really know any different. I resisted that future, not because there is anything inherently wrong with it, but because I had to hope there was something more to life. I wanted secure employment in something that I enjoyed doing, but what that would be wasn't clear to me yet and I was under no illusion that it would be easy to find.

At this point in time, my parents needed me to become less reliant on them. They were, as I said, just about managing. Having one fewer body to manage might enable them to better support me in other ways later on. I looked for work despite having no formal qualifications besides GCSEs. Successfully applying for anything other than a retail job seemed unattainable to me.

The idea of this filled me with anxiety: customer service deserves better than somebody like me, who is totally socially inept and would choke if somebody were to ask a question that I didn't know the answer to.

In order to avoid ending up there, during the beginning of summer in 2015, I joined an employment training course close to my home. It was a course designed to equip young people with necessary workplace attributes and skills, such as preparing a CV, professional mannerisms (to colleagues and clients both in person and on the phone) and effectively using a computer. None of us wanted to be there; it felt like endless, tedious pontificating from the facilitators. We were all in similar circumstances, each of us desperate to sidestep enlisting at a Jobcentre at all costs because of the *I, Daniel Blake*-style horror stories we had all heard of endless bureaucracy and the lack of the faintest amount of human empathy.

Fortunately, though the course was in its own way kind of terrible, it turned out that joining it was the right decision to make, and after six weeks, the facilitators of the course arranged for some interviews to take place between the group and employers. I was successful in one of them and it propelled me into a job placement in London.

This was the urban centre where I wanted to be. Four Tube zones away from the sodden bog of the suburbs that I grew up in.

The role itself was something that I hadn't heard of before. I was going to be a research apprentice at a research- and consultancy-based organisation. When explaining this to my family and friends, I was met with glazed expressions. This is what excited me though. I was breaking the mould, doing something different, and hopefully fruitful.

My first day was a disorientating experience for many reasons. For the first time, I wasn't going to London as a tourist. I was going as a professional. And I couldn't cope with it at all: the swathes of people rushing around with fierce intent, the *Evening Standard* being thrust into my face and the terrible humidity of stations and trains during August, none of it helping reduce the trepidation I was feeling for my first day.

When I arrived at work, I met with my line manager and was given an induction and a job description, which finally explained to me in full what being a research apprentice would entail.

I would be providing administrative support (making bookings, sitting on the reception desk and such) and I would also be involved in project work, which tended to be evaluations of programmes concerning mental health, local governmental policy and leadership development (working with organisations such as the NHS, the Department for Education and various NGOs). My new workplace was small and quiet, confined to one single floor in a big building of offices and with about ten members of staff in the office, only one other person being close to my age.

I didn't really know how socio-economic classes operated until I joined the organisation, but when getting to know my new colleagues, class signifiers suddenly became incredibly apparent. Everybody I grew up with lived in more or less the same-sized house, their parents probably hadn't gone to university and my friends all had a very similar world view and almost invariable similar areas of interests, the typical Twitter bio description generally being something like 'beer, birds and football'. At the time, whenever I attempted to cough up a word to describe my new colleagues, it was always 'eccentric'. They all sounded immorally well educated, capable of doing a crossword at record speed. And they were dressed in quite a casual manner, like students (at least compared to my rigid idea of professionalism at the time). Later I realised that it was actually just a very middle-class workplace. None of them had tattoos of their dead relatives' names on their body, nor were they buying energy drinks or speaking at all in a way that I was familiar with. Once, my friend and colleague had gone out to get 'snacks'. I was expecting chocolate or cookies of some sort, and I was mildly disgusted when she returned with grilled artichokes.

It was when fleshing out these class disparities, through talking to my new colleagues and spending a lot of time in London, that I learned why being at home had felt stifling in recent years. I was now among people that I felt were closest to who I 'wanted to be'. I pretty much wanted to emulate them; to continue to work in the research field, to engage in politics meaningfully through organising or demonstrations, to cycle around London without fear of an accident, and to read frequently, for pleasure I guess, becoming one of those people that I had always thought were pompous 'bookish types'. It seems strange to me now, that something like reading was an activity I'd wilfully written off as something that was nerdy posturing. It had all become so overwhelming that I began to have a sort of crisis of identity.

London had made me feel inadequate, a feeling that I think is very particular to being young and vulnerable. I'd always feel like there was something inside me that I couldn't quite express when talking to those around me. I'd pre-empt difficult situations, for instance, where somebody might talk to me about something that I didn't understand, by writing notes on my iPhone. They were effectively invocations which I would repeat to myself, to avoid the inevitable angst and confusion when I feared engaging with the people around me. In those first months of employment, when navigating social terrain that made me an anxious, blithering, incoherent mess, I would remind myself of this one particularly:

28 October 2015

I'm beginning to see that my insight is in no way substantially more insignificant than that of anyone else. While I know that we are all faced by the same existential questions and that our difference lies with the way we engage with them, I know that others have felt exactly the same as I have throughout history, that same fragility. I take solace from this. Still, I'm always acutely aware of the chasm between myself and others, and yet I'm always troubled by the nagging feeling that however understanding others are and however much I love them, they don't really get it. I don't even quite get it myself. What I have is a generalised sense of unease and a fascination with the fact of my own subjectivity. I thought it was neurosis, something wrong with myself and not everything around me. I can't ever explain, to my own satisfaction, to colleagues, family, and friends, what the problem is, so I have decided to write it down. I know that what I want to say and my deeper thoughts always need to be reflected upon in solitude.

Reading this would always contextualise what I was feeling, whether the feeling was brought about by being young in an older office space, finding out all the aforementioned 'new' things that I could be, or simply the change in me between London and home.

Over time, through commuting and the day-to-day of my research role at work, I began to oddly enjoy the very particular exhaustion that the city provoked, the cosmopolitanism and the sense of acceleration that was satisfying the ignorant feeling that where I had come to be was the centre of the universe, that this was where everything was happening.

But I also began to notice, despite the speed with which my life was moving, a significant deterioration in my mental health. I was increasingly compartmentalising what was going on for me, marking it out as a sort of vague continuous sadness. I wasn't prepared to give it a name.

Inevitably, as things got worse for me, I had to stop lying to myself. It was depression; palpable, possessing and physically prostrating. I spent my weekend waking hours lying in bed with my back in the shape of a question mark, watching mindless videos and vlogs, and being coarse with my parents.

19 March 2016

I'm so tired. I wake up already exhausted. My bones feel all metallic inside, cold, hard and brittle. I'm trapped in this rotting cage of a body. Artificial light is everywhere and it makes my skin seethe, I know that my grotesque blackened pores are visible and so I avoid eye contact, I don't want people to look at me. My back becomes hunched over from inaction, or maybe painting my nails at most, and then in the morning I wake up and do it all again.

I started to wonder, with some encouragement from colleagues (enthusiastic proponents of education), whether university might be a better place to really 'find myself', so after a year as a research apprentice, I started applying for courses. The plan was to find a university in London, get a student loan and find somewhere close by to live. Amazingly, during a tumultuous summer in 2016, when my depression was at its peak, I received an offer from Goldsmiths College to study a BA in anthropology. I spent a couple of weeks looking for accommodation, although frankly I didn't care what squalid ramshackle dwelling I would be living in for £650 per month. I just wanted to be outside of Zone 5 and to feel vaguely independent.

Eventually, in August, I found a home in New Cross, a Victorian terraced house with five bedrooms, which was being let as student accommodation. I don't really remember how it felt when initially moving in; I was too transfixed by my new circumstance and how much things were going to change.

I didn't miss being at home in the suburbs, I didn't miss having a dinner made for me, I didn't miss having a dishwasher and I didn't even miss home when I would break out into sweats on the walk from the shower to my room because the house in New Cross was built during the 'Little Ice Age' and essentially acted as a container for hot air during the summer. I didn't miss any of it, because now, rather than focusing on what I had left behind, I felt a lot of things had become accessible to me. So many avenues – LGBT+ culture, political activism and academia – that had previously been nebulous and out of reach to me were now on my doorstep. I felt that I could now finally engage with these things and finally escape the sheltered closet of conservative, heterosexual suburbia.

Finding my way in this new world was difficult at first, and this impacted heavily on my mental health, so I wrote a note to try and isolate and minimise what I was feeling as an individual and place it in the context of everything else that was going on in the world (climate change, elections and doctrines of absolute contempt and hatred gaining traction).

24 July 2016

The world we reside in is not good for us. In its entirety, capitalism has reduced it to this: smallness, shambling, anxious, segmented, hedonistic, unable to sustain interests in anything, unsure that life will remain valuable enough over the next few seconds to justify breathing any deeper. Fascists are overrunning everything and things only look to get worse because amidst the rubble which a liberal society has condemned us to, misguided masses look for some small amount of hope; but they're as fragmented and as worn-out as anything else in this dying world.

But set against these struggles with overbearing sadness was the joy of feeling able to plunge into the world of dating and explore my sexual identity openly. I was finally able to talk about it with my peers, as I had not been before. My peers agreed unanimously that online dating was a lot of fun; it was free of any kind of tangible obligation and you could meet people outside your immediate friendship circles. I took up their recommendation, joined Tinder and went on a hell of a lot of dates with men and women, which ranged from really good to really terrible experiences, as anybody should probably expect when dating. A man once followed me home after a pretty pernicious experience, and even asked me if I wanted to play on the swings that were outside my house… But for every sinister or uncomfortable encounter, there were many more affirming ones. When I told a colleague of mine how I was occupying my time, she remarked that it was all 'the seduction of youth' and urged me to revel in it while it lasted.

At first, I wasn't entirely sure what my colleague had meant by this. I was having a lot of fun in my new surroundings, but I was also taking SSRIs, suffering from insomnia, anxiety sometimes impeding my ability to function, and often drinking bottles of wine to knock me out so that I would be able to sleep. All this, while I was also sometimes subjected to explicit homophobic abuse, and once even a sermon – 'In all your ways acknowledge him, and He will make straight your paths' – in response to which I would ironically recite in my head and to my friends facing hardships, like an incantation, 'Youth, youth, baby.'

On reflection though, it's easy to understand the sentiment behind that phrase, 'the seduction of youth'. This is a period in your life which is full of fantastic contradictions, and existing between those is not an absurdity because you can (perhaps) glibly excuse yourself as trying to find your way in the world. Most of my problems before moving to London centred around the overwhelming feeling that I was just an observer of everything that I have described; I felt alone navigating many of the struggles that come with leaving the 'safety net' that I had up until that point, but no longer. I could now be a participant in whatever exhilarating (and often, frightening) opportunities came my way, whether in the form of student activities, political engagement or relationships and, sorry for the horrible word, networking. This year has reminded me that there are all sorts of ways to live, and all sorts of ways of being with other people. It has created a space in which I can be myself.

AN INTERGENERATIONAL CONVERSATION

Tom Greenslade

Liquid faeces cover my carefully gloved hands every day. Even worse, a living, breathing, thinking person spews this foul lava over me, adding humiliation to their other pains. Since their emergency admission to hospital, they must confront their new and troubling reality.

'God, when did I get old?'

'What happened – is this it?'

'How humiliating. My arse has to be cleaned by a kid in his twenties.'

They battle conflicting urges, alternately apologising for the vile work they've gifted me, yet silently thanking their guts for releasing that unbearable pressure. Once they adjust to our routines, things will be easier. They'll use their call-bells pre-emptively, knowing that it might take me a few minutes to get round to them. They'll flip onto their sides eagerly, waiting for the grating edge of the cardboard bedpan to be placed under them. I'll retreat with a few words of reassurance and no encouragement. This job is making me ill too. I work heavy shifts, during which I expect to be urinated on, covered in blood and faeces, and verbally and physically assaulted.

As graduation loomed, my job hunt became increasingly urgent. Like most of my year group, I was looking for something fulfilling. There's no rush to build a disappointing career – my generation has fifty years of working life ahead of them. I set up a few online alerts and when a job as a healthcare assistant came up, I went for it. We have an ageing population, so the future of health and social care is dominated by the needs of the elderly – this is where I could make a difference. Sadly, working for the NHS, I swiftly found that kind words don't pay the bills.

It takes surprisingly little to bring even the superfit down from the top of the world. No one expects ill health, but eventually it gatecrashes everybody's party, whether chairman or cleaner. The variety of patients means that hospital work continues to challenge my preconceptions about people. An obese father of three defied stereotypes. He was far from lazy, as he explained. Despite weighing 160 kg, he lived a normal life, but with the weight of an extra person strapped to his back. Trying to lose weight for life-changing surgery was one of the hardest things he'd ever done. Six attempts deep, this man just kept on trying. His addiction to food couldn't be tackled by going cold turkey, but every day he battled to control the calories.

Most dramatically of all, working as a healthcare assistant has changed the way I view old people. Secondary and higher education are bubbles of youth, where people stick close to those in their own age group. An isolated community of young people is cut adrift from older generations; the old and the young become inscrutable to one another. Part of the reason for this has to be exposure. Naturally, we become friends with the people around us, because we relate to them so easily. Older generations are at altogether different stages in their lives. There's a lack of empathy – we keep our distance.

Failure to spend time together stifles understanding, and it was this chasm I sought to bridge. Central to my job is the dismantling of stereotypes. Pigeonholing might sometimes be necessary to help me deal with new people and their needs quickly, but once I get to know them on a personal level, all that falls by the wayside.

Partly, disregarding older generations is a defence mechanism. I don't want to think about the ageing process and what it will do to me. I'm immortal, destined to make and unmake all aspects of my personality and body in a never-ending cycle. To be confronted with old bodies is to be reminded of my own mortality. We prefer these decaying vessels to remain alien. We no longer see the people they were as young men and women, so we create that false divide. It shouldn't be the case, but seeing a youthful photograph of a now decrepit figure restores their humanity to our eyes.

Curiously, our experiences are the same – none of these people planned to get old. It took them by surprise. One lady asked me how I could stand to be in her room. Confused, I asked her why.

'Oh, you know. I'm a smelly old lady.'

She was far from it – well turned out, propped up in an armchair, with various tubes fanning out of her body. This lady was recalling the experiences of her own youth. The stench of TCP and mothballs. The elderly as a poverty-stricken class, unable to meet their own basic needs. She'd spent so long thinking of older generations in this way that she'd condemned herself to live this role. What a pleasant surprise to be reminded that she was a fresh individual, whose company I enjoyed! A similar fatalism festers in grandparents who refer to themselves as 'silly old gits' or tell youngsters not to waste time on them, but to go out and 'enjoy themselves'.

As I wander into the hospital I consider the strangeness of orientating my entire being around these people. I try to present them with an easily accessible and uplifting character, maintaining a sense of youthful energy. It might encourage them to smile and get out of bed for the day. Essentially, I'm guilty of misrepresenting what it means to be young. I carry my age like an abundant fruit basket. To everybody I meet, I hand over a sweet and satisfying peach. This is the wealth of youth – there is no decay here. I am young and carefree. Student debt does not exist. I filter out anything which might confuse or irritate, erasing youthful slang from my speech.

Partly this is the necessity of professionalism – medical teams have weighty responsibilities. It's inappropriate to allow your personal life to affect the working day. Mostly, it's just the easiest way to interact. Presenting as that Nice Young Man smooths me out. I remind some patients of their grandsons. Others delight in telling me that if they were sixty years younger they'd steal a kiss.

The first patient to break through my professional defences was a woman of my age, also a recent graduate. Her first and only year of married life was spent being cared for by her husband. He'd wake three times at night to medicate her suffering and check on her survival. After several months, she was admitted to hospital in the hope that we could regulate things more effectively. Her similar age and background meant that I immediately identified with her. I was often flustered whilst caring for her, mumbling idiotic things as I fumbled through basic clinical routines. Beetroot red, I asked if she'd prefer me to stop talking.

She smiled, closed her eyes, and whispered: 'I am rather tired.'

Youth robbed of its future, while the patient next door rolled into their ninth decade. When this woman died it set off a firework in my mind, ricocheting inside my head. A bundle of sparks zipped around, too fast for me to process. It felt like the only way to release the energy was by burying my fist in a wall. On the surface I was still, eyes glazed. When my lunch break ended, I went back to work with my unfinished thoughts and stunted emotions. A traumatic experience, but one which provoked a more unsettling realisation. I'd been depersonalising my elderly patients.

Yet who are we to doubt the enormous value in these lives? Many have an undiminished eagerness to experience life. Beyond this, they're also a powerful repository of identity. There's a good reason why family history is so popular. People want to ground themselves, and revel in their proximity to thrilling stories about their nearest and dearest. Each generation becomes the guardian of the next. What if Grandpa's train hadn't been delayed? He would have been on that minesweeper which left Lowestoft during World War II and disappeared without a trace. Instead, someone else's kin was drafted into his coffin, and our line continued. The diversity of history enriches our lives and puts them in context, thanks to the storytellers of older generations.

Ageing is hard work for everyone, not least the old. I've had to perform CPR on a woman in her mid-nineties because, despite feeling ready to die, she was determined to care for her disabled brother. And there will be tears. Possibly my greatest misjudgement was against an elderly patient's husband. Sat by her bedside, unmoving for a few hours each day, he seemed oddly uncaring. It was only later that his daughter told me he cried all the way home because his wife no longer recognised him.

It's tempting to become overprotective of older folk. There's a tension between enabling independence, and recognising the risks inherent in declining physical and mental function. We encourage mobility, but then hover nervously as a patient recovering from a hip replacement walks to the bathroom. We 'act in their best interest'. Home isn't safe anymore, you need extra help. Take these pills, they keep you alive. As one patient declared, she was having a second childhood without any of the fun bits.

But the caring can be informal. It gives people meaning and purpose, allowing them to carry on. Mixed-age friendship groups can surprise us by sharing resources to spread the burden. One patient, Ada, had to give up driving when she was diagnosed with dementia. She loaned the car to a pool of friends, who used this sky-blue Honda to help their more dependent companions. Weekly big shops, hospital appointments, and outings to flower shows were now possible again.

There's a cruel irony in the job title of carer. Our work helps to liberate others, enabling them to live more independent and fulfilling lives. But, who looks out for us? Impairment does not always discriminate by age but, in my experience, paid carers are often young people caring for older generations. Meanwhile, our own lives are disrupted. My lack of care experience ensured that I was hired as an apprentice, irrespective of my degree. Such apprenticeship schemes allow employers to pay us below the normal minimum wage if they see fit. UNISON, a trade union for the public sector, has major concerns about the NHS using apprentices as a supply of cheap labour. We should be gaining valuable training over an extended period. This is the trade-off we make when accepting a lower wage. In reality, we perform the full range of duties within a few weeks of setting foot on the wards. Yet new starters in NHS healthcare assistant apprentice roles are paid what UNISON calls a 'poverty pay rate'. The most recent figures show an average wage of just £3.92 per hour.[*]

Care work is strenuous emotional, physical and intellectual labour. Shifts of more than twelve hours are thoroughly draining. One of my younger colleagues lives in cramped conditions with her extended family. She's the main breadwinner, but comes into work sleep-deprived when her baby sister cries through the night. Even then, she can't miss a beat. Vulnerable people depend on her.

For a lot of young people, unless we live a frugal life, we're screwed. Some things can be controlled – get a cheaper mobile phone contract, ride a bicycle (if you can afford to buy one) instead of the bus. But if we deviate – someone in our family becomes unable to work, or maybe we can't pay the rent one month – the penalties are severe. We face the same unexpected financial challenges as any other individual

* *You're Hired! A UNISON report on apprenticeships in the NHS*, UNISON, April 2016, available at https://www.unison.org.uk/content/uploads/2016/06/NHS-Apprenticeships-UNISON-FoI_report_final.pdf

trying to allocate their income, and the same consequences. Although I'm privileged to be financially secure, many of my colleagues have no buffer to soften these blows. The triple lock policy guarantees a minimum increase of 2.5 per cent a year in the basic state pension. This seems grossly unfair when I've just been given a 1 per cent pay rise for the year. That's not even in line with inflation – and NHS wage increases have stalled at this figure, or been frozen, for the past seven years.

It's tempting to take aim at older generations, but there's little mileage in that. Media voices and election pollsters delight in trying to split the electorate along easy to understand lines. Using age as a marker, they've given us the 'grey vote' and contrasted it with the 'youth vote'. We're led to believe that older generations have voted for policies that actively harm their younger counterparts. In the case of the Brexit vote, the over-fifty-fives were seen to have unfairly sacrificed young people's European future on the altar of small-minded nationalism. In reality, none of us are limited by blind allegiance to these mythical voting blocs. All issues are cross-generational, and we need to foster this belief by restoring an effective intergenerational conversation. As I learned through my work as a carer, ageism is a toxic force. Just like us, the elderly are individuals with their own hopes and fears for the future. We all make decisions based on an unknowable blend of self-interest, a desire to improve the lot of family and friends, and a hazy understanding of what might shape a better society.

Cyril is a good example of why I feel no animosity towards the older generations. He was born and bred a Londoner, raised his family there, and retired some twenty years ago. He didn't own his home in London, but had rented privately for decades. When the landlord decided to move back in, he simply gave Cyril the two months' notice required by law. Barely scraping by before, Cyril stumbled into a hostile rental market, with prices far beyond his reach. Searching for somewhere affordable and within driving distance of his London-based family, he settled for a damp mobile home in the rural South West. It was simple to guess the source of the nasty chest infection which had brought him into hospital. When he was discharged, Cyril joked that we could take on sky-high housing costs together if we topped and tailed. Torn out of his community, how could I see this elderly man as the cause of my generation's problems?

Current attitudes are driving harmful divisions between people, young and old. We have to resist this trend and pull the generations together. This may come through organised politics. As my fellow essayists discuss, disengaged youth needs to politicise itself. But we also need to make change happen on a personal level.

ACKNOWLEDGEMENTS

We would like to thank Rachael Kerr, DeAndra Lupu and everyone at Unbound. Thank you to Julia Kingsford at Kingsford Campbell. Thank you to Henry Palmer, Simran Randhawa and June Eric Udorie for early support. Thank you to Kate Foskett for editorial duties and sifting open submissions to the book. Thank you to Roseanna Dias, Vanessa Bellar Sprujit, Hannah Higginson and Victoria Tillotson and all the staff at Watershed, who worked so hard on making *Rife* the amazing platform it is. Thank you to Lesley Silvester and Terry Kahn, Helen and Peter Wilde and The Nisbet Trust for their generosity.

ABOUT THE AUTHORS

Charlie Brinkhurst-Cuff is a writer, editor and creative with focuses on race, feminism, media, youth culture and social politics. She is the deputy editor at *gal-dem* (a magazine and collective exclusively written and produced by women of colour and non-binary people of colour, pushing for diversity in the media), a writer and editor for *Dazed*, a columnist at the *i* newspaper, a *Guardian* freelancer and a regular panellist and speaker for the BBC. In 2016 her opinions section at *gal-dem* won the Best Online Comment Award against the *Financial Times* and in 2017 she won the Georgina Henry Award for Innovation in Journalism on behalf of *gal-dem*.

Kaja Brown, former *Rife* intern, is a writer who currently studies creative writing at Aberystwyth University. She enjoys experimenting with memoir, poetry and short stories, as well as editing her fantasy-novel manuscript. Her favourite themes to write about are LGBT+ life, nature, identity and mental health.

Shona Cobb is a writer, blogger and activist. She's written for *Metro* and the *Guardian*, spoken on TV and radio, and for seven years has written her own blog about disability rights, accessibility and ableism.

Alex Diggins is a writer and teacher based in Bristol. He won second place in the *New Welsh Review*'s 2018 essay prize, and he was shortlisted for the Armchair Mountaineer 2018 'Wild Writing' competition. His work has appeared in *Bristol Life*, *Bristol 24/7*, *Rife*, *Caught by the River* and *New Welsh Review*. He writes about literature, the environment and social justice. He is working on a book about writers and the sea.

Ailsa Fineron is a writer, photographer and improving potter living in Bristol. She is a contributor to *gal-dem*, former *Rife* intern and has been published in *The Colour of Madness*, *The Good Journal*, *GIRLS/CLUB* and *Nocturnal* magazine amongst others.

Olivia Fletcher is a motivational speaker for a youth empowerment charity, working between Belfast and London. After withdrawing from her studies at university, she has engaged in charity work and has worked for the Croydon Labour Party.

Ellie Ford-Elliott is a writer and poet. She has a degree in English with writing from the University of the West of England and has performed poetry across Bristol. Her articles have been published in *Wye Valley Life* magazine and *Rife*. She lives in Hereford.

Brandon J. Graham is a graduate of the University of Bristol. He is a writer and freelance digital artist. He currently lives in Bristol.

Tom Greenslade is a healthcare worker and writer. He lives in Bristol.

Rosalind Jana is an author, journalist and poet. She's written for places including British *Vogue*, BBC Radio 4, *Broadly*, BuzzFeed, *Suitcase* and *Dazed*, and her debut non-fiction book *Notes on Being Teenage* came out in 2016. She lives in London.

Sammy Jones is the written content editor of *Rife* and is a freelance journalist and copywriter. She has previously worked at *Crack Magazine* and *Bristol 24/7*, and currently covers Welsh entertainment for *Metro*.

Mariam Khan grew up in Birmingham. She is a feminist and is the editor of an anthology of essays by Muslim women published in 2019 by Picador.

Amber Kirk-Ford is an award-winning blogger and vlogger. She has written for the *Guardian* and MTV, and has appeared on Sky News and the *MailOnline*. She has also appeared in *Stylist* magazine and the *i* newspaper. She lives in Norfolk.

Chloe Kitching is currently production assistant for Kneehigh. She has also worked for a number of other cultural organisations in different capacities. This is the first essay she has published.

Liv Little is a writer, producer and curator. She is the founding editor-in-chief of award-winning publication *gal-dem*, which aims to push the creative work of women of colour into the forefront of British discourse and debate. She's also produced audio documentaries for the migration museum and written for a range of publications including ASOS, the *Guardian* and *Wonderland*. Liv has trained and worked in factual television, producing content for BBC Three and working on programmes for Sky Arts, Channel 4 and BBC One. She is obsessed with using documentary as a way to spotlight the stories that we don't normally hear about in mainstream media.

Ella Marshall is a writer and photographer from Bristol. In 2016, she founded Freedom of Mind C.I.C. to deliver events that would celebrate and facilitate important discussions about mental health and emotional wellbeing, for which she was recognised as the Enterprise Hero at Bristol Young Heroes Awards 2017. Her work has featured in the *Independent Magazine*, *Bristol 24/7* and *Rife* and she has previously served as a Member of UK Youth Parliament. Ella is currently studying International Relations and History at the London School of Economics and Political Science.

Chloë Maughan is a researcher, writer and photographer based in Bristol. She is an outspoken survivor of sexual violence, and writes regularly on gender, survival and mental health. She is a contributor for *The Skinny* and *Rife*, and was commended in the Foyle Young Poets of the Year Award in 2010.

Ilyas Nagdee is the current NUS Black Students' Officer. He has written on various platforms about institutional racism, the criminalisation of communities and his love for his home city of Manchester. He is a graduate of the University of Manchester, where he also worked extensively to widen access to education.

Katie Oldham is a writer and musician based in Brighton. She performs in the band Sit Down, and writes the blog Scarphelia, which she has kept since 2012.

Nicholas Preston is a student based in London and studies anthropology at Goldsmiths College. He's also an aspiring writer and blogs at This Dilapidated World.

Aniqah Rawat is a theatre and performance student at the University of Bristol. She has written articles for *That's What*

She Said magazine and is also a member of the National Youth Theatre.

Malakaï Sargeant is a freelance writer, producer and theatre-maker working to stretch the limits of performing arts, enabling the socially and politically disenfranchised to make a mark within the sector and beyond. He is the artistic director of participatory theatre company the S+K Project.

Nikesh Shukla is the author of three novels. Most recently, he authored the critically acclaimed *The One Who Wrote Destiny* (2018). His debut novel, *Coconut Unlimited*, was shortlisted for the Costa First Novel Award 2010. His second novel, *Meatspace*, was released to critical acclaim in 2014. Nikesh has written for the *Guardian, Observer, Independent, Esquire*, BuzzFeed, Vice, BBC2, LitHub, Guernica and BBC Radio 4. Nikesh is also the editor of the bestselling essay collection *The Good Immigrant*, which won the Readers' Choice Award at the Books Are My Bag Awards. He co-edited *The Good Immigrant USA* with Chimene Suleyman. He is the author of two YA novels, *Run, Riot* and *The Boxer*. Nikesh was one of *Time* magazine's cultural leaders, *Foreign Policy* magazine's 100 Global Thinkers and *The Bookseller*'s 100 most influential people in publishing in 2016 and in 2017. He is the co-founder of the literary journal *The Good Journal* and *The Good Literary Agency*.

Brenda Wong is a social media and content strategist. Originally from Kuala Lumpur, she now lives in London and works in customer operations for Monzo Bank.

ABOUT *RIFE* AND WATERSHED

Rife is an online magazine for young people made by young people. The platform was created in 2014 in response to a Bristol Talent Lab that identified a gap in the media – where were the young voices? By mentoring young journalists on a six-monthly basis from our offices in Bristol's Watershed, *Rife* aims to empower them with the skills to enter the creative industries. The majority of these young journalists are of colour and are non-graduates, and they've gone on to work at the *Guardian*, BBC, *Metro* and more. *Rife* also runs workshops, appears at festivals and talks, and now has a book. Read more at www.rifemagazine.co.uk

Watershed in Bristol is recognised for its internationally distinctive programme of invention and talent development; as a leading centre for film culture; and as Bristol's city centre cultural meeting and debating place of choice. Watershed delivers a diverse programme of films, events, festivals, artists' commissions, workshops and conferences. It supports the next generation of creative talent through groundbreaking engagement programmes like *Rife*, and develops talent and new practice in creative technology in its world-leading lab The Pervasive Media Studio. Visit or support us at www.watershed.co.uk

Unbound is the world's first crowdfunding publisher, established in 2011.

We believe that wonderful things can happen when you clear a path for people who share a passion. That's why we've built a platform that brings together readers and authors to crowdfund books they believe in – and give fresh ideas that don't fit the traditional mould the chance they deserve.

This book is in your hands because readers made it possible. Everyone who pledged their support is listed below. Join them by visiting unbound.com and supporting a book today.

With special thanks to Natracare for their support of this book

Tom Abba
Sharmin Abbasi
Naz Abdillahi
Liban Abdullahi
Martha Adam
Sara Nisha Adams
Yomi Adegoke
Mary Adeson
Charles Adrian
Mediah Ahmed
Jon Aitken
Nazire Ezgi Akarsu
Emad Akhtar
Shahmima Akhtar
Folarin Akinmade

Zakirah Alam
Georgie Aldridge
Max Alexander
Bisha K. Ali
Richard Allen
Linas Alsenas
Sophia Althammer
Tanuja Amarasuriya
Audrey Ampofo
Eric Anderson
Josephine Andrews
Marie Andrews
Carl Anka
Amy Annette
Tsveta Apostolova

David AR
Polly Arrowsmith
Richard Ash
Dylan Ashby Thompson
Richard Ashcroft
Owain Astles
Tim Atack
Nasri Atallah
Matthew Austin
Suzanne Azzopardi
Alisha Bailey
Jenny Baines
Jat Bains
Sim Bajwa
Sam Baker
Simon Baker
Emily Ball
Jenny Bangham
Sophie Barker
Sarah Barnard
Gena-mour Barrett
Layla Barron
Alison Baskerville
Emily Bater
Kathryn Beale
Mark Beechill
Hajera Begum
Mamataj Begum
Catherine Bell
Marns Bell
Vanessa Bellaar Spruijt
Beng & Paul
Ruth Bennett
Jendella Benson
Sarah Bentley
Bernie Bernard
BFI Film Academy Bristol
Alsasha Bhat
Arnika Bhupal

Nikki Bi
Elly Bill
Elizabeth Billinger
Sam Binnie
Melissa Blackburn
Amy Louise Blaney
Alex Booer
@BooksandJohn
Isobel Booth
Shane Boothby
Xavier Boucherat
Megan Bourne
Rachel Bower
Charlotte Brady
Corrie Bray
Richard W H Bray
Andy Brereton
Kristian Brodie
David Brook
Kaja Brown
Sarah Brown
Sarah Brownsword
Aoife Bruen
Nicholas Burman
Cai Burton
Rachael Burton
Virginie Busette
Aisha Bushby
Aslan Byrne
Tanya Byrne
James Caig
Kit Caless
Sophie Cameron
Charlie Campbell
Rosie Canning
Lauren Cantillon
Rebecca Carter
Rachel Cartwright
David Castle

Sarah Castleton
Lucy Catchpole
Cassie Chadderton
Gina Chahal
Ollie Chamberlain
Jaspal Chana
Vishakh Chandrasekhar
Laura Charlton
Tom Chatfield
Zoe Chatfield
Darren Chetty
Zen Cho
Vera Chok
Yousef Cisco
Caro and Cat Clarke
Laura Clements
Harry Clementson
Alexander Clover
Dave Coates
Mel Cockman
Adam Coffee
Rachel Coldicutt
Pete Collins
Kate Collis
Jane Commane
Louise Conlin
Jess Connett
Carla Cook
Rosie Cooke
Sue Cooper
Katharine Corr
Sarah Corrigan
Mark Cosgrove
Lauren Couch
Elaine Cox
Ellie Cox
Rosi Crawley
Create Studios
James Cressey

Kathlyn Crocker
Shannon Cullen
Hannah Curran
Kim Curran Goodson
Afshan D'souza-Lodhi
Dan Dalton
Bucker Dangor
Wasi Daniju
Rupert Dannreuther
Darren
Daniellè Dash
Rishi Dastidar
Nada Dastmalchi
Jonathan Davidson
Geraint Davies
Jonathan Davies
Alison Davis
Elizabeth Day
Susie Day
Becca Day-Preston
Richard de Lancey
Lianne de Mello
Devinda De Silva
Jennifer Dellner
Dominique Dennemont
Andrew Denner
Jo Dennis
Jill Denton
Anneka Deva
Sharan Dhaliwal
Becca Di Francesco
Roseanna Dias
Edward Dingwall
Claire Doherty
Lottie Donovan
Maura Dooley
Louise Doughty
Nina Douglas
Tiernan Douieb

Orlane Doumbe
Kristopher Doyle
Karen Drake
Rob Drummer
John Durrant
Jean Edelstein
Helen Edwards
Nicola Edwards
Alex Ekong
Chloë Elizabeth
Matthew Elliott
Sarah Elliott
Joanna Ellis
Lynne Elvins
Luke Emery
Eleanor Envision
Ayla Chandni Estreich
Ilana Estreich
Fergus Evans
Jane Evans
Bernardine Evaristo
Lee Farley
Megan Farr
Emmet Farragher
Peter Faulkner
L Felix
Heta Fell
Aimée Felone
Joanne Fenton
Saima Ferdows
Athena Fernyhough
Stuart Ffoulkes
Ed Finch
Becky Fincham
Stevie Finegan
Laura Fisher
Nathan FitzPatrick
Jean Flack
Molly Flatt

Louise Forbes
Leanne Ford
Susan Ford
Zoe Ford
Ellie Ford-Elliott
Charles Forsdick
Hannah Fort Teller
Aresa Foster
Ian Foster
Lucas Fothergill
Ceri Fowler
Jon Fox
Susanne Frank
Sarah Franklin
Rebecca Franks
Tim Fraser
Eve Freeman
Naomi Frisby
Melissa Fu
Eugen Furch
Elaine Gallacher
Cathy Galvin
Kate Gardner
Louise Gardner
Beth Garrod
Michelle Gately
Ella Gatfield
Steve Gatfield
Jo Gatford
Ryan Gattis
Jeremy Gavron
Aimee-Marie Gedge
Claire Genevieve
Miranda George
Will Georgi
Jonathan Gibbs
Phil Gibby
Mia Gilson
Amy Glover

Salena Godden
Emma Goldhawk
Matt Golding
Sophie Goldsworthy
Hayley Gorman
Niven Govinden
Brandon J. Graham
Dayne Grant
Lucy Gray
Michelle Green
Demelza Griffiths
Neil Griffiths
Niki Groom
Radiya Hafiza
Daniel Hahn
Emylia Hall
Lindsey Hall
Richard Hancock
Donna Hardcastle
Megha Harish
Sinead Harold
Jonathan Harper
Richard Harris
Abby Harrison
Kate Harrison
Kristen Harrison
Lisa Harrison
Uzma Hasan
Victoria Haslam
Carolyn Hassan
Fran Haswell
Morgan Hendy
Kate Hepplewhite
Rachel Herman
Sonja Herz
Philip Hewitt
Dan Higginson
Felicity Higginson
Hannah Higginson

Meredith and Peter Higginson
Richard Higginson
Bethan HighgateBetts
Matt Hill
Polly Ho-Yen
Sj Holgate
Tiffany Holmes
Tracy & Martin Homer
Sarah Honey
Becky Horsley
Ben Horton
Joseph Horton
Alex Hoskins
Deanne Howe
Lexy Hudson
Bex Hughes
David Hunter
Rebecca Hunter
Will Hunter
Ramla Hussein
Alice Hutton
Lizzie Huxley-Jones
Amanda Huxtable
Zamzam Ibrahim
Samuel Iliffe
Impact Hub Birmingham
Suzey Ingold
Lois Ireson
Ammara Isa
Jessica Jackson
Sara Jafari
Anna James
Lisa Jenkins
Louise Jennings
Simon Jerrome
Natalie Jester
Katherine Jewkes
Catrin John
Denny John

Catherine Johnson
Caitlin Jones
Christopher Jones
David Jones
Laura Jones
Sammy Jones
Katherine Josselyn
Zainab Juma
Fahima K
Wei Ming Kam
Prithi Kanakamedala
Varun Kanish
Jasminder Kaur
Sandy Kaur
Suzanne Kavanagh
Amanda Kelly
Andrew Kelly
Donna Kelly
Stephen Kelman
Cas Kemp
Ros Kennedy
Ross Kennedy
Callum Kenny
Laura Kenwright
Gemma Keyes
Stephen Keyes
Shazad Khalid
Farhana Khalique
Aina Khan
Aneeqa Khan
Irundeep Khatkar
Dan Kieran
Harriet King
Julia Kingsford
Sam Kinsley
Amber Kirk-Ford
Andy Kisaragi
Vanessa Kisuule
Emma Kitching

Rosie Klapac
Daniel Kramb
Laura Kriefman
Jess Kumwongpin-Barnes
Suhayla Kuri
Zainab Kwaw-Swanzy
Navjoyt Ladher
Lolita Laguna Crespo
Raj K Lal
Sookie Lalla
Sonya Lalli
Kirstin Lamb
Philip Langeskov
Jo Lansdowne
Maisie Lawrence
Rowan Lawton
Clare Leczycki
Gaby Lee
Mark Lee
Diane Leedham
Georgia Lennie
Sandra van Lente
Rhiannon Lewis
Emma Lewis-Kalubowila
Rachel Leyshon
Martha Limburg
Cath Little
Rebecca Livingstone
Lara Liz
Morgan Lloyd Malcolm
Kate Lockwood Jefford
Josie Long
Molly Pushpa Longden
Amy Lord
Caroline Lorimer
Jamie Lorimer
Sharmaine Lovegrove
Elinor Lower
Samuel Ludford

Barbie Lyon

Tamara Macfarlane

Peter Mackie

Seonaid Macleod

Anand Madhvani

Hannah Maguire

Sabrina Mahfouz

Churnjeet Mahn

Sammy Maine

Krishan Majithia

Jayan Makenji

Khawar Malik

Deej Malik-Johnson

Gautam Malkani

Ailbhe Malone

Halimah Manan

Perminder Mann

Rachel Mann

Sarah Manvel

Ellen Marsh

Ella Marshall

Laura Marshall

Pip Martin

Tim Martin

Will McConnell Simpson

Amy McCulloch

Heather McDaid

Kate McDermott

SarahLouise McDonald

Eleanor McDowall

Chrisy McFadden

Helen McGee

John McGee

Clare McGinn

Verity McIntosh

Marie-Anne McQuay

Glen Mehn

Louise Mei

Chloe Meineck

Joe Melia

Zak Mensah

Fidel Meraz

Etienne Michelet

Lidija Milic

Kiran Millwood Hargrave

Anjelica Minas

Sam Missingham

John Mitchinson

Lucy Moffatt

Georgina Morley

Charlotte Morris

Jackie Morris

Ed Morrish

Andrea Morrison

Miss Morse

Angela Morton

Joanna Moult

Ian Mousley

Amrita Mudan

Matt Muir

Kim Mulholland

Karen-Babette Müller

Bethan Mure

Mike Murphy

Andrew Murray

Charlie Murray

Georgia Murray

Phil Murwill

Holly Muse

Carlo Navato

Louise Marie Neal

Kate Neilan

Louise Neill

Rachel Nelken

Katie Nelson

Jenni Nock

Agnes Norbury

Caroline Norbury

SUPPORTERS

Laura North
Alice Nuttall
Kevin O'Connor
Jenny O'Gorman
Anneliese O'Malley
Hilary O'Shaughnessy
Rachel Oakes
Antonia Odunlami
Natalie Ohlson
Musa Okwonga
Ayomide Oluyemi
Ellen Orange
Katharine Orton
Adam Osborne
Fiz Osborne
Alice Oseman
Tenelle Ottley-Matthew
Dolapo Oyenuga
Siena Parker
Radha Patel
Vinay Patel
Zsofia Paulikovics
Holly Peckitt
Naomi Peel
Bianca Pellet
Dick Penny
Rebecca Pickets
Jennifer Pierce
Luisa Plaja
Eddie Playfair
Hazel Plowman
Katherine Pole
Justin Pollard
Patricia Pollock
Emily Poole
Beki Pope
Nina Pottell
Alex Poulter
Dan Powell

Nicola Powell
Amy Powis
Alex Preston
Cheryl Price
Stephen Price
Maddy Probst
Tim Pushman
Kalaiyashni Puvanendran
Alice Quigley
Arusa Qureshi
Iman Qureshi
Sadiah Qureshi
Sarrah Qureshi
Suhan Rajkumar
Angus Ramsay
Polly Randall
Nimer Rashed
Leila Rasheed
Fiona Razvi
Clare Reddington
David Redfern
Jo Reid
Kerry-Jo Reilly
Jessica Richards
Jane Richardson
Jo Richardson
Ruby Robinson
Simon Robinson
Will Robinson
James Robson
Paul Rockett
Katie Roden
Courtney Rodrigues
Stuart Roper-Marshall
Amy Rose
Becca Rose
Mandy Rose
Mot Rotciv
C.N. Rowen

Giulia Rüegg
Lydia Ruffles
Davina Rungasamy
Alex Rutherford
Evi S
Amna Saleem
Sonia Sandhu
Karen Sands-O'Connor
Bhavithrah Satkunarasa
Jonathan Saunders
Billy Saxton
Bareerah Sayed
Hamish Scadding
Mel Scaffold
Juliet Scott
Wilf Scott
Andreas Sedlatschek
Rani Selvarajah
Sophie Setter Jerrome
Sarah Shaffi
Muj Shah
Mim Shaikh
Samantha Shannon
Lucy Shaw
Andrew Shead
Carla Shepherd
Ashley Shield
Nikesh Shukla
Grace Shutti
Jess Siggers
Julia Silk
Anthea Simmons
Claire Simmons
Josh Simons
Leilah Skelton
Niall Slater
Slimpickins
Stephen Slocombe
Steve Slocombe

Wendy Smithers
Ishaan Sood
Amy South
Annabel Sowemimo
John Sparkhall
Duncan Speakman
Margaret Spillane
Kirsty Stanley
Anna Starkey
Katarzyna Stawarz
Cathryn Steele
Robin Stevens
Poppy Steward
Claire Stewart
Roz Stobart
Jan Stocker
James Stockhausen
Katie Stone
Anna Stothard
Louie Stowell
Alexandra Strick
Suky Stroud
Laura Summers
Dan Sumption
Alice Sutherland-Hawes
Chelsea Swift
Susie Symes
James Taljaard
Zeba Talkhani
Amy Clare Tasker
Richard Tatnall
Helen Taylor
David Taylor-Matthews
Jaspreet Tehara
Teobesta Tesfa Endrias
www.thebookbag.co.uk
Alice Thomas
Amy Thomas
Fiona Thompson

Tim Thornton
Clare Titley
James Touzel
Madeline Toy
Angelique Tran Van Sang
Anthony Trevelyan
Nick Triggs
Matilda Tristram
Edward Trotter
Michele Trusolino
Sian Tukiainen
Debbie Turner
Eleanor Turney
Wendy Tuxworth
Alex Twose
Harriet Tyce
Akane Vallery Uchida
Jack Underwood
Deepti Unnikrishnan
Victoria Uong
Mayur Upadhyaya
Fatih Uzuner
Mark Vent
Akshitha Victor
Richard Vigars
Johanna von Fischer
Vic Wakefield-Jarrett
Jonathan Wakeham
Damon L. Wakes
Stephen Walker
Victoria Walker
Kat Wall
Kamina Walton
Rhea Warner
Ellie Warren
Emma Warren

Beth Watson
Alex Webb
Katherine Webber
Dom Weinberg
James Westby
Simon White
Helen Wilde
Will Wiles
Gethin Wilkinson
Harriet Williams
Helen Williams
Morgan Williams
Christina Willmore
Emily Willsher
Johanna Wilson
Sarah Wilson
Stephen Wilson
Chlo Winfield
Robbie Wojciechowski
Amy Wong
Brenda Wong
Daniel Wood
Nicholas Wood
Katherine Woodfine
Sal Woodward
Laura Wright
Martin Wroe
Matthew Xia
Rukhsana Yasmin
Sairah Yassir-Deane
Steve Yates
Daniel York
Talia Yousef
Martin Zaltz Austwick
Helen Zaltzman
Samar Ziadat